M. L Cowles

Redbank:

Life on a Southern Plantation

M. L Cowles

Redbank:
Life on a Southern Plantation

ISBN/EAN: 9783337001421

Printed in Europe, USA, Canada, Australia, Japan

Cover: Foto ©ninafisch / pixelio.de

More available books at **www.hansebooks.com**

REDBANK:

LIFE ON A SOUTHERN PLANTATION.

By M. L. COWLES.

"*We often do more good by our sympathy than by our labors.*"
                                                                CANON FARRAR.

BOSTON, MASS.:
Arena Publishing Company,
COPLEY SQUARE,
1893.

Copyrighted 1893
By
M. L. Cowles,
All rights reserved.

ARENA PRESS.

THIS SKETCH OF SOUTHERN LIFE

IS DEDICATED

TO MY FOUR DAUGHTERS,

WHOSE HEARTS FIND NO DIVIDING LINE

BETWEEN NORTH AND SOUTH.

REDBANK.

CHAPTER I.

"What an amount of patience one needs in this world! Here I've been waiting fifteen minutes, at least, and it is probable I shall have to wait fifteen minutes longer before he comes. The lazy boy! But I will *not* call him. I will not remind him of his appointment, if he does not care to keep it."

As she spoke she tapped the end of her foot with her riding-whip, in vexation.

"And the day is so beautiful, too—just the thing for a ride through the pines. O, Harry! Harry! if only you could be made over! if you had a little less physical beauty and a few solid virtues! Such as punctuality, for instance." Jessie Holcombe looked almost tearful as she spoke these last few words; they evidently came from the bottom of a very full heart—a heart not merely filled with momentary annoyance, but deeply wounded by the faults of another.

She was a handsome girl, and her riding habit became her well; it revealed not only beauty of form, but a certain clear outline of character. She was simple and stately—a little sedate in manners, a little severe in morals. Her complexion was very pure and beautiful, with the rich, warm undertone which betokens perfect health. Her features were clearly and beautifully chiseled; about the mouth especially, there were lines of sweetness and strength which were in themselves a revelation of character. Her large dark-brown eyes, veiled by delicate lids and long lashes, were full of that strange radiance which we call soul. As you looked into their wonderful depths, you recognized a strong and lofty spirit, already trained to tenderness and patience, in the stern school of life.

For ten or fifteen minutes longer she stood almost motionless; at length, weary of waiting, she gathered up her skirt, and walked slowly down the steps of the piazza out into the yard. Turning a corner of the house, she got a view of the stables in the rear. Yes, the horses were both ready; Peyton was standing quietly, —holding the reins and waiting for the riders to come. She moved down the broad carriage-way, nodding pleasantly to the groom.

"Well, Peyton, did you think I was never coming?" she asked.

The man only grinned; he was a negro, and with him a grin meant all kinds of things. As an answer, it was far better than a long string of words. Its ambiguity was faultless. If language was invented to conceal one's thoughts, how much more perfect, for such a purpose, is the negro's grin.

"How is Dolly to-day?" she inquired after a moment, approaching a beautiful black mare, and laying her hand lovingly on the glossy mane.

"She's all right, Miss Jessie—jes' ready for a gallop dis minute."

"I see she is. You do take splendid care of her,

Peyton," continued the girl; "she is always perfectly groomed. I thank you more than I know how to express."

Again the negro grinned, but there was a difference this time. Before, he was slightly deprecating the necessity of waiting so long when there was so much work to be done; now, his dusky countenance was illumined with veritable pleasure at the lady's approval. He had a great admiration for his beautiful young mistress, and a word of praise from her lips was worth more to him than his month's wages.

"She is a beauty, isn't she?" said Jessie, after caressing the horse for a few minutes.

"No use ter talk 'bout dat—no horse like her roun' dis plantation," replied the negro. "Ef you wants ter sell her, dere's plenty would like to buy her, I can tell you dat, Miss Jessie."

"Money could not buy her, Peyton,—I love her too dearly to sell her for any price. You know she used to belong to my brother—the one who was killed in the war. She was a mere colt then. He was riding her in a cavalry charge, when the ball struck him. She is not as young as she once was. Ah! Dolly, you are growing old." And again the hand was laid lovingly on the animal's shapely head.

"Come, Peyton, lead her to the block; I will get up and arrange myself. Perhaps by that time my cavalier will come."

She was just ready to start, when a young man, whistling gayly, came out of the back door of the house, and rapidly crossed the grass to the stables.

"Have I kept you waiting?" he cried, quickening his pace.

"Look at your watch and see. It must be an hour

behind the time. Fortunately I am your sister, or you would not escape punishment."

"A thousand pardons!" he exclaimed, removing his hat and bowing gracefully. "I was writing a letter, and it was a devilish hard task. Casting my eyes up to the ceiling for an idea, I happened to catch a glimpse of the clock—and, behold me."

"Well, pray don't keep me waiting any longer, or the sun will be ready to set," said the young lady, smiling and accepting his apology without any comment.

The gentleman vaulted into the saddle, and the two cantered off together. Peyton stood still, a few moments, watching them as they went down the long avenue to the road; then, turning away, he said to himself in a low tone—"I'd never take dem for brudder and sister, if dey didn't look so much alike. Now, dere's Miss Jessie—I'd like to work fur her always, 'thout any pay; but Marse Harry——" here he shook his head, and left the sentence unfinished.

Once in the open road, the two riders dashed off in a gallop, and were soon lost to sight.

"Which way?" asked the young man.

"By the mill."

When they were in sight of the mill, they slackened their speed, and came down to a walk.

"I do like this dear old mill so much," said Jessie; "the building itself is just as picturesque as it can be, with that creeper running all over it, and the group of fine old sweet-gum trees growing so near. Then the big pond, and the waterfall and the stream rushing so madly over the rocks—the clatter of the wheels and grinding-stones, - and the cool drip, drip, drip of the water. The last touch of beauty is added by the low-roofed cottage of the miller up there on the slope under the trees. It is just the loveliest spot on the whole plantation. I feel as if I must have a glimpse of it every day, or else I've been defrauded of something."

"Somehow, I don't like it," said her companion; "I never come this road, if I can help it; I have an uncanny feeling about it, especially at night: as if something dreadful had happened here, or were going to happen. I don't know which."

"Why, something dreadful did happen here, ever so long ago," answered Jessie. "Perhaps your feeling comes from that."

"Perhaps," he answered carelessly.

"You have heard all about it, haven't you?" she asked with quickened interest.

"In a vague kind of way," he replied; "but I'm not fond of dreadful things, even in story books, so I've never heard the full account."

"Why, it was in the lifetime of the Colonel's grandfather, who was a dreadfully wicked old man, they say. He used to beat his slaves and maltreat even his wife and daughter. Well, it was summer-time, and there had been a long and terrible drought; for many weeks, not a drop of rain had fallen, and the cotton was burning up in the fields. The old man was in a rage from morning till night because it did not rain. He used to walk the piazza, and curse and swear at the heavens. At last one day a little cloud appeared in the sky, and soon grew into great masses, black with thunder and lightning. The storm broke with perfect fury over the country; the rain fell in torrents, beating down the cotton into the very ground; the wind was like a hurricane, uprooting trees, and sweeping away buildings. The millpond rose so fast and high that the miller was frightened, and rushed home to his family, but he never reached them; he was blown into the pond and drowned. The mill went down with a great crash; the miller's house, his wife, and five little children were all carried off by the flood. It is a story that Aunt Lucy loves to tell. The old man was ruined, and he died soon afterwards. The only daughter was Colonel Winston's mother, and that's the way he happens to own this plantation. He himself rebuilt the mill, many years ago."

"Yes, I've heard it all before," replied Harry Holcombe, in an absent way. By this time they had passed the mill, crossed the rude bridge over the stream, and were in the woods beyond.

"Come, let's have another gallop," said the gentleman.

"A trot this time," cried the girl, as the two horses started off. Soon they were dashing over the white sandy road which wound through a wood of tall pines, such as are often seen in the eastern portions of the Southern states. For simple and imposing beauty, no forest equals that of the noble pine; the tall and stately trunks, the crown of dark feathery foliage; the absence of undergrowth revealing the massive pillars, together form a vast natural cathedral, which produces an impression of solemnity and awe. The prolonged moan that lingers forever in the lofty aisles seems to come from an invisible organ.

When they reached the depths of the wood, both riders felt this, and brought their horses to a walk. For a long time they rode side by side without speaking. Jessie broke the silence.

"Harry," she said in her simple, direct way, "I wish you would not manage to vex the Colonel so."

"Why, what have I done now?" he asked, impatiently, removing his hat and tossing back his hair.

"I don't know; only I heard him say, this morning, that, if you were his son, he would give you a good thrashing."

"I daresay he would. Thank heaven that I am not his son!" cried the young man with levity and indifference.

"But, Harry, since you are in his house and eat his bread, you ought to try to please him."

"An angel could not do that, Jessie, far less a poor sinner like me."

"Well, you might try, dear, not to put him in a rage as you often do."

"I don't put him in a rage, he puts himself into one. If he finds his overcoat hanging on the second instead of the third peg from the hall door, he gets into a rage and begins to abuse me. If his riding-whip is found lying on the hall-table, instead of standing handle down in one special corner, he gets into a rage and abuses me."

"Well, if he gets angry so easily, you ought to be careful not to disturb anything that belongs to him. Harry, *you* are not exactly perfect."

"If I don't know that already, it isn't because you haven't told me often enough. Damn the fussy old Colonel," he exclaimed after a moment's pause.

"If you feel like that, you ought not remain under his roof. Why don't you go somewhere else?"

"Where the deuce am I to go?"

"The world is all before you where to choose," she answered.

"Well, what if it is? I know precious little about any of it—only a small portion of Virginia, and this little cotton-patch in Georgia."

"How little adventure you have about you!" she exclaimed impatiently. "Oh, if I were only a man!"

"What would you do, pray?"

"At least, I'd earn an honest living, and not live on other people."

"How would you do it? Let's hear, please."

"There are ten thousand kinds of service by which a man can make himself useful in the world, and thus earn his own bread."

"Which one would you choose?"

"The one I liked the best—the one that would help me to grow nobler and better every day."

"How clear and definite you are!" he answered. "You would go *somewhere*—do *something*—*the* something that would help you to grow nobler and better every day. Now, if I had come to you for advice—which I haven't—I would go away mightily aided by what you have said,"—and he began to whistle softly.

"Well," she continued after a short pause, "if you do not know where to go and are determined to stay here, why don't you try to help the Colonel. There are many ways in which you could do that, now he has no overseer."

"The old fool, to send away such a good fellow as Sam Griffin! Why, Jessie, he won't let anybody help him. As for me, he does not think that I have sense enough to turn over an ash-cake."

"He does not think that you want to do anything but ride around, and smoke, and hunt, and read novels. Prove to him that he is mistaken. He did give you the charge of the mill at one time, and how did it turn out? That surely was your fault, not his."

"Yes, set me to watch a thief of a nigger! I value my brains too much to waste them on that kind of work. Besides, you know I hate the very sight of that infernal old mill; its clatter drives me almost mad."

She made no reply to this remark. After all, what was the use of talking?

Presently he turned to her, and said, "I know perfectly well what's the matter with the Colonel just at present."

"What is it?" she asked, quickly; "he seems to have lost all his old geniality of manner."

"It is only the lack of money, my dear. It is amazing how a little ' filthy lucre ' in one's pocket improves one's temper. But he need not quarrel with me. If he only knew it, I could give him profound sympathy, for I'm in the same box myself."

"But do you think that he is really in debt? He must be rich—he has so much land—thousands of acres."

"Yes; but land does not enrich one at this time. It is the very cause of his embarrassment. If he would sell half of it, he would be far better off."

"But he spends money so freely," said the girl; "surely that does not look as if he needed it."

"That only shows what an old fool he is. He would have enough, if he did not pitch it out in the road."

"You are right," she said, slowly and sadly, "but I suppose he has always been accustomed to scatter it around freely, and, at his age, it is hard to change."

"Well, I'm sorry for him," replied the young man, "but I don't see how I can help him."

"I am sure you could if you would only try, Harry dear," she said, very gently; "and you would be so much happier, and I would, too." She looked at him with a world of tenderness in her dark eyes, but he did not respond to the appeal.

"Do let's go faster," he exclaimed, after a short silence, as if weary of the conversation, and they galloped on again until their horses were well-spent.

When, at length, they fell into a walk, Harry said, very quietly, " Look here, Jessie, you need not bother your pious little soul about me. I suppose I ought to feel complimented to be the object of so much solicitude, but, to tell the truth, it makes me confoundedly uncomfortable. Would you really like to know what I am going to do?"

" Indeed I would," she answered.

" Now, this is a secret between us two, remember," he continued. " I would not tell anybody else in the world but you." Here he paused as if reluctant to speak.

" You need not be afraid that I will betray any secret of yours, Harry dear," she said, looking at him wistfully.

" I know that well enough, but there are some things a fellow does not care to talk about, even to his sister. However, I want to relieve some of your excessive anxiety—I'm afraid it keeps you awake at night; so here goes. You know Alice Brooks, of course. Well, I have serious intentions in that direction. She is a nice little thing, and rich for these times in the South—a plantation or two, and some bank and railroad stock. I know all about it. Now, I'm going to fall in love with her, and win her pretty little hand, sure as shot."

" But she will never marry you, Harry."

" Yes, she will; she likes me right well now, and I know I can make her like me better, if I try."

" But surely, Harry, you are not going to marry her for her money."

" By no means would I do such a very wicked thing," he said, with a low laugh. " I am going to love her with all my might, and marry her in spite of her money!"

" Then I hope you will try to make yourself worthy of her, for she is a lovely girl," said Jessie.

"Yes, I know that," he replied, and then relapsed into silence.

They had now made a wide circuit around the mill side of the plantation, and were nearing the house. As Jessie thought of her brother's words, her heart grew lighter and happier than it had been for a long time. The knowledge that he was really in love with a high-minded girl, made her have hopes of his salvation. A man generally shows what is in him, when he selects his wife. If Harry could only win Alice Brooks, Jessie felt convinced that such a wife would have great influence over him. But how about Alice herself? Would there not be a terrible risk for her in the union? Assuredly there would. But if they truly loved each other, there would be a holy power around them which would save them both, for Jessie Holcombe believed in the divine source of human love.

These thoughts were in her mind when the horses stopped in front of the house; with her brother's assistance she alighted, and ran up the steps of the piazza, humming an old song, her cheeks glowing, and her heart full of bright hopes for the future.

As she was crossing the broad hall of the old plantation house, on her way upstairs, she met her little niece, Lilian, who was crying bitterly.

"What is it, darling?" asked Jessie, seating herself on the steps and taking the child in her arms; "tell me all about it, and I will make it right again."

"Papa has kicked Tasso," cried the child. "And broken his leg."

"Oh! dear, what shall we do?" exclaimed Jessie, springing up with an angry flash in her eyes. "Come, let's go right away and see what can be done. Does mamma know about it?"

"Yes," answered the child, sobbing still louder, "she is trying to mend it now out in the gardener's house."

They went together to the garden where there was a small house in which the gardener kept his tools. There was a lady within, and a colored man who held a dog in his arms; the former was trying to bandage the broken leg, which the latter was holding firmly in place between the splints.

"Oh, Eleanor!" cried Jessie, "do let me help you!"

"It is done now," said the lady, quietly. Her voice suited her face and her manner, both of which were very sweet and serene. "But I do not think he will live through it—he is such a restless creature. Can you tie him up now, Reuben, so he will not be able to get these splints out of place?"

"I'll try ter, mistis; but I'd jes' kill him, ef I was you, an' save him from all de sufferin', fur dis is a mighty bad break."

"We will wait until to-morrow, at least. Perhaps you can give him something to ease the pain, and put him to sleep to-night!"

"Let me take him ter my house, mistis. I'll do all I can ter help him along."

"Thank you, thank you, Reuben, I'm sure you will," exclaimed the lady, the tears coming into her eyes.

"Lor! mistis, dat's nothin' at all," replied the man; "I'd do more'n dat fur you any day."

"Uncle Reuben," said Jessie, as the negro began to move off with the dog in his arms, "don't kill him unless it is absolutely necessary."

"I won't, Miss Jessie; you may take my word for it."

Here Lilian began to sob anew, and it required all Jessie's tact to subdue her grief. She carried off the child into the house, and up to her own room, where she managed to amuse her until the bell rang for supper.

CHAPTER II.

REDBANK was an old Georgia plantation house, in one of the counties which lie along the Savannah River. It was built on a generous scale; square and substantial, it rose to a goodly height in a grove of fine old trees. It was painted white with green blinds, and entirely surrounded by broad piazzas. A large hall with a handsome staircase ran through the center of the house. Spacious rooms were ranged on each side of this hall; an upper hall and rooms corresponded with those below.

Colonel Winston, the owner of Redbank, had been a very wealthy man in the old days before the war, and this had been his favorite residence. Here he had entertained his friends with princely hospitality. In all the country around, there had been no house so handsome, no yard so full of choice plants and flowers, no stables so filled with fine horses and carriages.

The Colonel had been young and fast in those days, and had enjoyed life very keenly. Now he was almost fifty years old, and things did not move so smoothly as they had once done.

He had lived through the war, and had helped to fight the battles of the South. He had suffered defeat, and humiliation, and loss of property. All this had made him hard and bitter. The pain of old wounds robbed his days of ease; the thought of what he had lost, robbed his soul of peace. He was a stout old rebel, not yet reconstructed; every bone in his body was stiff with pride and defiance. Just before the war began, he had married a woman much younger than himself. How it ever happened, no one knew,—they were so unlike.

They met at the Virginia Springs one summer; in the autumn they were married. He had carried her away to Redbank, where she had lived ever since—through the long years when her husband was fighting on the banks of the Potomac or the James, and through the longer years that had since followed. He had been wounded more than once, but never so badly but that he could come to her; it had not been necessary for her to go to him. The colorless plantation life had dulled her once buoyant spirits, and subdued a nature that had been proud and wilful. Six children had come to them, but one by one they had died in her arms; only two were now left—Lilian a delicate girl of seven, and a fine baby boy, still in the cradle.

Several years after the war was ended, the father of Mrs. Winston in the distant Virginia home, had died; the mother had soon followed. By these bereavements, a brother and a sister, both much younger than herself, were left orphans. Then the heart of Eleanor Winston awoke within her. She yearned for the love and companionship of her kindred. She wrote them to come and henceforth make their home with her; they gladly accepted the invitation. More than a year had since passed. Harry Holcombe, the brother, was a young man of twenty-five, Jessie, the sister, was twenty; and yet to look at them one would have felt almost inclined to reverse their ages. Harry, though possessing a remarkably fine physique, was so lighthearted, so pleasure-loving, so boyish in all his ways, that he could easily have passed for twenty; while Jessie, unnaturally developed by that stirring period, possessed the manners and character of a mature woman. It is strange that the same outward circumstances should so differently impress two human souls. One year of service in the Confederate Army before the final collapse, had tinged the brother with an *insouciance*, a reckless dash, which he promised to carry with him through life. To the sister that year of terrible anxiety and suffering had given an earnestness of thought that had transformed the little maiden into a woman.

Existence at Redbank was by no means congenial to either of them. The loneliness of the plantation and the absence of social gayety, together with the irritability of their brother-in-law, and the sadness of their sister, made the current of every-day life far from smooth and pleasant in its flow: but they possessed only a small fortune between them—not enough to make them independent and able to choose a home elsewhere in the world. Jessie realized the situation more keenly than her brother did, and often urged him to go away, and find some congenial employment for himself. She would have been content to remain and bear the frictions of her lot, if he had only decided to leave Redbank and make for himself a career and a name in the great world. She loved him and was ambitious for him; it grieved her to see him waste his youth and talents in inglorious ease. But her efforts were all in vain; she could not arouse him from the torpor of inactivity. He would listen to her tender chidings with an amused expression upon his handsome face, and then continue to follow his easy and aimless course.

．．．．．．．．．．．

It was long after dark when the supper-bell rang, and the family assembled in the large square dining-room. It was mid-winter, and a wood fire was blazing on the hearth. Jessie and Harry came first; soon Lilian bounded in, followed by her mother. They all stood around the fireplace, chatting pleasantly, for ten or fifteen minutes, before the Colonel appeared. Then a hush fell upon them; even Oliver, the old butler, straightened himself up and grew more solemn in manner; for the master was evidently in a bad humor. Lilian alone seemed unconscious of his imposing presence.

Colonel Winston was tall, thin, and erect, with spare gray locks and a long gray beard. His eyebrows were very thick and still black, standing like a hedge over small but brilliant black eyes. His whole face had a keen, proud, *distingué* air; he looked more like a foreign nobleman than a Southern planter. Impatient, irascible, exacting at home, he was polished, suave, and genial in society. His character was full of inconsistencies, which one, who was not brought into familiar intercourse with him, readily forgot in the indescribable charm of his manners and conversation. Though quick to anger and entirely devoid of self-control, he had a kind and generous heart; as husband, father and master, he was at times very indulgent.

In silence, the family seated themselves at the table. It was an attractive board, with its snowy napery, its old china and silver, and its wax candles in tall silver candlesticks. This evening meal, commonly called supper, was almost a dinner in the profusion of its viands. Cold meats, jellies, and jams were accompanied by hot breads of every kind, from the light roll to the flannel-cake.

Lilian sat on the right hand of her father. In her

childish innocence, she was unconscious of the chilling atmosphere around him. She broke the silence by asking—"Papa, did you know you broke Tasso's leg, when you kicked him?" No response came, and she quickly added, "It was a very bad break too—Uncle Reuben said so. Perhaps Tasso will die; you would be sorry then, wouldn't you?" Still her father made no reply. He appeared more awful than ever; and, looking up at Oliver, he said severely, "Why don't you attend to your business, sir? Don't you see I want some butter?" The servant moved quickly, and passed the desired dish.

At the other end of the table, Mrs. Winston and her sister were talking in very low tones about the last Harper, which had just come, and which contained some articles they wished to read together. Harry was eating his supper with great enjoyment, apparently oblivious of the presence of any one else. He had nothing but contempt for his brother-in-law's weaknesses, and always managed to make the latter understand the fact. His own faults were of a different character; he felt a kind of superiority on this account. Though every day, he broke at least half the laws of the decalogue; yet, in the small affairs of family life, he was always gracious and obliging.

Presently Lilian spoke again. "Papa," she said, "you know Tasso belongs to me. Uncle Hal gave him to me, and I love him dearly. If he dies, I'll cry my eyes out. Do you hear?"

"Eat your supper," answered her father, sharply; "it seems to me you talk too much for a child of your age."

Such a reproof was rare to her, and she looked up at him with a surprised expression in her brown eyes.

"Well, I don't think you talk enough for a gentleman

of your age," she said, laughing; " does he, Uncle Hal?"

The remark was too amusing not to excite a smile. Even old Oliver moved off into a corner to hide the irrepressible grin. Pleased with the effect of her words, Lilian continued,· " Papa, what's the matter with you to-night? Has somebody kicked *you?*"

Before a reply could be made the door opened and the nurse entered with Master Francis, the baby. He was a fine boy of six months. Glad to be out of the dull nursery, and in the midst of this cheerful company, he began to shake his little hands and feet, and to crow with all his might.

"What in the world did you bring him down here for?" asked Mrs. Winston. "He will get so wide awake that he will never go to sleep."

"Well, mistis," the nurse replied, "he jes kep' frettin' so I was afeerd he'd begin ter cry, and dat would worry you."

"Do let me have him," pleaded Jessie. "I know he will be good with me." Mrs. Winston assented, and it was amusing to see the little gentleman's appreciation of the situation.· He laughed and gurgled, and snatched at things in a charming way that soon attracted the attention of every one, and partially dispelled the gloom that had settled upon the family party. Knives and forks and spoons were sent rattling to the floor; at· last, when a plate followed, it seemed time to put a stop to the fun. Eleanor arose, and taking him in her arms, said, " Well, baby, you have done mischief enough now. You must come back to the nursery with me, and go to sleep like a good boy."

She bore him away, while the others got up from the table. The Colonel went into the library, a large front room connected with the dining-room by folding doors.

Here he kept his books, his desk, his papers, and here he smoked and sulked to his heart's content. Jessie, Harry, and Lilian crossed the hall to the back-parlor, where they usually spent the evening together.

"Give us some music, Jessie," said her brother. "Music hath charms to soothe the savage breast, you know."

She seated herself at the piano, while he threw himself lazily upon the sofa. Lilian came and sat down beside him. While Jessie played *Mendelssohn's Songs without Words*, in an endless succession, these good comrades had a delightful time with each other. Lilian pulled his hair, pinched his nose, blew into his ears, and tickled him with a broom-straw, while he pretended to be asleep and snored most fearfully. Now and then, he would jump at her like a hungry wolf, and she would run away as if terrified beyond measure. When he subsided and lay down again, she would return slowly, and the same play was repeated. At length she grew tired of this game; then he took her in his arms and began to tell her stories. It was sweet to see them together. The understanding between them seemed perfect, and the love unutterable.

Finally, the eyes of the child grew heavy and the little head fell upon his breast, where it nestled tenderly, while again and again he softly kissed the pretty red lips. At nine o'clock he arose, and gently carried her upstairs to be put to bed. Then he returned to the sitting-room for a talk with Jessie—perhaps, to be scolded by her, which he generally bore with great patience. He did not mind it much; it was like the patter of the rain-drops to him, scarcely arousing him from his own thoughts and fancies. At ten o'clock they both retired. This was the usual order of events in the household at Redbank.

CHAPTER III.

THE next afternoon, Lilian came to Harry, who was dozing on the sofa in the back-parlor with a handkerchief over his face, and, arousing him, asked if he would not go with her to the Quarter to see how Tasso was. He arose with a bound, shook himself, and said—" You naughty Puss! What did you wake me for? I was dreaming about my sweetheart. She was going to say something very nice to me and now I shall never know what it was!" She laughed heartily at this.

"But, say, won't you go with me?" she cried. "Aunt Jessie is busy reading to mamma, and you know I cannot go alone."

"I am your most obedient servant," he said, with a low bow. Then he took her up in his arms, and kissed her. "Run and get on your things, and we will be off. I'll take my gun along, and perhaps we will kill some birds."

The Quarter was a kind of negro village such as was found on every large Southern plantation. It consisted of one long street with a row of log cabins on each side. At Redbank, the Quarter was half a mile in the rear of the house, and was situated in the midst of a beautiful oak grove. The road that led to it was called the red lane. Lilian was very fond of this walk; there was a noisy little brook to be crossed, which always afforded her much excitement. She was soon ready to start, and came bounding out of the house to join her uncle.

He was standing on the back piazza, with his gun upon his shoulder and several eager dogs around him. He took her little hand in his, and they went across the back-yard, out of the gate, and down the red lane, chatting all the while like good comrades, unmindful of any difference in age or condition. Harry Holcombe loved his little niece better than any one on earth. Her perfect confidence was inexpressibly dear to him. She always had a welcome for him, and a smile and a kiss.

He felt happy this afternoon as she skipped along beside him. Presently he raised his gun, as if to fire at a little bird that was sitting on the fence. "May I kill him?" he asked. "No," she answered with a shake of the head, "not that one. Wait a while." Soon the question was asked again. The reply was always the same—"No, not that one." He seemed to understand her perfectly, and smiled under his dark mustache, while a soft light shone in his eyes. In a little while they came to the brook; then they had a merry time; she was greatly excited about crossing it; there was no bridge, only a narrow log spanned the few feet to the other side. She watched the dogs go over, and then stepped upon the log very bravely; but her heart failed her and she jumped down again. Her uncle looked at her lovely, innocent face, flushed with exercise and excitement, and thought he had never seen anything so beautiful. "Let me carry you over on my shoulder," he said at length, when he saw plainly that her courage was not equal to the occasion. "Oh, no!" she replied, shrinking back, "you would drop me."

"Well, then, you walk on the log, and I will hold your hand and see that you do not fall. Look, I have on high top boots, and the water is not deep; I can easily wade." This plan seemed to suit her, so they were soon on the other side.

The Quarter was very quiet, as they entered it; only a few women were moving about and a few children playing in groups here and there.

The young man had a pleasant greeting for every one. As they approached the cabin of Uncle Reuben, they heard the buzz of a wheel. "Aunt Lucy is spinning!" cried the child. "Oh! how nice! I love to see her spin! Don't you think the rolls are pretty, Uncle Hal?"

"Of course I do," he answered.

The old negress gave them a cordial welcome, and brought them stools near the half-open door. But in a moment she exclaimed, as if in a kind of panic—"Look, here, Marse Harry, you jes, take dat gun outer dis house. You suppose I'se gwine ter be shot, ef I can help it?"

"Why, Aunt Lucy, I'm not going to shoot you," the young man answered, with a smile.

"I dunno 'bout dat," she said, doubtfully; "ef you don't look out, 'fore long, you'll shoot yourself or somebody else; Marse Harry, you ain't haf 'ticular 'nuff ter suit me."

To please the old negress, he got up and set his gun outside.

Aunt Lucy was an odd-looking little woman, with a turned-up nose, and a little set-back to her head, that gave her an aggressive air. She had a brisk way of stepping around, and was rather hard on those whose movements were more measured. Among the negroes, she was not popular, having the reputation of being very proud, and inclined to interfere with the affairs of other people. It was said that Uncle Reuben was dreadfully henpecked.

"How is Tasso, Aunt Lucy?" asked Lilian, almost before they were seated.

"I knowed dat dog brought you here," the old woman replied, with a hearty chuckle. "Tasso's 'sleep over dere in that corner; Reuben, he gin him somethin' ter put him ter sleep, an' he's dat quiet, you'd never know he'd a leg broke. I reckon he'll git over it. Ef anybody can help him, Reuben can."

"May I go and see him?" asked the child, timidly, for she was a little afraid of Aunt Lucy.

"Course you can, honey," was the reply; and Lilian crept softly to the corner where the dog lay. He was in a low basket, and the splint to which his leg was bound fitted tightly into the bottom of the basket, so that he could not move the wounded limb in the least. He was dozing quietly, and the child turned away, perfectly satisfied that nothing more could be done for him.

While this little scene was taking place, Harry had fallen into easy conversation with the old woman.

"Well, how wags the world with you to-day, Aunt Lucy?" he asked.

"Why, I'se right smart, Marse Harry," she replied, her dusky face illuminated with pleasure at his interest.

"I must say you look pretty comfortable," he continued, surveying the room on all sides. "I wouldn't be ashamed to live in such a house myself." The cabin was very neat, and even possessed some touches of beauty. In one corner, there was a little cupboard, with a few blue cups and saucers displayed upon its shelves; and a bright square of rag carpet lay in the middle of the room. Near the door, was the spinning-wheel with a pair of cards and a pile of cotton rolls lying on the floor. At one end of the cabin, there was an immense fireplace, where a few chunks were slowly smouldering away. A great iron pot suspended from a crane, swung over the fire, and a savory odor escaped from its lid. Aunt Lucy, to whom idleness was odious, soon took up her cards and began to turn off the beautiful rolls, while she talked to her company. Lilian watched her with intense delight, and begged now and then to hold one of the fleecy things in her hands. This amused the old negress very much, and she laughed heartily at the child's innocent interest in what was to her a commonplace employment.

"How good your supper smells, Aunt Lucy!" said Harry, with an appreciative sniff. "Do tell me what you have in that great pot?"

"Why, Marse Harry, dat's only a chicken an' some rice. I'se gwine ter give Reuben some pillau for his supper. Reuben likes dat sometimes for a change. I raises chickens, you know."

"Please invite me to the feast," said the young gentleman; "pillau is my soul's delight."

"De lor'! Marse Harry, as if you'd eat anything in dis house."

"Just try me and see. I'm sure there's enough in that big pot for Uncle Reuben and me too."

The old woman laughed and said, "I s'pose you don't consideh Dinah and Milly,"—referring to her two daughters.

"Oh! that pot holds enough for us all," he replied, gayly, for he dearly loved to joke with the negroes, with all of whom he was a great favorite.

"De lor'! Marse Harry, I isn't got plates fitten fur de quality to eat out'n," she exclaimed with another chuckle.

"Well, I see plainly you are not in a hospitable mood to-day," he said, rising to go.

"No, don't go yit," she pleaded; " I'se hardly got a good look at you an' Miss Lilian."

He sat down again, saying pleasantly, " I declare, Aunt Lucy, you do look immensely comfortable."

"Pshaw," she answered, "you knows well 'nuff dere's allus plenty ter want. I keeps pretty busy a-wantin' all de time,"—and she laughed again.

Her wholesome chuckle formed a kind of running accompaniment to the conversation.

"That's the way with most of us," said Harry; " but what do you want in particular just at this time? It seems to me you are better off than most of the darkies. You've got the best house in the whole Quarter."

"An' not much of a house at dat," returned the old woman in a very dry tone. "Dat chimley it do smoke fitten ter drive a body out o' doors, an' I'se got ter habe a winder dat I can see out'n—not dat plank in dar, but rale glass like dat in de white folks's houses. Why, I has ter work winter well as summer, an' how can a body see wid de door shut in sich a house as dis, an' how can I habe de door open in de winter?—Mought pritty nigh as well live out in de road."

"Well, those are real grievances," said the young man, with a genuine touch of sympathy.

"I reckon dey is," she replied, with emphasis; " besides, Marse Harry," she continued, not having yet finished the list of her wants, "I doesn't hab clo'es 'nuff ter keep an ole critter like me warm in de winter."

"Well, winter is almost over now," said Harry, " in the summer you don't need much."

"He's a-comin' agin, sure," she returned—speaking of winter.

"But you are not old, Aunt Lucy."

"Yes, I is, Marse Harry; I'se nigh on ter fifty."

"I must say you are pretty smart for your age. We heard you spinning as we came up the red lane. Do you really spin on that old shackley wheel?" he asked.

"What else is dere ter spin on?" she answered. "Why, I spins an' weaves nigh 'bout all de clo'es I gits. Reuben, he don't gin me nothin'—he jes buys 'bacco—chaws all de time, Reuben does."

Harry caught sight of a corn-cob pipe on the bench of the wheel, and was bold enough to ask, "Well, don't you smoke, Aunt Lucy?"

"'Course I does," she answered, briskly; "I'se not gwine ter let Reuben chaw an' I not smoke."

"Perhaps if you stop smoking, he will stop chewing," said the young man, enjoying the conversation immensely.

"Now, Marse Harry," exclaimed the old woman emphatically, "you don't know nothin' 'tall 'bout Reuben. He wouldn't stop chawin' ef I stopped eatin'; he'd jes, be glad I'd lef' all de wittles fur him."

The gentleman could not help laughing, and Aunt Lucy joined him most heartily.

"I think I shall have to see Uncle Reuben and give him a lecture; he is evidently in a very bad way."

"Well, Reuben, he likes fur de white folks ter notice him," said the old woman, "but I tells you, Marse Harry, he's a hard case. Eben Brudder Jerry, he can't move Reuben. Reuben he won't eben go ter hear Brudder Jerry pritch. Sometimes I axes him whar he specks he'se gwine when he dies; in de groun' he says, an' dat's all he knows an' cares 'bout de matter. He'll fin' hisself in a part o' de groun' whar it's pritty hot, I'se afeard." The inevitable chuckle followed these remarks.

Seeing that Lilian was no longer playing with the pretty gray kitten, and thinking that she must be tired, Harry now arose to go.

"You mus' come agin ter see me," Aunt Lucy said, as she shook hands with them both and wished them good luck.

The walk home was delightful beyond expression to the little maiden. Harry took her round by the long road, as it was called by the negroes. It skirted the edge of a dense forest on one side, and the broad and now brown cotton fields on the other. The dogs were all the while rushing into the woods and barking furiously at the abundant game. This excited the child beyond measure, and she kept asking her uncle what was the matter with them. At length, a rabbit ran across the road, and before Lilian could cry out, the dreadful gun was fired, and the poor little creature dropped dead. She laid her hand gently on its soft fur, and looked at its beautiful eyes, still wide open; but she said nothing, for she realized that it was now too late to remedy the mischief.

Presently they passed a persimmon tree, and the young man shook down some of the well-dried fruit, of which she was very fond. He even hunted in his pocket for a piece of paper, in which she could wrap up some to carry home to mamma and Aunt Jessie.

They were obliged to cross the little brook, three times, and each time on stepping-stones. She was merry over it all, and did not realize that she was getting tired; but, that evening, after supper, there was no play in the back parlor with Uncle Hal. The little head had grown heavy before the meal was over, and had sunk wearily upon the table. Then Harry had taken her up in his strong arms, and carried her off to the nursery. He even helped to undress her—taking off the little shoes with the gentleness of a woman, and kissing each of the dear little bare feet. When she was snugly tucked into bed he closed the door softly, and went downstairs. That evening, he dozed on the sofa, while Jessie again played the *Songs without Words*.

CHAPTER IV.

"There is no jovial companionship equal to that where the jokes are rather small and the laughter abundant."—W. IRVING.

A FEW weeks later, Mrs. Winston gave a dinner-party to her friends and neighbors. The twenty-second of February was the Colonel's birthday, consequently it had always been duly celebrated by a big "dining," such as the planters of the South delighted in. Now, when Mrs. Winston gave a dinner, the hour was always five o'clock, and a long evening of gayety for the young people followed.

On the afternoon of the twenty-second, the guests began to arrive a little after four, and so rapidly and promptly did they appear that the front parlor was soon filled, and old Oliver, with great solemnity, opened the massive sliding-doors into the back parlor. These rooms were well-furnished for those days, and looked thoroughly comfortable with the beautiful wood fires that were blazing on the generous hearths. It was rather a dark afternoon, threatening rain, but the gloom outside was effectually excluded by the closed blinds, and the heavy crimson damask curtains. Lamp-light and firelight together made a brilliant interior.

The company consisted of eight or ten gentlemen and as many ladies. With the exception of a few of the young men, they were all old and familiar friends. Some were neighbors on adjoining plantations, and some were from the city, which was ten miles distant. The greetings were cordial, and conversation flowed easily. A confused hum of voices, mingled with occasional peals of laughter, filled the rooms. The host and hostess moved here and there among the guests, and exchanged a thousand graceful civilities. In this atmosphere of light, social gayety, they seemed to be breathing their native air; smiles, laughter, gestures, conversation, were all alike delightfully spontaneous. Soon the company began to break up into groups, standing under the chandeliers and around the tables. Colonel Winston became the centre of a party of gentlemen, all of whom were in a most genial mood. There was something really boyish in their bantering tones and hearty laughter. One of the number was a gentleman of striking appearance; he was tall and finely formed, with a massive, statesman-like head adorned with long gray hair. His manners were easy and dignified, with now and then a touch of playfulness. This was Judge Brooks, a friend from the neighboring city. The other gentlemen were less notable. Major Allison was a large but unsuccessful planter. Dr. Crump was the leading physician of the county. The Rev. Mr. Hunter was the rector of a fashionable city church which Mrs. Winston and the Colonel sometimes managed to attend.

"Well, Major," said the host, "it seems an age since I have seen you. We are immensely glad to have you with us again. How did you find the roads?"

"It took us just two hours and a half to drive ten miles—think of that."

"Ah! the roads must be rather bad, then," said Mr. Hunter.

"Perfectly abominable! A disgrace to the state.

But it is only one of the abominations of this abominable age in which we live."

Every one laughed at the Major's emphatic manner. He was known far and wide as an incorrigible pessimist.

"Well, who is responsible?" asked some one.

"Who is responsible for anything nowadays!" exclaimed the Major, with a touch of scorn; "that is more than I can tell, I'm sure. With free niggers on one side, and ruined Southerners on the other, everything that ought to claim attention is let alone. Where the general let-alone system is going to land us, I'm sure I don't know."

"So you don't like these degenerate times, Major?" said the Judge in his calm, smooth tones.

"Like it?" cried the Major, his delicate nostrils quivering with indignation, "who does like it, I want to know? Things were different when I was young. I'd like to go back to those days."

"Most of us would like the fun of being young again," replied Judge Brooks, smiling pleasantly and glancing at the other gentlemen.

"Well," said the Major, still hot and flurried, "you people of the city, professional men, lawyers and doctors, don't feel the full weight of these hard times; but we planters do. We are simply ruined." It had always been hard times with the Major, who had an extravagant wife and several daughters who were following in their mother's footsteps.

"But are you not getting used to being ruined?." asked the Judge. "You have been singing that old song ever since I first knew you. The tightest shoe becomes comfortable after it has been worn a long while."

" That depends upon the foot," said the Major with a laugh. " Now my foot is too old, and too full of corns for a tight shoe ever to become comfortable ; and just so, I'm too old and crotchety ever to get used to being poor, and I seem to be coming to that very fast. I don't know how to wait on myself, even if I wanted to."

The Major had the floor, and continued to pour out a dismal story of his trials and troubles. Judge Brooks presently joined a group of young girls who were clustered around a center-table in the back parlor.

" Well, what are the pretty magpies chattering about now ? " he asked, embracing them all in his kindly smile.

" Spring dresses, of course," answered Miss Nettie Hunter, a *petite* and pretty blonde. She was the only daughter of the clergyman ; but in spite of the spiritual atmosphere in which her life had been spent it must be confessed that she was somewhat worldly and strongly imbued with vanity and coquetry. " You have a judicial mind, Judge Brooks ; can you not help us in our decisions ? " she asked.

" As if you needed any help on a subject which you have all mastered long ago," he replied ; " why, I feel so ignorant in your presence that I cannot even listen intelligently. You speak in an unknown tongue."

" How I pity a person who has never experienced the delights of shopping," exclaimed Miss Bessie Allison, a dark-eyed girl who, although not pretty, was exceedingly well-dressed.

" And who never felt the sweet consciousness of looking like a bit of rainbow, fallen down to the earth," said Miss Nettie Hunter.

" Poor fellow !" cried the doctor's young and beautiful wife, whose toilette was always a marvel of style and color.

"Don't pity me too much," replied the Judge, laughing; "I can at least admire the bits of rainbow when I see them floating along our streets."

"Do tell me," said Miss Nettie, "what is your favorite color, for I am very anxious to please you."

"That you always do, my dear," he answered. "I don't think it depends in the least on the dress you wear. A simple maiden in her prime is lovely in any dress."

"But," persisted Miss Nettie, with a coquettish turn of her head, and a saucy smile, "I'm not a simple maiden—most people consider me a very affected one; and I'm not in my prime either—I'm over twenty—that's *passée* isn't it? So I insist upon knowing your favorite color."

The Judge looked at her with an amused twinkle in his gray eyes. "My preference changes like a woman's moods," he answered in his bland tones; "now it is blue, now it is red, now it is yellow, and now it is all seven colors combined. Everything depends upon the person who wears it."

"You do not assist us in the least," exclaimed Miss Bessie Allison.

"On the contrary, you add to our perplexity," said Miss Hunter; "it is just like a lawyer to make confusion doubly confused."

"There, I shall have to retreat in order to preserve my reputation for wisdom," he replied, with a smile. At that moment, a young gentleman approached the table, and Judge Brooks resigned his place. "Here, Mr. Miller," he said, "cannot you aid these fair ones? If you have an eye for color, now is the time to prove it."

Mr. Miller was a slender youth, with a large mouth

and a faint mustache, but his soul was gallant, and he slipped with delight into the place vacated by the Judge, and the chatter went on. Soon other gentlemen joined the group, and they became almost noisy in their merriment.

As Judge Brooks turned away, he noticed a lady and gentleman seated alone, near a distant window, partially concealed by the heavy curtains. They seemed so absorbed in their *tête-à-tête* that they were entirely oblivious of the presence of others. A shadow passed over the Judge's face as he recognized his niece and Harry Holcombe. He felt very much like interrupting their conversation, but he did not. He went to a distant corner, sat down beside a table littered with newspapers and magazines and began to turn them over mechanically. Presently he got up and went into the next room, again seating himself in an easy-chair apart from the other guests. He was evidently waiting for some one; occasionally, he looked through the open door into the hall; he was watching the staircase, and listening for a light footstep. The signal for passing into the dining-room had been given, and the company were moving onward in pairs, when Judge Brooks caught the sound for which he had been listening. A young girl in white descended the staircase; he stepped into the hall to meet her, and gave her his arm with the greeting —"The *late* Miss Jessie Holcombe."

"Don't speak of it," she said, shaking her head; "I'm very sorry, but really it was not my fault. Eleanor would have me arrange my hair in this way, and Lizzie fussed and fussed over it. I could not get away from her. She declared before I came down that I looked like a perfect fright. Do I?" she asked, looking up into his face with the innocence of a little child.

"A dreadful fright!" answered the gentleman soberly, standing off at a little distance and surveying the crimps and curls, which in truth he thought amazingly becoming. "If I were not a very brave man, I would turn my back and run away."

"Now I know you are jesting," she said, breaking into a little laugh; "I thank you ever so much for waiting for me. On your arm, I shall be able to face the crowd without any sense of shame,"—and she smiled up at him as a daughter might have smiled upon her father. They moved on into the dining-room, where the guests were now seating themselves around a table, heaped with fruits and flowers, and sparkling with glass and silver. Miss Holcombe nodded her greetings to each friend, and found her place; she was glad it was beside the Judge.

There was a little silence while the napkins were unfolded, and then the ladies began a conversation about the flowers. In the center of the table there was a great vase filled with the choicest roses; at a little distance from this, there were slender antique pitchers of silver from which sprung creamy hyacinths with ferns and ribbon grasses waving among them; at the corners of the table, in low glass dishes, were heaps of English violets. Each lady was eager to say something about her conservatory or pit, and to tell about her own particular method of managing bulbs and slips.

When the hum of voices somewhat subsided, Major Allison, whose seat was some distance from the Colonel, called out in his high, harsh tone,—"How do you like your new overseer, Colonel?"

"Oh! he's a right good fellow," was the reply; "but he has departed this life."

"What! dead!" cried a chorus of voices.

"Yes, dead to us," said the Colonel, with a touch of

mock solemnity. "He died of disgust of free niggers and cotton. I only engaged him for a year on trial, and his time was up a few weeks ago. Neither of us wished to renew the engagement. He's gone back where he came from. The truth is, he did not know anything about planting cotton, or managing the hands. He is a city fellow. I believe most of his life has been spent behind a counter, measuring calico. Why under the heaven he wanted to turn overseer, I cannot guess. His talents certainly do not lie in that direction. In fact, he is made of superfine clay—has nice white hands and little feet. My wife thinks him a very superior young man." Here the Colonel laughed.

Mrs. Winston answered with some warmth, "Indeed I do; Mr. Griffin is not only well-bred and well-educated, but he has the best heart in the world."

"You see," continued the Colonel in a jocular tone, "he used to cater for my wife—ride around the plantation, and buy up eggs and chickens and such things, and go off to the city for her whenever she wanted a lemon or a nutmeg. In return, she used to overwhelm him with delicate attentions. Of course, he thought her an angel. Don't you think it was time for me to send him off?"

"What! because he thought your wife an angel!" exclaimed the Judge; "then, you'll have to send a few more of us off. All the ladies are angels, are they not? That used to be the good old orthodox opinion."

"You must put that question to our reverend friend," Colonel Winston replied, waving his hand towards the clergyman; "he knows more about heavenly things than a miserable sinner like me." Mr. Hunter smiled and held his peace.

"Silence gives consent," said the Judge; "it must be so, since the clergy maintain it."

"Are you not getting too old to talk nonsense?" asked Miss Holcombe, looking up at Judge Brooks with an amused expression. "You set a bad example to us who are younger."

"Of course, I'm too old to talk nonsense if you say so, my dear; but it is all on account of being seated near you. When I'm classified with the young, I'm young too, and commit all the follies of youth; when I'm classified with the aged, I'm a very oracle of wisdom."

The young lady made a little motion of rising. "Well, to save you from further folly, perhaps I had better vacate my seat in favor of some one older."

"A thousand times *no!*" he exclaimed, laying his hand upon her arm; "as if all the wisdom of all the sages could weigh in the balance with one moment of delicious, nonsensical youth! My dear, I've been hard at work all day—I've been a very owl for wise looks and wise words; do allow me to be as foolish as I please to-night."

"Indeed you shall!" cried Miss Hunter across the table. "When we return to the drawing-room, you shall have a seat upon the sofa, and we angels will hover around you and whisper and giggle after our usual angelic fashion, and you shall drink the very dregs of folly, if you wish."

"By proposing to all of you at once?" he asked.

"If you like," she answered, gayly; "but being the eldest, I shall take precedence, and be the first to consider and reply to your proposal."

"But you would have to reject me, because you are already engaged."

"Temporarily!" she replied with a laugh—"until a better fellow presents himself. You know perfectly well that you are considered the greatest catch in the city."

"Gracious heavens! is that the way the angels speak of me!" and he clasped his hands and raised his eyes to the ceiling.

"Never mind," said Miss Holcombe, "you know there is no danger unless you yourself take the first step in folly."

"My dear," he replied with mock gravity, "with pitfalls everywhere, I shall be afraid to take any step at all. My only safety is in standing still. To a man of my temperament, that is very tiresome."

"Miss Nettie," said Colonel Winston, "I cannot allow you and my venerable friend to flirt across the table. There must be some sacred spot on this green earth where flirting is not permitted, and I hold out for the dinner-table."

"I suppose you would reserve that sacred spot exclusively for politics," said Miss Hunter with a light laugh.

"Yes, Miss Nettie, you are right as usual," the Colonel answered. "There is nothing quite equal to politics for making a man enjoy the delights of a good dinner, nor for helping him to forget the weak points of a bad one. A man gets so warmed up that he could swallow and digest cobble-stones."

"Well, Colonel," exclaimed Mrs. Allison, a large, showily-dressed lady, "I think that politics are perfectly odious. It was politics that brought on the war, and the war has ruined us all."

"Saved us, you mean," said the Judge in his calm, emphatic manner.

Judge Brooks was a broad-minded man, and was known to hold heretical views on many subjects, but the present company were scarcely prepared for such an utterance as this. Every eye was turned upon him with surprise and inquiry.

"Yes," he continued with a pleasant smile, "I mean exactly what I have said—the war has saved us. We were in a very bad way before the war and now I really see signs of improvement."

"*Par example?*" said the Colonel, in an interrogative tone. "Explain yourself, my dear Judge or our good friends will take up the idea that you are deranged, or worse still, a dotard."

"Well, things are bad enough now," replied the Judge, "but there are signs of improvement all around us. As a nation we have been aroused from our bed of roses, and forced to take part in the struggle for existence. Our young men and our fair maidens are beginning to feel the dignity of labor. The discipline is severe, but the result will be fine."

"And a whole nation must be ruined that a few dandies and dollies may grow sensible," exclaimed the Colonel, impatiently. "Is that your meaning?"

"Not exactly," said the Judge with his genial smile which always seemed to extract the bitterness from opposition; "the ruin you speak of is material, and every day we are moving on slowly towards recovery. The good I speak of is the moral good which always comes to a nation from a life-and-death struggle such as ours has been."

"Moral good, indeed!" cried Major Allison, who was growing somewhat excited. "So far as I can see, there is only moral evil from it."

"Everything depends on our point of view, Major," said Mr. Hunter.

"Well, I confess mine's in a fog," replied the Major, trying to laugh with good-humor.

"Perhaps the fog will lift after a while," said the hostess.

"No, madam," he exclaimed with deep feeling. "I'm sorry to disagree with you on any subject, but my fog gets thicker and thicker every day. Sometimes, when I think of the condition of our country, I'm actually sorry that I was ever born."

"Oh! Major Allison, how can you feel so!" exclaimed Jessie Holcombe, her eyes flashing with intense emotion. "If there is one thing for which I feel thankful, it is to be living at this very time—neither sooner nor later, but right now."

"Miss Jessie, you astonish me," said the Major. "What can you mean? How can a lovely girl like war and bloodshed and anarchy?"

"I do not like bloodshed and anarchy," she replied, still aglow with fine feeling, "but I do admire heroism, both active and passive. I am glad to be in the world at a time when noble passions are aroused, and great deeds are done."

"Now, Jessie has mounted Pegasus," whispered Miss Hunter to Dr. Crump who was seated beside her.

The gentleman adjusted his eyeglasses, and turned them on Jessie for a moment, then in a low tone he replied, "It must be confessed she looks remarkably well on horseback."

"Miss Holcombe is right," said Judge Brooks; "in times of peace, a nation has no history. We have been making a chapter of history."

"Say rather a folio volume!" exclaimed the clergyman.

"If our enemies write it, I'm afraid we shall not figure in it as heroes, but as very sorry knaves," said Harry Holcombe, who up to this point had been too much occupied with his fair neighbor, Miss Alice Brooks, to pay much attention to the general conversation.

"We must leave that for posterity to settle," replied Mr. Hunter. "A modern historian has said that there never was a dispute between two parties, in which all the right was on one side and all the wrong on the other."

"Right or wrong, we made a gallant fight, and some good will come out of it," remarked Harry Holcombe.

"That is true," said the Judge; "heroic effort is never wasted. Wherever there has been the spirit of manly struggle and sacrifice, there has been some good from it. Patriotism, courage, self-devotion are worth more to a nation than gold or silver, or factories, or ships, or anything else. Our Southern land has been plowed up from end to end, and planted with a new seed for a new harvest—finer far than cotton, Colonel."

As he spoke these words, Jessie Holcombe looked up at him with delighted approval in her dark eyes.

"Yes," said Mr. Hunter in a quiet, impressive tone, "I am beginning to see that the war has done a great work for the South. I believe the future will prove that defeat was better for us than victory would have been."

"He raves!" cried the Colonel; "put blisters behind his ears."

There was general laughter at this remark, and the discussion ended. Soon the hostess arose from the table; all followed her example, and passed with her into the drawing-rooms. There they again scattered into groups, talking and laughing with charming abandon.

The young girls gathered around the Judge. "We are going to execute our threat," said Miss Hunter. "You must come with us."

He looked down upon them with an expression of great amusement in his eyes, saying, "I have no thought of resistance. What are you going to do with me?"

"We have not yet decided," was the answer, "but you can surely trust yourself with the angels."

As they were moving off with him, he turned and saw that Jessie was not with them; she was standing near the door, talking with several gentlemen.

"Miss Holcombe," he cried, "do you not intend to join us?" The young lady thus addressed, smiled and shook her head.

"Leave Jessie alone," said Miss Nettie Hunter; "the division will be long enough without her. She thinks her share would be too small to be worth accepting."

"But I do not like a single one of the divine creatures to turn her back upon me," replied the Judge. He looked again at Jessie, but she was unmoved by the mute entreaty of his face, and went on with her conversation. It was easy to see that her presence would have made his captivity sweet.

"Well, what are you going to do with me?" he again asked helplessly, as they marched him into the back-parlor.

"We will allow you, perhaps, to decide your own fate," answered Miss Bessie Allison.

"That would not be at all wise," he said.

"Why?" demanded Emma Allison, who was very young and very pretty.

"If a prisoner is allowed to decide his own fate, he invariably pleads for release."

"You need not think for a moment that we will listen to any such pleas as that," said Miss Clara Stevens.

"No, indeed!" exclaimed Nettie Hunter. "You are an exceedingly wise old bird, but at last you have been caught with chaff, and now you need not imagine that you can get away."

He joined their laughter, saying, "I'm curious to see what you are going to do with the old bird, now he is caught."

"Let me see," said Miss Nettie, with a reflective turn of her pretty head; "he has so often laughed at our snares and broken our nets, that he deserves a dreadful fate, but we will not be too severe. Your sentence is to dance with each one of us in an endless succession."

"Mercy! Mercy!" cried the Judge; "I do not know how to dance."

"Then we will teach you."

"But I have no capacity for learning," he urged.

"We will lend you a little of ours," they replied in chorus.

"But it is too soon after dinner; such exercise would be bad for my health."

"You are a clever pleader," said Miss Nettie; "but your sophistries are unavailing; you shall not be released this time. If you cannot dance, you shall play a game of cards with us."

"But I detest cards!" he exclaimed.

"Surely not, with such angelic partners," said Miss Bessie Allison.

"Yes," he answered, "even with such angelic partners. To play cards will demand some concentration of thought. How can I concentrate myself upon anything with so many fair women around me? I shall be as distracted as a bee in a flower-garden."

"Then we'll win the game and you'll pay the stakes," said Miss Bessie.

"And what are you going to stake?" he asked; "my poor worthless life?"

"By no means," was the reply. "We will play for candy—the very best that can be bought in the city."

"Very well," he answered. "I'll agree to it."

The card-table was soon brought out and the game went on merrily. Whether by luck or by design, the Judge lost all the time, and the girls scolded him for his bad playing, and congratulated themselves on the heaps of *bonbons* they were winning. Finally, when the gentleman declared himself a miserable bankrupt on the verge of suicide, the merry creatures allowed him to stop. Then they called on Miss Holcombe for some music, and insisted that he should take a turn in the waltz with each one of them. He was too polite and good-natured to rebel, and though his movements were so ungraceful that they called him a dancing bear, he performed his part to the end. At length, Miss Hunter released him from his bondage, with the words, "Now, I hope, I have impressed upon you the danger to which you expose yourself when you jest with our good names, and mockingly call us angels."

He bowed gracefully, and replied, "Rest assured I shall never offend again. I am thoroughly convinced of my error, and am deeply repentant."

Every one laughed, even the young ladies against whom the remark was aimed. "Judge Brooks, you have a tongue which no woman can ever hope to tie," exclaimed Miss Hunter. "It is the only thing in the world that I'm really afraid of."

"Well, my dear," said her father, who was near enough to hear the remark, "I'm sincerely glad that there is one thing of which you have a little wholesome awe. It makes one feel that you are not quite beyond hope."

When the Judge was released, Miss Holcombe, was still at the piano. "I am quite exhausted," he said in a low tone; "do play something slow, and sweet, and soothing to rest me."

. Jessie smiled, and began "The Whispering Wind," but Nettie Hunter came up immediately with the exclamation, "Do stop that, Jessie, and give us something lively. You know I don't like anything but dance music. That piece you are playing now is worse than a schoolgirl's scales."

"You should not speak so irreverently of what you do not understand," said the Judge.

"I know well enough that I do not understand it," she answered, gayly, "but it's the music that's to blame, not myself—I'm all right." This speech and the bewitching little air with which it was spoken, was received with peals of laughter; but the imperious creature could not have her way now. Judge Brooks told her that Miss Holcombe was playing for him, and he could not allow any one to interfere with her selection.

"When this is finished, you shall have something gay," said Jessie; "I feel in a very amiable mood tonight, and will strive to suit the taste of each one of my friends by turn."

Perhaps she enjoyed her position at the piano, because it gave her an occasional view of a lady and gentleman who were slowly promenading up and down the long hall. From the expression of the lady's face, Jessie knew that her brother was making good use of his opportunities.

"Well, when you are ready, please give us a waltz," replied Nettie, "for we are going to dance again. Now, we have got rid of the bear, we are going to have some real fun," and she looked at the Judge with a mocking little gesture. He smiled, but made no response. "Mrs. Winston," she cried, "may we dance in the hall?"

"Of course you may," the lady answered. "Call

Oliver to remove anything that is in the way."

"A thousand thanks," she said, and flitted into the next room. The dancing went on with slight pauses until almost midnight. Judge Brooks sat beside Miss Holcombe, and kept up a pleasant conversation with her while she played the lively music, whispering pretty compliments about her hands and arms, and commenting upon the changing expression of the shadow she cast upon the wall. Several persons tried to tempt him away from his post, but his reply was always the same, " Miss Holcombe is making a martyr of herself, playing the whole evening for our entertainment, and I feel as if it were my duty to stand at her elbow and encourage her." Every now and then he got a smile from the beautiful pianist which would have repaid any man for a much more disagreeable task.

It is a law in this world that everything shall pass away, and so this delightful evening had an end.

CHAPTER V.

March had now come, and winter seemed ready and willing to yield his throne to spring. It had been raining all day—a warm rain that had descended gently as if afraid of hurting the tender young things that were beginning to peep up out of the ground. When evening came, and the curtains were drawn, there was something restful in the monotonous patter outside.

Colonel Winston and his wife were alone in the library. A large fire was burning on the hearth and it gave a cheerful air to a room otherwise shabby, solemn, and sombre. The lady and gentleman were seated on opposite sides of a center table, on which stood a large lamp with a soft shade over it. The table was loaded with books and newspapers, but neither of them seemed inclined to read; they sat silently gazing into the fire, absorbed in thought. He was lying back in an easy-chair with his feet upon a hassock, smoking the end of a cigar. When at length it became so short as to endanger his fingers, he tossed it into the fire, arose from his seat, and taking a match from the mantel, lighted another. His heavy black brows, together with several sharp vertical wrinkles between the eyes, gave him a very disagreeable look. He was evidently in a bad humor. Something was radically wrong about him—whether it was his liver, that potent source of ill-temper, or not remains to be seen.

Mrs. Winston was as calm and colorless as usual. She was far from being beautiful, but there was something striking about her face from its breadth of brow and the expression of firmness about the mouth. Her hair was still sunny brown without a strand of silver; it waved back from the forehead and was knotted rather too low for the fashion of those days. She was smaller than her sister, but there was a strong family resemblance between them. It was more in manner than in face; there was about them both a certain quiet dignity which repelled familiarity and commanded respect. To-night she had left the nursery, where she usually spent her evenings in reading, and had descended to the library, a room which she did not often invade at this hour. That she had a purpose in view was evident to her husband, but he seemed determined not to give her any assistance in making known her wishes, whatever they were. They were both so silent that one might have fancied some spell had been laid upon them.

Mrs. Winston always found it hard to speak with her husband on matters of business, because he repelled her curiosity and ignored her advice. Like many women she had been content for a long time to remain in profound ignorance, believing that all was well; but of late she had begun to have some suspicion that the Colonel's affairs were getting into a tangle, and she realized her right to inquire into the matter. She knew that he had managed badly since the war, but she could not guess the extent of his difficulties.

"Francis," she said, as he threw away the end of his second cigar, "I do wish you would not smoke so much. I think it makes you very nervous."

"That's all you know about it," he answered, sharply; "I don't smoke half-a-dozen cigars during the day. I cannot afford to smoke any more, even if I wanted to."

"Well, then, what is the matter with you, of late?

Do you know you are getting almost unbearable in your family? You slam the doors and kick the dogs, and scold the servants. It seems to be growing worse every day. Only this morning, Oliver told me that he did not think he could stand it much longer."

"Then let him clear out, immediately," exclaimed the Colonel, fiercely.

"But he is invaluable to me—I cannot spare him. He is the best servant I have ever had in my life."

"He used to be, but, like all the rest of them, he has been utterly ruined by freedom."

"I don't agree with you; he has some self-respect, and objects to being treated like a boy. If he left us, I am sure we could never supply his place."

"I wish to heaven the whole kit and cargo of them would leave! They are a dead weight upon the South."

"You don't know what you are saying, Francis; your words are as unreasonable as your conduct. We could never get along without them."

"I say we could!" he exclaimed in loud, impatient tones. "I'd like to pitch every one of them into the Atlantic Ocean, and all the good-for-nothing white folks too. The South needs workers now more than ever before—not idle, lounging, drinking, sporting gentlemen."

"I know you refer to Harry," she replied, very gently. "I can see that he annoys you by his carelessness, but you ought to be able to make excuses for him; he had very bad influences thrown around him during his early youth. He has a good heart, and I hope some day he will prove himself a man. Certainly he has been behaving very well of late."

"Yes, but how much longer will it last? You can never be sure of him; by the time you begin to think him a good fellow, he is off on another spree."

"Well, I do not think you are very wise in scolding him so much as you do. You can never hope to influence him, in that way."

"Hope to influence him!" exclaimed the Colonel. "I would as soon hope to influence the moon and stars. He seems a sorry case to me. If he only manages not to disgrace the family, I shall be thankful."

"You are not quite just to Harry," said Mrs. Winston. "I believe if he had some congenial occupation, he would do as well as most of men."

"Then why don't he find one? He is not lacking in brains."

"You forget that he has never been trained to do any thing, and is now completely at a loss. If you were without property, I daresay you would find it hard to know what to do for a living. I wish that you were generous enough to help Harry in the right way."

This remark evoked no answer, so she continued: "Francis, I cannot believe that Harry's carelessness would annoy you so, if there was not something else at the bottom of it. I am sure you are in want of money."

"Then if you are so sure, why do you bother to ask?" he said, impatiently.

"Because I may be able to help you, if you will really tell me the whole truth about your affairs."

He thought in a moment about the small fortune settled upon her at marriage, and which, being securely invested, had not suffered from the war. This made him ready to confess his difficulties. But the proud man could not sit still while the tale was told—he arose from his seat and began to pace the floor. "Well, then," he said, "I don't know how under the sun I'm going to run this plantation another year. Cotton is so low that it is ruinous to raise it with free labor. I am at my wits' end, and feel like throwing up the whole thing."

"Sell part of the plantation," she said. "It is altogether too large for you to manage alone, and you cannot find an overseer to suit you. No reasonable man needs five thousand acres of land. I am sure you would make more money, if you did not plant on such an extensive scale."

"You need not give me any such advice," he replied. "I shall never sell a single acre of this plantation. I will not part with my birthright. I will not become a miserable little farmer, holding a garden patch for a living."

"Then borrow money from your factor," she suggested.

It angered him to see that she had no idea of placing her own small fortune in his hands. His voice was loud and sharp as he said, "That's all you know about business affairs. I should think you would have better sense than to give me that advice. I already owe him more than I shall ever be able to pay. Besides, he is a rascally fellow. I would like to give him a kick this very minute. He has grown rich on his loans. He is not much better than a common swindler." The Colonel grabbed another cigar from the mantelpiece, lighted it, and threw himself into an easy-chair.

It was some time before she suggested anything else, but at length she said, "Well, why don't you borrow from Judge Brooks? He has plenty of money, and would be willing to lend you some if he knew you needed it. He has the kindest and most generous soul of any man I ever met."

"Such an idea is utterly humiliating to me," replied the Colonel. "I do not think that I could possibly bend myself so low. Judge Brooks and I have always been friends. No word or thought of money has ever come between us. I cannot bear to have our friendship poisoned by business relations. Let me keep the few friends I have, as long as I live."

Eleanor Winston was proud herself, and she could understand the feelings of her husband. In money matters it is better to apply to strangers than to friends. It is a strong tie that can stand that strain. The situation was indeed perplexing, and she gazed in vain into the fire for some kindly inspiration. Suddenly she looked up and said, "Francis, why don't you write to Philip, and frankly tell him about your difficulties? He is rich now."

The Colonel smoked on in silence as if he had not heard the words of his wife; he tapped the ashes from the end of his cigar into the bronze dish which was meant to receive them; he stroked his beard again and again; he ran his hand through his scanty hair. Perhaps, he was ruminating on this new idea with the intention of accepting it; perhaps, it was too odious for him to find any expression for his feelings. Finally he said with an effort, "I have thought of that myself more than once, but it would be awfully hard for me to beg from Philip. I don't exactly know why I should feel so, for I have done enough for him in the past to have some claim upon him now; but the truth is, I can never think of him as rich and prosperous—he used to be such a spendthrift."

"Yes," said Mrs. Winston, "but the war changed him. He was different when he came out of it. Do write to him immediately and tell him all about your difficulties. As you say, you have done enough for him in the past; he ought to be willing to make some return now that fortune's wheel has carried him to the top."

Mr. Philip Winston was a brother of the Colonel. He was much younger, being the son of a second wife. In his youth he had been very wild and worthless. At the close of the war, he went west, settling in one of those large cities on the Northern Lakes. Here he soon found scope for his energy and talents, both of which he had hitherto recklessly squandered. In the course of a few years, he made a large fortune. He was unmarried, and had no nearer relative on earth than the Colonel. Occasionally, the brothers had exchanged letters which were always frank and affectionate. The younger spoke freely to the elder of his prosperous condition; he even boasted of the brilliant social position that he had earned for himself. The thought of Philip's success was far from agreeable to the Colonel, when he remembered his own losses. He was too proud and sensitive not to feel the humiliation of applying for help to one whom he had been accustomed to regard as an inferior. Yet as he revolved the idea in his mind, to-night, the expression of his face slowly changed. The wrinkles on his brow were smoothed out, and he began to talk about his boyhood, and the many scrapes out of which he had assisted his brother. It did him good to go back and review the gay scenes of his youth.

It was late—the clock was striking eleven—before Mrs. Winston left her husband, and ascended the stairs to her own room.

After she was gone, he seated himself at his desk, drew a sheet of paper in front of him, took up a pen, and dipped it in the ink-bottle. Then he paused a moment. Soon he flung the pen aside, and springing up, began to walk the floor.

"Confound it!" he exclaimed, "to be reduced to this beggarly strait! I don't believe I can do it after all. I wish to goodness there was some other way. The truth is, I don't know how to work, and I don't know how to beg." After pacing back and forward for a full half-hour, he again sat down at his desk, and dashed off a hurried letter. Then he sealed and addressed it. The next morning it was sent.

CHAPTER VI.

"There is no use in trying to sew or read either," said Jessie, folding the tiny garment on which she had been at work, and laying it in her dainty work-basket; then she transferred a book which had been lying upon her lap, to a convenient chair, arose from her seat, and began to pace slowly up and down the piazza. Every now and then she drew a long breath of delight. The afternoon was mild and spring-like, and she felt the charm of earth and sky. "The day is too beautiful for anything but idle enjoyment," she continued, speaking aloud to herself, as she moved hither and thither; "they talk about the languor that comes with spring weather—I have never experienced it; on the contrary, the spring always makes me restless—I feel just as the birds of passage must feel,—a wild longing to soar away somewhere to other lands. The current of life in my veins seems swifter and stronger, impelling me to greater activity. Oh! for a fuller and richer existence than this!"—and she panted as if for more air.

Soon she descended the steps of the piazza, and went out into the yard, looking carefully at the trees and shrubs for signs of reviving life, noting with a throb of pleasure the up-springing crocuses and daffodils, and the swelling buds upon the rose-bushes. She stopped and gathered a handful of violets, pressed them to her lips, and then fastened them on her bosom. Yes, the great heart of Nature had begun to throb anew—the sap was once more ascending to form the leaves and flowers, and her young soul felt a strange thrill of delight, as she thought of the beautiful possibilities of the future. Suddenly she heard the tramp of horses in the distance, and saw a phaeton coming up the avenue. It was drawn by dark gray horses—she knew them well. The Judge was coming for a call upon his friend, the Colonel. Jessie thought immediately of some urgent business with her brother-in-law. She stood and watched the approach of the carriage with the interest which is usually given to a visitor in the country. When the horses stopped, and the Judge alighted, she went forward and gave him a cordial greeting. There was something joyous in her light movements, and a flush of pleasure was on her face. She conducted her guest into the house, leading the way into the library, which looked more quiet, dusky, and glum than usual after the bright warm sunshine outside. Only the friends of the Colonel were received in this room; believing, as she did, that the call was for him, she had dared to enter his sanctum. As soon as her companion was seated, and she had opened a window to admit a little more light and air, she turned to him and said, "Now do excuse me, and I will go and see if I can find the Colonel."

"Pray don't trouble yourself," replied the visitor. "I know he is not at home; I met him on the road several miles from here, and had a little chat with him. My call to-day is not on the Colonel, nor on his wife. I have come on purpose to see you, and am very happy to find you alone. I scarcely expected such good fortune."

"What an honor!" she exclaimed. "I am overwhelmed! You must have something very important to say to me."

He smiled upon her in his usual gracious way, and rising from the seat he had taken, he led her to a sofa where they sat down side by side.

"Yes," he answered, "you are right; I have something very important to say to you—quite awful in fact." She was too familiar with his playful manner to be alarmed by such an assertion. "But first let us talk a little about the weather. What a charming day it is! One would think that a May day had gotten lost and turned up here in March. The spring makes me feel quite young again. I really could not endure the city. I had to come out into the open country, where I could get the smell of the fresh earth and the odor of bonfires. My drive of ten miles has been one long draught of delicious enjoyment."

"Yes," said the girl, quickly, "I understand it exactly. All day I have so longed for a ride on horseback, but Eleanor is not willing for me to go alone, and Harry went off hunting early this morning, and has not yet returned."

"How would you like a drive in the carriage with me?" he asked.

"Ever so much!" she answered with a gasp of delight. "Are you really in earnest? How good you are!"

"Yes, to myself," he said with a tender smile. "But, first, let me dispatch my business—we will ride afterwards. I could not talk and attend to the horses, too, and my man, Jim, would be *de trop*."

"Well, do hurry," she exclaimed, impatiently. "What can it be? Have you a message from Alice? Does she want me to come and stay with her?"

"No, not that. I have not seen Alice for several weeks. Guess again."

"I cannot guess—please be good and tell me at once, for I long to be out of this solemn place. I think the Colonel leaves at least half of himself in this room even when he goes out of it. Don't you feel his personality a little?"

"Yes, it is rather stuffy; perhaps, if the windows were all opened, the air would be better."

"Now, you are laughing at me as you always do. I cannot say that I am enjoying your call very much. You are more provoking than usual."

"Am I? That's a great pity, for I was trying to be particularly agreeable."

"Then for once you are a hopeless failure."

"Don't say that please," he exclaimed.

"If you wish me to retract my words, you must tell me immediately what important business you have with me. Has there been a dreadful failure? and is my poor little fortune lost?"

"Not that either," he said, very solemnly, "guess again."

"No, I will not make another single effort. If you do not hurry and tell me, I shall run off, put on my hat, and get Jim to take me to ride. How beautiful those gray horses are!" and she glanced longingly out of the window, and heaved a little sigh.

"No, you cannot escape; for the present you are my prisoner—I am between you and the door, and could easily arrest you."

"Well, I am at least sure that you are the bearer of some message from somebody. Perhaps Nettie Hunter is going to give a party? Is that it?" she asked, eagerly.

"No; your wits are dull to-day."

"They always are."

"I deny that," he said with a grave smile. Then there was silence for a few moments, while she looked out of the window in a composed way, as if quite determined to await his pleasure. Soon he moved a little closer to her and spoke. "Jessie," his levity was all gone now; there was something solemn and tender in his manner; "I do not know how to say it to you without making myself very ridiculous, perhaps; but the truth is, I like you very much. Is it possible you have never guessed my secret?" She had a dim perception of what he meant, and her face became very white and cold. She did not answer and the gentleman continued, "Don't let me frighten you, Jessie; I know you consider me a very old man—quite old enough to die, and you have treated me always with a charming innocent, confiding sweetness which would be becoming in a great, great grand-daughter; but, in your presence, I often find my old heart beating in a very youthful way. My darling, I want you to come to my home, and live with me always." She was trembling violently, and her eyes had a terrified look as she raised them to his. She could not speak—the words died on her lips. She had often heard the girls jest about the Judge, and call him a great catch, but their chatter had made no impression upon her. She knew that he was a widower and very rich, living in a handsome home in the city over which no mistress presided. His duties as guardian of his niece often brought him to a neighboring plantation, owned by the widow of his brother. His fondness for this niece was known to every one, and it was said that he desired to bring about a marriage between her and his only child, a young man at present travelling in

Europe. These thoughts now came to Jessie, together with the idea of his being full of years and honors. In the confusion of her mind, every item she had ever heard of him combined to produce a vague feeling of remoteness. She seemed entirely outside the world in which he moved; did he indeed wish her to enter it, and henceforth become its central figure? The idea was incredible, and she simply refused to accept it.

"I'm afraid I do not understand you," she said, fixing her large eyes upon him. "I can easily believe that you like me, and enjoy the banter we always indulge in, when together, but——" and her voice died away in a faint and unintelligible whisper.

"Jessie," he answered in his low, calm tones, "I want you to be my wife—surely you can understand that. Does it, indeed, seem so incredible that I should dare to love you?—an old man like me? My darling child, old as I am, I still have something to offer you—a heart full of tenderness and love. Despite the difference in years, we seem suited to each other. You know we always enjoy being together: the companionship is just as sweet as if I were many years younger. Jessie, I can give you many things that you are made to enjoy—I can place you in a world of beauty where every wish of yours shall be gratified. Come, my darling, say that you will consent to be my wife."

Again she looked up at him with that frightened expression in her eyes. "I cannot," she gasped; "I cannot marry any one. I like you very, very much, but——" and again she paused.

"But what?" he asked.

"I do not know how to put it," she said. "I cannot think of you in that way. You seem so far above me—so great, so learned, so——"

"So old!" he exclaimed, somewhat sadly. "Say it out, my dear. You have always thought of a young man, an Apollo with curling locks and god-like strength."

"I have not thought much about it," she answered, timidly. "If I ever marry, it will be because I cannot help it, because I love somebody better than myself and really belong to him. Even then, I shall yield reluctantly, for, to me, marriage seems like bondage." There was a flash in her eyes as she said this. Neither of them spoke for a while; the ticking of the clock upon the mantelpiece sounded loud and strange to the young girl, as she sat almost motionless beside her grave suitor.

"I will not accept that as an answer," he said at length. "I want to tell you something about yourself and your future, as I see it; perhaps then you may feel differently. Jessie, you are an orphan, and in a sense dependent upon the care of your sister and her husband. From certain rumors, which I have recently heard, I fear the Colonel has managed his affairs very recklessly since the war, and is now deeply in debt. These difficulties will not improve his temper, my dear—I know all about it. Your life cannot be very happy now, and I'm afraid it will be less so as time goes on. Have you ever thought of this?"

"No," she answered, frankly, "I do not think much about the future. I dare say I shall be able to bear whatever comes."

"Yes," he said, "in your girlish innocence and ignorance, you think lightly of it now—you feel capable of devoting yourself to others; but long years lie before you in which to live and endure. I would save you from the trouble that lies before you. Let me save you, Jessie," he pleaded tenderly, reaching out for her hand which was lying idle upon her lap. She innocently gave it to him. She felt his goodness and the truth of his prophetic words so strongly that she could not speak. "Will you not give me the right henceforth to protect you from all suffering?" he asked, folding her little hand between his own soft palms.

"You could not do that," she answered, the tears coming into her eyes; "no human being can save another from suffering. We must drink the cup poured out for us, however bitter it may be. It is our common lot."

She paused a moment, and then continued, "You are very, very kind, and I thank you with all my heart; but indeed I cannot marry you. You have always been my friend since the first time we met, and as a friend I love you truly; but marriage means something more to me than that."

"What does it mean, Jessie?" he asked.

"The union of souls—the perfect music, set to noble words!" She looked at him with her child-like solemn gaze.

"Sometimes, perhaps," he said, slowly, "but not often in this world of ours."

He was thinking of his own youthful marriage, which had been a fatal mistake, and which had left him hungry for love all through his long life.

"It must mean that to me, otherwise it will be an intolerable yoke. You understand me, do you not? You would not have me sell myself for ease and comfort and protection, would you?"

As she spoke, her sad eyes were full of mute entreaty, and there was a quiver of pain about her sweet mouth.

"Yes, I understand you, my darling child," he said in a tone that sounded far away; "I understand you perfectly, and it only increases my love and reverence for you. It is hard to tell you all I feel; perhaps, if I could, you would not care to listen to me. It would sound like the folly of an old idiot."

"No, no," she cried, "believe me, it is not because you are old—I never think of that. But I do not want to marry any one. Surely I ought to respect such a feeling, and be true to the voice within me."

"Yes, you are right," he said; "I have been very foolish, but it is over now. Forgive me. You look so white that I almost feel as if I were the villain in some play."

"There is nothing to forgive," she answered. "You are very kind to care so much for me. I hope you will always be my friend."

"Yes," he said, "I will; if I cannot be more, I will not be less. There, we will not talk any more about it," and he raised her hand to his lips. "Will you come now for the ride?"

"Oh, no," she said, "wait till another day."

"Well, good-bye, then."

"Good-bye," she echoed faintly.

She sat very still, listening as he crossed the hall, and went down the steps of the piazza. From the window she watched him as he entered his carriage and drove away. Then she got up from the sofa, like one who walks in sleep, went upstairs to her room, and threw herself heavily upon the bed. Only a long sleep restored her to her usual self. When she awoke, it was dark. She sat up, rubbed her eyes, and for a moment wondered what disagreeable thing had happened to her. As soon as she recalled it all, she smiled to herself and said—"My first suitor! What a pity I could not love him and say 'yes.' But it shall not change things between us—I like him too well for that. Dear old Judge!

Of all the men I ever met, I like you best. Your nonsense is just delicious. At your age, I do not think you will die of love, so it is not worth while for me to feel very badly over it. Dear me! there's the supper bell! What a long nap I've taken!"

She arose hastily, shook out her dress, smoothed her hair in the darkness, and descended to the dining-room. She had made up her mind that neither the Colonel nor Eleanor should know anything about it, but the fates were against her. Almost as soon as she had seated herself, Colonel Winston, in a most unsuspecting mood, said:

"Well, you ladies have had a call from Judge Brooks —haven't you? How handsome those horses of his are! He drove them all the way from the city in less than an hour, and they looked perfectly fresh."

"Why, has he been here?" asked Mrs. Winston, quite innocently; "I didn't see him—did you, Jessie?"

"Yes," said the girl, a tell-tale color springing to her cheeks. "He made only a short call, and left his regards for you."

Mrs. Winston and her husband looked at each other, —a flash of intelligence passed between them.

"I hope you treated him with the courtesy that such a gentleman deserves," said the Colonel, a little severely.

"I do not think I failed in politeness," Jessie replied in a cold tone, without lifting her eyes.

"I'm afraid, like all women, you are a perfect simpleton," exclaimed the Colonel, with a shade of annoyance in his manner.

"Perhaps I am," she answered, simply; "at least, it is better to be foolish than to be false." That ended the matter, but it was long before Jessie Holcombe forgot the words and tone of her brother-in-law. They had left a sting.

CHAPTER VII.

One morning, when Jessie came down to breakfast, she found a dainty note lying upon her plate. She tore open the envelope and read it eagerly. "It is from Alice," she said, after she had restored it to the envelope; "her mother has taken cold, and is quite sick. She wants me to come over and spend a few days with her. Can you spare me, Nell?"

"Of course, you must go," Eleanor answered. "It will be very pleasant for you. What time do you want to start?"

"As soon as possible after dinner. Harry, you will go with me, won't you? We can go on horseback, and the ride will be delightful."

"Oh! yes. I will go with pleasure," he quickly answered.

"How many miles is it from here, anyway?" asked Jessie; "I've travelled it often enough, but I have no idea how far it is."

"Why, it must be four or five miles," Harry replied.

"I should think you could be more exact than that," said the Colonel, smiling. Of late his temper had improved somewhat, and this morning he was in a very genial mood. Everybody reflected his good-humor, and the meal was more cheerful than usual.

"Why do you think so?" asked Harry, turning his attention from his plate. He had a very bold, black eye, and was never afraid to look any one straight in the face. He now fixed his gaze intently upon the Colonel, who replied :

"It seems to me of late you have travelled over that road often enough to know the distance between here and there to an inch."

"Perhaps I have," the young man answered carelessly; "but generally I have something pleasanter than miles to think about."

"Well, Alice Brooks is a mighty nice girl," said the Colonel,—"one of the quiet kind, such as I like. They seem to be going out of fashion these days. Nettie Hunter is the style now. I would not have such a daughter for fifty thousand dollars, much as I need the money."

"Now I think she is immensely amusing," said Harry; "though how in the world she ever got into that nest I can't imagine."

"Nor I, neither," exclaimed the Colonel. "Sometimes I am almost inclined to believe that there are human cuckoos,"—and he laughed heartily.

"I'm always curious to know what Nettie is going to do next," said Jessie; "she is so full of whimsical notions that she keeps one on the lookout all the time."

"I prophesy that she will marry some day, just like other girls," said Mrs. Winston, "and settle down into a very commonplace woman—a little cross, too, perhaps, for she will never find a husband as indulgent as her father."

"I, for one, wouldn't like to marry her," said Harry; "she loves powerfully to have her own way, and knows how to kick up a row when she can't get it. I have seen her sometimes when she was slightly thwarted. I tell you she can look dangerous."

"Alice Brooks will make a much better wife according to my opinion," said the Colonel. "She is a sweet-tempered creature, and will accept whatever comes with proper resignation."

"I'm not so sure of that," exclaimed Jessie, who saw the drift of the conversation. "Alice is amiable, but she is a girl of very strong character. She has her ideal of what is right, and woe unto those who depart from it."

"She does not strike me that way at all," said the Colonel; "she looks as sweet and tender as a ripe peach."

"I think I know her better than you do," was the reply. Jessie could not resist the impulse to give Harry a slight warning. If he were indeed bent on winning this girl for his wife, it would be necessary for him to hold himself with a strong rein. No one pursued the conversation farther, so it ended here.

That afternoon as the brother and sister were riding along slowly over the miles between Redbank and The Grove, as the plantation of Mrs. Brooks was called, Harry broke the silence by saying, "Well, little sis, I really think I'm making some progress in a certain direction. I'm sure she likes me; in a month she will be madly in love. She's one of the kind who will go into it deep."

"And how about yourself, Harry? Surely you are not going to win her heart without giving yours in return?"

"Don't afflict yourself on that score," he answered. "If she is satisfied with what I give, that's enough, I reckon. You may be sure I shall have to think a good deal of a woman before I consent to tie myself down to her. It's an awful sacrifice."

"Yes, on her part," said Jessie. "I've never seen much on the man's. He comes and goes at pleasure, in spite of the marriage vows. With the woman it is altogether different—she is the one who is tied."

"Now, you are not a man, Jessica, and you don't know anything about it," he answered, lightly. "I insist that a fellow gives up his freedom when he marries. He no longer dares to get on a little spree, however dry he may be."

"That is superlative nonsense!" she exclaimed; "he sprees just as much as he pleases, and if his wife doesn't like it, why, she may go to Jericho."

"You are the most knowing little woman that I ever did see," he said, with a laugh. "One cannot start any subject of conversation but what you are ready with an opinion. Now, I call that being very *opinionated*, and you know what father used to say about such females."

"Father was very old-fashioned on some subjects. I have not inherited his ideas about women—I think you have. You ought to have been born fifty or a hundred years ago, Harry. You came into the world too late for your own peace of mind. Women are no longer going to bow down and worship men; they are going to claim equal rights with them."

"Do you think the great era of emancipation has come?" he exclaimed, immensely amused.

"I *do*," she answered, emphatically. "I read a good deal more than you do, and so I catch a breath of air from the outside world. This is not the eighteenth century—it is the nineteenth, and the latter half, too."

"I wonder if Alice Brooks holds such views?" said Harry in his lightest mood. He was only amused by Jessie's little feminine flashes.

"Alice Brooks is a very superior girl, Harry," said his

sister; "she is remarkably well-educated, and has read a great deal. Though she is so quiet and talks so little, she has a very clear head. If you want to marry her you must begin a course of training right away."

"If she marries me at all, she will have to take me as I am," he answered, carelessly.

"If you can say that, and really mean it, you are not worthy of her," Jessie replied.

After this they rode on in silence. Just before they reached The Grove he turned to his sister—

"Well, Jessie, if she should say anything about me, I trust you'll speak a good word for me."

"I will say all that I can truthfully say," she answered.

They found Alice Brooks on the piazza waiting for them. She looked almost radiant as she welcomed them, and conducted them into the house. Something had surely come over her since Jessie Holcombe had last seen her. What was it? Love, perhaps. Her blue eyes shone with a new light, and there was a certain vivacity and playfulness of manner which Jessie had never seen in her friend before. Alice was growing like her uncle, the Judge; the resemblance was so strong that both the brother and the sister felt it.

"Mamma is in bed, Jessie," said the young hostess, "but she wants very much to see you; so you must run right upstairs, and go to her room."

Jessie obeyed, and Harry and Alice were left alone in the parlor. The young man stayed until it was almost dark; then the lady went out on the piazza for the parting, and waved him a final adieu with her handkerchief.

Jessie Holcombe found herself much interested in the conversation of the invalid, and did not go down until the supper-bell rang. Alice met her friend at the foot of the staircase, threw her arms around her in a warm, impulsive way that almost startled Jessie, and exclaimed, "I am so very glad to have you with me, dear. I have such lots of things to talk about. I am going to keep you a whole week, if you will stay."

"Of course I will, if you want me. I'm of no particular account at home."

"Then you had better stay a month."

"Oh! you would get tired of me in a month, you would never want to see my face again."

"Try me and see," said Alice, "I don't get tired of my friends. When I once choose them, they are a part of myself forever."

Jessie turned and kissed the glowing cheek. She understood what this confession meant, just as well as she understood it a few hours later, after they had had that long talk before going to bed.

They were seated side by side upon the rug in front of the dying fire. They had been talking a long while on various topics, discussing the news of the neighborhood, and the nice books they had been reading, before the subject nearest to the heart of Alice, at length, came to the surface.

In a pause, she said, very quietly, "I invited your brother to stay to supper and spend the night with us, but he would not consent. Do you know why? Did he have some other engagement?"

"I don't know," Jessie replied; "he does not tell me much about himself. In a certain way, he is very reticent. I never know where he is going, nor where he has been. Sometimes he goes over to Dr. Crump's for a game of whist, and stays until bed-time, but not often. Perhaps he had promised to go to-night."

"Perhaps so," Alice answered, "he said he would like ever so much to stay, but had an engagement which he could not break. Of course, I did not urge him after he said that. He admires the doctor's pretty wife very much, does he not?"

"Why, yes, everybody admires her," said Jessie, "I think she is the most beautiful woman I ever saw—don't you?"

"Yes, she is perfectly beautiful, physically, but, do you know, I think she is very shallow. She has but two ideas in her pretty head—one is, how adorable I am! The other is, how beautifully I am dressed!"

"I believe that is Harry's opinion of her too. He often says that if she could talk, she would be divine, and all the men would be ready to fall down and worship her."

"Does he really say that?" asked Alice. "I'm glad, for, do you know, I thought that he was quite fascinated by her."

"Oh! no," said Jessie, "I don't think any woman has ever yet fascinated Harry. He loves to flirt, but he is very fastidious, and will not be easily captivated. I am sure that he has never yet been seriously in love."

"I am so glad to hear you say that," exclaimed Alice, giving the dying coals a poke with the tongs, and putting the chunks up together as if desirous to rekindle the fire. "Do you know, Jessie, your brother puzzles me a good deal. I cannot exactly understand him. Sometimes I think he is very much in love with a girl, and the next time I see them together, he hardly notices her."

Jessie laughed. "That's the true complexion of a flirt," she said, rather surprised at the innocence of her friend.

"You don't really mean to say that he trifles with girls, do you? I should despise him, if he did."

"Yes, with some girls he really does trifle and flirt; but he knows very well with whom he can play that game. Besides the girl usually begins it. Alice dear, he would never flirt with you—he has too much respect for you."

"Do you think so?" she asked, while the color deepened on her cheek. She was evidently stirred by some over-mastering emotion, for one moment her face was all aglow, and the next it was almost as white as her night-dress. "Jessie," she said, softly, after a long pause, "perhaps I ought not to talk to you about it, but somehow I cannot help it. Will you let me ask you frankly just one question?"

"What is it, dear?"

"Do you think your brother is really in earnest? He comes here continually, and treats me in a fashion altogether new. Do you think he means anything by it?"

"I am sure he does," said Jessie, very solemnly. Noble woman that she was, her heart was beating quickly now. She wished to be true to her friend and true to her brother. Was it possible to be true to both?

"Well, I would like to know the very truth," said Alice. "Jessie, I am sure you will keep my confidence sacred, or I would not talk to you as I am doing. You must never let your brother know that I have spoken a word to you about it. You will not, dear?"

"Never, never! Wild horses could not wring it from me."

Alice continued, "I sometimes feel as if I were standing on the edge of a precipice, ready to fall. I must reach out my hand to some one. I cannot speak to mamma, because, you know, she wants me to marry my cousin Waverley. Jessie, I am sure you can help me. I am afraid that I am beginning to love your brother. Tell me, please, tell me!—do you think he is worthy of my love?" She paused a moment, and buried her face in her hands as if ashamed of the confession that she had been constrained to make. Presently she looked up at her companion, and with a touch of pathos in her voice: "Forgive me for asking such a question. It must be very hard for you to answer it; but, Jessie, you must know that there are many rumors in the county about your brother. Some people say that he is good for nothing; some say that he is very dissipated—that he gets drunk and gambles; others says that he is in love with the doctor's wife, and will run away with her some day, if he can get the chance. Now, of course, I do not believe all this idle talk, but I would like to know if you think that I can safely give way to the impulse of my heart. Do you think him worthy of my love?"

Jessie Holcombe looked into the soft, almost tearful, eyes that were fixed steadfastly upon her, and answered, "Alice, I hope he is. It would be hard for me to rob him of such a treasure as your love by saying that he is not worthy of it. I will be very candid with you, dear; not for the world would I deceive you after the confidence you have given me. Harry has some grave faults —I will not deny it. He was only a boy when the war began. During those four years my father and my eldest brother were both away in the army, and Harry had very little restraint of any kind imposed upon him. Off and on, he was himself a great deal of the time in camp and was thrown into the midst of dreadful things. I cannot bear to think of it. But, in spite of this, he has many noble qualities. At home he is very amiable and gentle—kind and obliging to every one. You know in battle he proved himself the bravest of the brave. He was the spoiled darling of his regiment."

Her words had been very rapid, for she was eager to say all that she could truthfully say in defence of her brother. After a short pause for breath, she continued,

"I wish you could see him with Lilian—he is very fond of her. She goes to sleep in his arms every night while he sings to her or tells her stories. Then he carries her upstairs to bed as tenderly as a woman could. If he ever marries, I know he will be devoted to his wife and children, for he has a vein of true chivalry in his nature. I know he drinks sometimes, but I have never seen him drunk. I am afraid that he gambles too, but I think it is because he is restless and unhappy, rather than because he cares for cards. Alice, I think he intends to ask you to marry him, and, if you truly love him, I am sure you can do much to help him to be better than he is. His greatest fault is that he does not know what to do with himself. He seems perfectly at sea, and plunges first into one thing, then into another. It makes me very unhappy to think of it. I hope I have not made the impression upon your mind that he is better than he really is. He is full of faults, Alice —I cannot deny it, but I do believe that there is something truly noble in his nature."

"Jessie," whispered the girl, "I know that I could love him madly—he is just the man to inspire a grand passion. He is handsome, brilliant, and light-hearted; he fascinates me strangely. He seems a kind of hero— a splendid cavalry officer who could ride at the head of a regiment and throw his life away. But, dear, I am afraid of him. Sometimes I almost hope that he will never ask me to marry him. It would be very, very hard to reject him and yet I could not accept him without disregarding a warning voice within me."

The little French clock on the mantel-piece struck twelve.

"How late it is!" exclaimed Alice, "I did not dream that we had been talking so long. I suppose we ought to go to bed now."

In a few minutes, the lamp was blown out, and soon they were both asleep. The friendship between these two young girls had been of slow growth, but it had taken deep root in the heart of each, and promised to be as lasting as life itself. They were much alike in many ways. They both were fond of books, of music, of riding, of walking. Both had ideas about the philosophy of life, the moral structure of the universe, and all the other high things that young ladies handle nowadays. But, in character, there were some points of difference between them. The life of Alice Brooks had been one of unclouded sunshine. Her delicate maidenhood had been sheltered from all the rude winds of heaven. Having seen but a small side of human existence, her sympathies were not so broad as Jessie's; having been reared with rigid ideas of right and wrong, she had but little indulgence for the erring. Jessie Holcombe's soul had been stirred to its lowest depths by sorrow. She had an almost infinite pity for all those who go astray; she could have gathered them in her arms of love and helped them to rise again. Not so with Alice; it was her impulse to cut them off forever like branches that cumber the ground.

The two friends enjoyed every moment of their stay together. They rode, they read, they walked, they talked, they played chess, they practiced duets on the piano. This visit was to both a kind of revelation of themselves, each to the other. Alice had not before guessed the heights and depths of Jessie's nature, nor Jessie the heights and depths of her friend's. The days had passed very quickly in this sweet companionship—the week was already gone, and still the young hostess of The Grove would not consent for her guest to depart. Mrs. Brooks continued ill and urged the loneliness of her daughter as an argument for this prolonged visit. Harry came over frequently to inquire about the invalid, and also to ask about the plans of his sister. Jessie could easily see that he was pushing his suit with tact as well as boldness. She could not but hope that the course of this love would run smooth, and yet she well knew that it would encounter opposition from both the mother and the uncle of the young girl whose fate was at stake. Their very hearts were bent upon the union of Alice with her cousin.

Waverley Brooks was expected to return from Europe some time during the coming summer. Alice talked freely about his return, and all the plans that had been made by her uncle. They were all going north in July, to be absent several months. Waverley was expected to land and join them early in August, and they were to make a tour of the pleasant summer resorts of the Northern States. Alice did not seem to be at all enthusiastic over this prospect. Once she said to her friend:

"I do wish that I could be left behind. It would be ever so much nicer to stay here at home with my books. How much I could read. I do hate the idea of being dragged around from place to place, of having to dress, and dance, and laugh, and talk, when I would prefer to be silent. I do not seem made for such a life. After a while, it really disgusts me."

"Now, I would like it immensely," exclaimed Jessie. "It must be delightful to travel, and see sights, and meet famous people, and go to brilliant entertainments. Sometimes I long with my whole heart for such pomps and vanities."

"Then do let's change places," said Alice.

"I wish we could. Do you know, Alice dear, that you seem to me the most enviable person I have ever met in my whole life."

"Do I, Jessie? Ah! I have my little troubles as well as others,"—and a slight sigh escaped her lips.

Jessie's visit lengthened itself to three weeks, but in spite of the ever-increasing intimacy between the two friends, nothing more was said by either of them about Harry. Long years passed away before the heart of Alice Brooks was again unveiled.

CHAPTER VIII.

SPRING was slowly advancing, and life was moving on at Redbank in its usual monotonous course. The weather continued to be remarkably fine, tempting every one out of doors. The Colonel was wholly absorbed in the planting of cotton. Having no overseer, he spent much of his time on horseback, riding around, inspecting the vast fields, and overlooking the busy negroes. Eleanor found many things to claim her attention; the garden, the orchard, the poultry-yard, the dairy, the nursery, each daily demanded a share of her time.

Harry came and went, in a lazy and aimless fashion. Sometimes he would ride away and not return for several days, while the household were left to wonder what had become of him; sometimes he would go off with his gun on his shoulder, and spend hours in rambling through the lonely woods and swamps. Though it was not the season for sport, and he did not even carry a game-bag with him, still his gun was always the mute companion of these solitary walks.

Jessie spent much of her time on the broad piazzas; here the baby came with his playthings, and here Lilian brought her books for the daily lessons with her aunt. Jessie read and sewed, with the glad heart of spring-time beating in her bosom. The earth seemed too beautiful for any thought of sorrow or trouble. She often accompanied her brother-in-law in his rides to the mill and over the fields, and she was never so happy as when mounted on the back of Dolly. The Colonel was now as genial an escort as any lady could desire. He had received generous pecuniary assistance from his brother, and was a changed man. Adversity may refine the gold, but prosperity molds and polishes it.

One morning, when Jessie came down, equipped for a ride, she was disappointed not to find Dolly at the front door, ready saddled, beside the Colonel's horse. She immediately went in search of Peyton. She found him in the stable, busy grooming the carriage horses. Though they were now too old to be often used, Colonel Winston insisted that they should receive the same attention that had been formerly lavished upon them.

"Peyton," the young lady cried out on seeing him, "I thought you knew I was going to ride this morning. Where is Dolly? I am ready, and the Colonel is waiting for me."

"Well, Miss Jessie," said the negro, after a short pause, in which he showed great reluctance to speak, " you mustn't blame me, but de truf is, Dolly's gone."

"Gone where?" the girl exclaimed aghast. "What do you mean?"

"Why, las' night, 'bout ten o'clock," said the negro, "Marse Harry, he came to my house an' ordered me to go right straight to de stable an' saddle Dolly for him. I didn't know but you'd said dat he mought hab her, tho' de truf is, I could see dat Marse Harry he wasn't fitten ter ride a horse las' night. But, you see, Miss Jessie, 'twasn't my part to say so, or to 'spute wid him; an' arter de horse was saddled wid his ole cavalry saddle, he jes' rode off, an' I ain't seen Dolly sense!"

"But where is Harry's horse?" she asked.

"Lor! Miss Jessie, dat horse o' his'n is pritty nigh used up. She's got de sore back, an' de spavin, an' is lame in de lef' fore leg. Marse Harry, he bin ridin' like lightnin' lately. I dinno what bin de matter wid him; when he gets on a horse he rides him pritty nigh to de'f."

Jessie said not a word, but she turned away and went into the house. She sat down quietly in her own room and tried to calm her violent emotion, for she was very angry. It had been a long time since she had felt such indignation. This, then, was what could follow the recent good conduct of her brother. It was indeed impossible ever to trust him. He could be respectable and gentlemanly for a while, but there was no abiding strength to his character. It seemed almost incredible that he should take her horse without even asking permission, and go off in that clandestine way, under the shelter of darkness. His want of honor wounded her deeply. She was ashamed of him, ashamed that he bore the good old name of which she had always been so proud, ashamed to think that she had told Alice Brooks that he was worthy of her love. And then her horse—the horse that Richard, her noble brother, had been riding when the fatal bullet pierced his brain!—the beautiful, gentle creature that she had loved and caressed for years! Would Harry care for Richard's horse as she did? Would he see that no harm came to her? He had been drinking probably,—yes, Peyton as good as told her he was drunk; if that were true, Harry would care for nothing—the fire within him would consume both heart and conscience. She had never seen him drunk, but she could guess how wild and mad drunken men might be. How could he so debase himself! A vague dread came over her—a dread of some awful catastrophe to follow. All day long, with a heavy heart, she watched and waited for her brother to return, but he did not come. As the afternoon waned and twilight approached, she grew almost sick with anxiety. "What can it mean?" she asked herself again and again. She went to bed with the thought that perhaps, as he had gone in the night he would return in the night. In the early dawn, she got up, dressed herself hurriedly, and went out in the stables to see if Dolly was safely back in her stall. No, she was not there. Peyton only shook his head when she asked the question.

Another day passed away, and yet Harry did not come; and another and another, until the feverish anxiety of the young girl had changed into a dull and heavy heart-ache. She no longer dared to imagine what had happened—it must be something dreadful, and every footstep in the hall seemed to belong to the bearer of ill-tidings. The Colonel and Mrs. Winston had both been surprised and indignant, when the knowledge of Harry's conduct had come to them. They knew him too well to think that all would be well with Dolly. It pained them to see Jessie's white face, so full of silent suffering. She had not discussed the matter with any one. How could she bear to speak of it, when her own brother was the culprit? A common thief could not have done worse. It would have been even better for Dolly if a common thief had broken into the stables, and carried her off. Such a criminal might have been pursued, arrested, and forced to surrender the horse. It would have been for his interest also to take care of the animal that he had stolen. But Harry could not be pursued, and he would never think of poor Dolly, except to bury his sharp cavalry spurs in her glossy sides to make her go faster.

At length one morning, a week after his disappearance, Lizzie, the maid, rushed excitedly into the room, while her young mistress was dressing, and told her that "Marse Harry had come back in de night." Jessie threw on her clothes with feverish haste, and hurried out to see if her horse was safe and sound. Colonel Winston met her on the piazza; he was looking very grave; her heart sank within her. "Is anything the matter?" she asked, eagerly.

"Yes, my dear," he answered in a very kind tone, "I'm afraid your horse is ruined. She is very lame, her shoulder is sprained, and she is all used up." With a spasm of pain at her heart, the young girl hurried out to the stables.

"Peyton!" she called, as she entered the stable door, "where is she? quick, I must see her."

Peyton guided his mistress to the stable where Dolly was standing before a full manger.

"She won't eat nothin', Miss Jessie," he said, with a note of pity in his honest voice. He laid his dark hand gently on the animal's mane, and began to smooth out the tangles. The excited girl pushed by him, approached the wounded creature, put both arms around her neck, and laid her own fair cheek against the glossy head.

"Dolly! my poor, dear Dolly!" she moaned; "you cannot even tell me where the pain is and so I can do nothing for you." The horse shivered as if in agony, and stretching out her neck, uttered a faint whinny. "I am sure you know I love you, dear," she said, tenderly; "it breaks my heart to know that you are suffering. Oh! do not die, dear, dear Dolly. Eat just a little for me, and I'm sure you will feel better." But the horse turned from the measure of oats which Peyton held out to her and the shivers grew more frequent and violent.

"Perhaps she will drink, Peyton," said the young girl. Some water was quickly brought, and Dolly buried her nose deep in the bucket, and drank long draughts as if consumed by some inward fever.

"Can't you do something for her, Peyton?" The wail of those words went straight to the negro's heart.

"Miss Jessie," he replied, "I think she's had a fall; look here, both her knees is skinned, an' I think she's hurt inside. I'se a gwine to wash off her knees with arniky, an' de Colonel he has jes' ordered a drench fur her. I'll do what I ken fur her you may be sure; but I'se mightily afeard dat 'tis all over wid her."

Jessie felt that she could do nothing for the poor suffering creature, and so she turned and left the stables. She went to her room, and threw herself upon the bed in an agony that convulsed her slight form. Burying her face in her hands she exclaimed, again and again, "How could he do it! How could he do it! The only creature on earth that was wholly mine. Oh, Harry, how could you be so cruel, when you knew how much I loved her?"

While she lay there, the minutes were like years. She seemed to grow old under the intense strain of grief. At length, her emotion spent itself and she grew calm, seeming to contemplate her suffering at a distance, as we do after years have passed away and blunted the keenness of pain. When the breakfast-bell rang, she got up mechanically, smoothed out her dress, bathed her face and went down to the dining-room. Harry came in just before the meal was over, looking very old and wretched and red-eyed, but wearing his accustomed *nonchalance* of manner. The family greeted him coldly as he seated himself in their midst—all but Lilian; she sprang from her chair, threw her arms around his neck, and kissed him again and again. "I'm so glad you've come back, Uncle Hal!" she exclaimed.

Colonel Winston, after a while, looked up at him with stern displeasure in his face and voice, and said, "I would like to know what you have been doing with your sister's horse?"

"Why, riding her, of course," was the answer, given in a hard and careless tone; "horses were made to ride, were they not? Or were they only made to be petted by young ladies, and fed with lumps of sugar?"

"I am astonished beyond measure," exclaimed the Colonel, "that you should take your sister's horse out of my stable without her permission, and after a week's absence, return with the animal lamed and ruined."

"I did not know that any act of mine could astonish you," said the young man, with perfect indifference; "I think I have heard you make such an assertion more than once."

It was evident that nothing could be gained by words, so all were silent. After the meal was ended, as Jessie was going to her room, her brother stopped her in the hall, and said, "Forgive me, Jessie; I'm awfully sorry, but upon my honor I don't know how it happened."

She was about to turn away from him, feeling herself unfit to make any reply, when she caught an expression of intense pain upon his face. In a moment her heart was touched—"What is it, Harry?" she asked. "Is anything the matter with you?"

"Yes," he exclaimed in a tone of bitterness, "I'm afraid the devil has got me for good now."

"What do you mean?" she said, frightened by his strange manner.

"If you cannot guess, I shall not tell you; only I feel as if I could ride every horse in the stable to death."

"Oh! Harry! you have been drinking," she cried, wounded beyond measure to think that he had fallen so low as to appear before the family in such a condition. Was his self-respect indeed all gone?

"Of course I have," he exclaimed, looking at her defiantly.

"How could you! How could you!" she said, approaching him, and laying her hand lovingly upon his arm. "Do go up to your room and lie down, dear. You look so tired and worn-out."

"So I am, but I cannot rest," he answered, in a hoarse tone. "I'll get my gun, and go out into the woods."

"Harry, do tell me what is the matter with you," she begged piteously.

"Go and ask Alice Brooks," he replied bitterly, his blood-shot eyes flashing with anger.

Jessie stood still and looked at him tenderly, while tears of sympathy gathered upon her lashes. This, then, was the end of love's young dream. After all, he did care enough for Alice to become desperate and be ready to throw away his life when she rejected him.

"I know she loves me," he said after a moment; "but it is her mother and that meddling old Judge. They have told her something about me that has hardened her heart."

"I am so very sorry for you, dear," Jessie whispered. "I did hope it would be different." He turned away as if to escape from her sympathy. Soon afterwards she heard him calling the dogs, and, looking out, saw him going down the red lane with his gun upon his shoulder.

For some days, poor Dolly continued to grow worse. She lay down and they could not get her up again; she seemed to have no strength to stand. The faithful Peyton used every remedy within his reach, and nursed her with self-forgetful devotion, but all in vain.

At last one morning, the news was brought to the house that Dolly was dead. Peyton came himself to tell his young mistress. "I done all I could to save her, Miss Jessie," he said.

The girl put out her white hand—"I know you did, Peyton," she answered, "and I thank you with all my heart. I shall never forget your kindness." She did not know that the touch of her soft hand, more than repaid the negro for days and nights of watching over the dying horse. Peyton had a worshipful feeling for his young mistress, such as we give to the saints and angels whose dwelling-place is in the remote heavens.

Jessie grieved silently. The loss of Dolly revived the keenest sorrow of her life. She lived over those terrible days that followed the death of Richard, her oldest brother. She remembered the home-coming of the soldier's horse, saddled and bridled, but without a rider. She saw again the long procession, the hearse with its awful trappings, and the beautiful black charger walking behind with solemn tread. She heard the rattle of the sabres and empty pistols that hung at the saddle-bow. Night after night, she laid her hands upon her burning eyes to shut out this vision, which robbed her of sleep, and left her unrefreshed when morning came. Richard had been her ideal of all that was manly and noble—the *chevalier sans peur et sans reproche*. Even now she had no other standard by which to measure manhood. It was a perpetual grief to her that Harry should fall so far below this splendid type.

The loss of her horse made a great change in Jessie's habits. Henceforth there were no more delightful gallops through the green woods, and, without this healthful exercise, this pleasant variety, the days were dull and dreary. Her cheerfulness became less spontaneous

and her step less light. Every one was too busy to
notice the change. At last, one morning, Mrs. Winston
was shocked beyond measure to find her sister prostrated
with a burning fever. Jessie had felt it coming; for
many days the weariness and listlessness had been increasing, but she had struggled silently against it.
Malaria had chosen her for its first victim.

With all the outward attractions of Redbank, it was
not healthy in summer. Situated not far from a large
river, with brooks and creeks flowing sluggishly across
its fields in every direction, and swamps encircling it on
three sides, there was always more or less fever among
its inhabitants during the warm months. This year the
spring had been unusually early, and, by the middle of
June, the thermometer had mounted to the nineties.
The heat was somewhat relieved by continual showers,
but the freshness imparted to the air was only tempo-
rary. This weather was just the thing for the cotton,
which grew with marvellous rapidity, but it was very
far from being favorable for humanity.

Jessie's sickness was not of long continuance; within
a week it had yielded to the powerful influence of quinine, but a shadow had fallen over the whole household.
Other members of the family fell ill in quick succession,
and there were several deaths among the negroes. In
the midst of this general depression, Harry disappeared
in his usual mysterious fashion. He left without saying good-bye to any one, or even informing Jessie where
he was going, or when he expected to return. She was
accustomed to his careless ways, and yet such conduct
always wounded her.

Many of the neighbors on the adjoining plantations
had also taken their flight to cooler regions. Through
June, July, and half of August, the long hot days fol-

lowed each other with wearisome monotony. When evening came, and the sun went down behind the distant pines, proclaiming the approach of night-fall, a prayer of thanksgiving for the darkness ascended from many a heart in that fair Southern land.

CHAPTER IX.

"Through every web of life the dark threads run ; Oh! why and whither ? God knows all. I only know that He is good."—*Whittier.*

LILIAN was very ill. Even Mrs. Winston, who seldom allowed herself to show any anxiety about anything, was now alarmed, and bent over the little sufferer with deep solicitude. It was a hot evening in July; the light from a full moon, shining in a cloudless sky, poured into the room. The muslin curtains were parted to admit this radiance, which fell in floods upon the floor, casting shadows of the oak leaves that hung motionless outside near the closed windows. Even in this sultry weather, the windows could not be left open at night, for miasma entered like some stealthy creature in search of prey.

Mrs. Winston was seated near the bed where the sick child lay, fanning and soothing her as she tossed restlessly from side to side. There was no lamp in the room—only the moonlight. Jessie entered softly, looking almost unearthly in her long white dressing-gown, her dark hair unbound and falling over her shoulders. She approached the bedside noiselessly, and said in a low tone—"Do let me relieve you now. I am quite rested." "No," was the answer; "but come and sit down beside me and comfort me, dear." They both moved away from the bed. The child seemed at last to be sleeping. In a distant corner of the room, away from the glorious moonlight, they seated themselves side by side upon a lounge. Jessie put her arm around her sister, and whispered—" Poor tired darling! go to bed, and I will watch over Lilian. If there is the slightest change, I will call you immediately. It is killing you, dear,—the watching night after night, and the terrible anxiety. You *must* rest, or you will be ill yourself."

Mrs. Winston grasped her sister's hand, and with a low half-suppressed sob exclaimed, "Oh! Jessie, I am so unhappy, dear. I feel as if something dreadful were going to happen, and as if somehow I were to blame for it. I know my darling is going to die, and I cannot bear it—I cannot bear it. My heart will break."

"Hush, dear," said Jessie, "you must not say that. It is because you are tired that you feel so."

" Yes," she answered, wearily, "I *am* tired of everything, but most of all I am tired of life. It is such a hopeless puzzle—I am weary of trying to make anything out of it."

" I know how you feel, dear," said Jessie, "but you must not lose heart. There is surely some meaning to it all."

"*Perhaps*," she replied; "only I fear that I shall never find it. I do not know what is the matter with me, but somehow I lack interest in whatever I do. I go through my daily tasks like a machine; my very heart seems freezing within me. If I could only get rid of this dreadful feeling. Sometimes it seems as if I were dead even now."

Jessie could say nothing to this sad confession. Mrs. Winston continued—

"The Colonel's faults weigh upon me so—his petty exactions, his frequent ill-temper, is almost unbearable. If I could only run away from it all! but that's the point—I cannot—I must stay right here and endure it in silence. If I were only single like you! If there were no chains around me, binding me hopelessly to others!" Again she sobbed as if her heart were breaking. "Jessie," she exclaimed, suddenly, "never, never marry unless you love the man well enough to bear all things for his sake. Then you will not feel the terrible weight of the yoke. I am glad that you did not accept the Judge. In a worldly point of view, it would have been a fine thing for you; but it is a mistake for a young girl to be mated to an old man—nothing but trouble comes of it. And yet I thought you liked him, and would probably marry him."

"I do like him very much," said Jessie, "and I realize all the advantages of the position he would give me. But I cannot marry him. I cannot get rid of the feeling that he wants me, like a bit of statuary or a picture, just to fill a vacancy in his elegant home, and the thought of being bought like a piece of merchandise is horrible to me."

"But, dear, he loves you truly—it is easy to see that."

"Yes, as a father loves a daughter. I can and do respond to that affection. But, Nell, that is not what marriage means. We are told that the woman was given to the man for a help-mate. How could I ever help him? He is heights above me; he needs no help from any one—he is so strong and proud and wise and good. Eleanor, I could not bear to stand like a dummy and be loaded with costly presents. It would dwarf my own soul. I must be something more than that to the man I marry."

"What would you be?" asked Eleanor.

"I do not know; but I have a vague feeling that a wife should be a perpetual inspiration to her husband, helping him in all noble purposes, strengthening him when his faith is weak. I have been reading about Vittoria Colonna. She was a grand woman. Even her friendship was an inspiration to Michael Angelo."

"Yes, dear, but there are few women like her in the world."

"There ought to be more," said the young girl; "I wish that women did not care for such paltry things."

"You are right, Jessie; most of them will sell themselves for a velvet gown or a diamond necklace. They do not yet know their own value."

"A woman should love the best and holiest things on earth," said the girl; "she should keep her heart 'as chaste as ice, as pure as snow.' She should not dare to marry until she loves with her whole soul."

"But if she loves unwisely?" asked Eleanor, "what then?"

"If it be love, who shall say that it is unwise? Let her trust her own heart and God," answered Jessie in a solemn tone. She thought of Alice Brooks, and her words were a plea for her brother.

"I believe you are right," said Mrs. Winston, "but the world seems to have outgrown such old-fashioned notions. I will tell you a bit of my own history, dear. When I was very young, I loved, or rather I felt the first stirrings of a mighty love, but I crushed its growth because the man was poor. He went to California, for it was when the gold-fever was raging. He went to make a fortune for me, and there he died. I can never tell you how I suffered when I heard that he was dead. I did not realize until then how strong was the feeling

I had been struggling to crush. It has lived on ever since; like a limb bruised and maimed long ago, there are still times when the scars ache. I often feel that I would have been a different woman if I had married him. He was full of tender and poetic sentiment. I could have given the practical element to the union, and we would have been very happy together, and perhaps successful. Colonel Winston has not been really unkind, but I know that I have been suffering from a hardening process ever since I married him. My true mate was lost to me by my own fault. I was not worthy of him." Tears glistened on her lashes as she spoke. Jessie reached out for her sister's hand, and clasped it in her own.

"Did father know anything about it?" she asked.

"No," said Eleanor, "father was ambitious for me, and I never dared to tell him. The man I loved was quite outside our set. He was the tutor in the family of one of our neighbors. I was very intimate with the young girls of the family, and used to meet him in an informal way. He always assisted us in getting up our charades, and tableaux, and fancy-balls, for he was very clever, and knew everything about history, and historical costumes. He was a Northern man. Ever since those days, I have had a tender spot in my heart for New England. He was finely educated and full of talent, but bashful and ill-at-ease in the aristocratic society of Virginia. He never showed to advantage, —no one but myself knew how much there was in him. I was just the wife for him—I can see it plainly now. If I had only put my hand in his, it would have inspired him with hope and confidence. I was the belle of the neighborhood, a bold, dashing girl who would have infused her own proud spirit into her husband.

He was very timid in pleading his suit; he felt his poverty, and he knew my pride. I was tender and haughty by turns, enjoying my power over him. I knew that he was really worth more than any of the young men in the county, but I could not resist the girlish impulse to trifle with his love. One night at a party, he told me that he was thinking of going to California to make his fortune. He asked me with a searching look if he should go. I answered with emphasis—'Yes; if I were a man, I would go myself.' Soon I went off to dance with some one else, and forgot all about it. The next day, I left home to visit a friend in Richmond, when I returned, he was gone. He wrote me one long, passionate letter before he sailed around the Horn for California. I could not reply to it, for I had no address. A year afterwards I heard of his death. A paper was sent to me from the North; by whom, I never knew. I realized then, that I could never love any one else. I felt too desperate to care what became of me. In less than another year, I was the wife of Colonel Winston. I accepted him because my father wished me to, and because it seemed to offer some escape from my aimless, wretched life. It was wrong, and I have been punished for it. Jessie, I have never told this to any one before. I would like to save you from making such a mistake as I have made. Be true to your own heart, even if the whole world condemns you."

The young girl was deeply moved, and only pressed the hand of her sister in silence. After this they could talk no more; the emotion of both was overpowering. The sick child stirred and moaned in her sleep. Mrs. Winston went to the bed and felt the hot hands and head; then she poured out some medicine, and gave it to the little sufferer. She sighed deeply as she resumed her seat. Her heart was heavy with anxiety and sorrow. Presently, she went to the window and looked out; but there was no comfort in the beauty of the world.

"Eleanor," said Jessie, "I do wish you would consent to go to bed. Your face is perfectly haggard. I will sit up the rest of the night, and watch beside Lilian."

"No," Eleanor replied, "I could not sleep. I feel too nervous and excited. There may be some change about midnight, and I cannot bear to leave my darling for a single moment. It seems as if she were slipping away from me, and I were reaching out my arms in vain to hold her. Oh! Jessie, motherhood is full of bitterness as well as joy. To think that she is a part of my very self, and yet I cannot suffer for her. If she dies, I know I shall not be able to live without her."

"She will not die," said the young girl, with quiet confidence.

"How can you know!" exclaimed the mother impatiently; "you must not cheat me with such promises."

"Eleanor," said Jessie, "God is good. He is Our Father—He loves us. In moments of agony, I have learned to cling desperately to this simple creed."

"You are better than I am," replied Mrs. Winston, "there is nothing I doubt more than the love of God for us poor mortals. To me He seems a cruel tryant. Only count the little graves out yonder in the corner of the garden—there are four of them, side by side. Why did God give me those children, just to take them away as soon as I had learned to love them?"

"We cannot tell why such things happen, but still we must believe. There is no other hope for us."

Mrs. Winston shook her head sadly. "I used to have a little bit of superficial religion," she said, "but I have flung it away long ago—it was of no account. I really hate to go to church now—to bend and bow and call on the good Lord, when I don't believe at all that He is good."

Jessie felt shocked to hear her sister speak thus, but she only answered—" Please do not talk so, Eleanor. He will hear you—He seems so near to-night."

She was thinking of the awful midnight stillness, the almost unnatural glory of the moonlight outside, and the Angel of Death bending over the sick child. She could not talk—she laid her tired head against the corner of the lounge. Eleanor's words filled her with horror. They revealed a desolation of soul such as she had never before seen—a waste place filled with ruins. In the silence she began to pray. She did not fall on her knees—she did not even clasp her hands; but her lips moved unconsciously without the utterance of a sound, while she pleaded for her sister.

The hours were slowly passing. The distant clock struck again and again. Still Lilian slept; her breathing seemed to be growing fainter and fainter. Nothing more could be done. Human wisdom was of no avail now. A soul was drifting out alone upon a dim and shoreless sea. The awful mystery of Death filled the room like a great shadow. The sisters sat silent and motionless, awaiting the final moan. Gradually they were overpowered by utter weariness and the sultry atmosphere of the night. They, too, were drifting away from the visible world into a land as mysterious as Death. They both fell asleep.

Suddenly, Jessie opened her eyes and sprung from her seat. The day was breaking. The sky was all aglow with the splendor of the rising sun. She went softly to the bed and bent over the pillows. Then she uttered a low cry.

"Wake up, Eleanor! wake up!" The words came with a great sob. There is an agony of joy as well as of sorrow. "Lilian is better, dear. She is much better. Only see the moisture on her face and hands. The fever has left her. She is not going to die. God is good!"

Mrs. Winston fell almost helpless upon the bed beside her child, whose eyes were wide open and full of intelligence.

"Yes," the mother whispered faintly, "God is better than I thought."

. . . . .

Jessie was dispirited and heartsore. The long weeks of Lilian's convalescence had taxed her strength almost beyond endurance. Eleanor was too weak and worn out to share in this task. The child had been very fretful—calling continually for Uncle Hal, asking again and again where he was, why he had gone away, and when he was going to return. He alone could tell her stories that she liked. Jessie's fairy tales were very insipid to her. What did she care about two kings that went to war over a princess with long golden hair, or about a magician who, by his incantations, made the earth open and reveal its treasures? "I do not like that story," the child would often say; "tell me about the little dwarf with the big spectacles on his nose."

"But, dear, I do not know that one," the patient girl would reply. Then Lilian would call for Uncle Hal to lift her from the bed to the sofa, or to carry her down to the piazza and swing her in the hammock, and sob as if her heart would break because he did not come. Jessie felt equally at a loss how to comfort and amuse the child, and how to bear the daily weariness of such a life. She longed for some escape. If something would only happen! If somebody would only come!

One afternoon, late in August, when there was a little coolness in the air, she put on her hat and left the house for a walk. Lilian was asleep in the care of Lizzie, and would not miss her for a while. A desperate impulse had come over the young girl to fly from everything—to go on and on and on, until the fever of impatience and longing within her had consumed itself. As she crossed the back yard she called Tiger to accompany her. He was a fine English mastiff, and would be a fitting escort for a solitary maiden. She had long ago won his savage heart by her kindness, and he came bounding over the grass to join her. With a quick step she went down the red lane. The little brook was now entirely dry, and she walked over the pebbly bed, stopping to pick a sickly flower that was growing on the other side. When she came to the Quarter, she paused a few moments to speak to the women and children who were sitting under the trees. There was Aunt Nancy, fat and placid, seated on a low stool, dozing in the afternoon sun; there was Aunt Harriet, with a piece of knitting work in her hands, walking up and down her little garden patch, driving out an invasion of pigs and chickens; there were Rose and Hester; and Dinah with her baby in her arms; and Rena, the tall beautiful mulatto girl who had just married Big Jake, already the father of ten children. Jessie had a pleasant word for each one of them. As she passed Aunt Lucy's house, a cheery voice called to her,

"How d' you do, Miss Jessie? Where's you gwine, honey? Can't you stop an' see me a minute?" The old woman was sitting near the open door, carding as usual. The girl did not enter the cabin, but seated herself outside on the doorstep.

"'Pears it's a long time sense I'se seen you, honey," said the negress; "de sight o' yer face is good for sore eyes. I ain't seen you fur nigh onto two weeks. Miss Lilian's better, I knows. You looks sorter white an' tired. Is you well, honey?"

"Yes, I believe so," answered Jessie; "and how are you, Aunt Lucy?"

"Right smart, thank 'ee," replied the old woman. "I'se scarcely ever sick, Miss Jessie, an' does you know why?"

"No, tell me, please," said Jessie.

"It's all kase I won't sot around like dese tudder colored folks. Now, ef I'se got a pain, I never hopes to sot it off—I walks it off. Up and down, side o' dis ole wheel I goes, a-singin' de very bes' tune I can find in dis ole head, an' de pain it gits better right off."

"Perhaps that's a good plan, Aunt Lucy," said the girl, with a smile; "I know it is not always well to yield to one's feelings."

"Dat's true as gospil, honey. I don't b'lieve in a-humorin' myse'f any more dan I b'lieves in humorin' tudder folks, an' dat's not a speck. Now, when my gals says dey's got de fever, I jes' gins dem de cards an' a pile o' cotton', sted o' quinine. Dey knows better dan to tell me dey's got de fever. Haf de talk 'bout de fever is lazeness, an' dat's wusser dan all de fevers in de worrel, kase dere's no medicine fur to cure it—'les 'tis a hick'ry stick,"—and Aunt Lucy lay back in her chair and laughed heartily. It was impossible not to feel the contagion of her cheerfulness. Jessie laughed too.

"Dere's times, I can tell you, when a hick'ry stick is

rale good medicine; you 'plies it to de back in de shape of a blister," and she laughed again.

"I'm sure you, at least, never need such medicine," said the girl; "you are always busy. Why do you work so hard, Aunt Lucy? You are free now."

"Now you knows well 'nuff, Miss Jessie," exclaimed the negress, "dat freedom ain't made no diff'rence at all to de niggers. Dey talks a heap 'bout freedom as ef 'twas a-gwine to sot us all up in fine houses an' dress us up in caliky, an' put fans in our hans ter fan off de flies and skeetos wid; but dat kind o' talk is all shucks. I'se got no more patience wid it dan I'se got wid lazeness. Freedom's jes' gin us de right to work fur ourse'f; it's not gin us de right to be lazy. I foun' dat out purty quick —I did. I was jes' fool 'nuff, Miss Jessie, to sot roun' myse'f a while; but den I see, plain as de nose in a nigger's face, dat I'se got no smoke-house full o' meat, an' ole Marster's smoke-house it was locked up arter freedom. I'se jes' got to be smarter dan ever steppin' roun', or dar'll be no bacon nor cornmeal eder in dis house. Don't talk to me 'bout freedom." And the old woman gave a contemptuous grunt.

"But you are glad to be free, Aunt Lucy, are you not?" asked the girl.

"Yes, Miss Jessie, I is; it makes me sorter proud to feel dat I b'longs to myse'f, an' dat nobody ken tuck up my chillen an' carry dem off an' sell 'em. But den I'se allus had a good marster, an' I'se not agwine to cuss him now I'se free. Ole Marster's gin me 'nuff ter eat all my life, an' good clo'es to wear—better 'n I'se got now to save my soul. No, I'se yit to see what freedom's done so much fur de niggers. P'raps you can tell me, Miss Jessie," said Aunt Lucy, looking at the young lady with her small keen eyes.

"You may never see the difference, Aunt Lucy," Jessie answered, "but your children and grandchildren probably will. The negroes are now free to make what they can of themselves. They can learn to read and write, and, if they are industrious, they can save money and buy land for themselves, and get comfortable homes. But these things cannot be gained without hard work."

"Jes' what I says!" exclaimed the old woman; "ef I'se free, I'se got to work all de harder, an' I specks to go on cardin' an' spinnin' all de same till I dies. But, Miss Jessie, offen I'se full o' doubt 'bout de time when I gits too ole to spin. Who's gwine to look arter me den? Reuben he'll chaw all de same, an' never hab no money to buy nothin' but 'bacco. Dat's de question, honey, dat offen bothers me."

"Take no thought for the morrow, Aunt Lucy; do your duty now and leave the future alone."

"I know dat's gospil truf, Miss Jessie, an' the Lord allus looks arter his'n; but all de same, He specks us to step roun' purty spry fur ourse'f. Brudder Jerry, he says so. He prays loud an' strong, but he hoes de cotton an' de corn all de same."

"That's very true, Aunt Lucy, but after we have done our best we must not worry about what is going to happen. I am sure Colonel Winston will never let you suffer in your old age."

"I knows dat, an' I only hopes ole Marster may live jes' as long as I does."

Jessie made no reply; she did not feel like talking, and left the old woman to continue the conversation. Presently Aunt Lucy looked up and said, sharply:

"'Pears to me you'se mighty quiet to-day, Miss Jessie. You looks tired an' whiter dan I likes to see you. What's de matter, honey?"

"I *am* tired, Aunt Lucy—very tired. I came out for a walk, hoping the fresh air and the exercise would rest me. I must go on now; I want to go to the mill this way through the woods and come back by the road. Good-bye,"—and she arose from her seat.

Aunt Lucy laid down the cards and reached out her hard black hands; she took the soft white ones between her palms and stroked them tenderly. She loved this fair young creature, and felt a pang to see her droop. "Honey," she said in a tone full of sympathy, "you jes' mustn't git faint-hearted—'taint no use. I'se all feard you doesn't pray 'nuff. Now, I doesn't never stop a prayin' an' a-singin'. I prays when I cards, an' I sings when I spins. I likes de music o' dis ole wheel—it's jes as good as de piany any day. De truf is, I likes it better—kase you has de music an' de broach o' cotton, too,"—and once more she laughed her hearty laugh. Jessie joined in, and Aunt Lucy seemed delighted to have chased the sadness from that sweet young face. "Dat's right—I loves to hear you laugh; you looks more like yourse'f now. Good-bye, an' don't you stay out too late, honey."

Tiger had been lying at the feet of his young mistress, watching her face with intense interest. When she arose, he got up also, and wagged his tail as if to express his readiness to follow her wherever she might choose to go. She laid her hand upon his collar, and they started off again together. Presently they entered the wood and hurried along the narrow road. It was so sweet and cool under the trees that the tired girl felt inexpressibly refreshed and almost skimmed the ground. Broken bits of sunshine fell through the thick foliage, and made a lovely mottled pathway for her.

After a while, she came to a bend in the road, and

through a long leafy vista she caught a glimpse of the
great pond, shining in the sunlight. She heard the fall
of the water over the dam, and the noisy clatter of the
wheels. Then she reached an opening in the trees, and
stepped out into the main road that led to Redbank.
She crossed the bridge over the mill-stream, lingering
to look up and down at the rushing water, now brighten-
ing in the sunshine, now darkening in the shadow, and
ever hurrying onward " to join the brimming river." On
the other side, at the foot of a green slope near the road,
she found a convenient stone, and sat down. From this
point she could take in the whole scene. She was very
weary and needed to rest. As she sat there all kinds of
thoughts were hurrying through her tired brain. It would
be impossible to follow them as they came and went in
an endless procession. She could not help thinking of
her own strange, sad life, and wondering if she would
ever reach a goal of happiness, as some did. More than
ever before, she was beginning to dread dulness and
monotony—to long for variety and excitement. Then
she recalled the words of the Judge and found herself
surprised at the truth of his prophetic vision. Would
it have been better to have accepted his offer, and found
escape in that manner? No, she could not believe that:
and yet the way which he had presented to her looked
more attractive now than it had done a few months ago
when he had offered himself to her. She was beginning
to feel uncertain of herself; she wondered if the time
would ever come in the future, when she would be so
weary of everything that, like Eleanor, she would marry
in desperation. " Oh! no!" she exclaimed aloud, clasping her hands—" anything but that, I must be strong—I
must be true. God help me!" Her passionate words
aroused Tiger; he looked up at her with amazement in

his sleepy eyes. Was her question addressed to him? She answered his mute inquiry by putting her hand upon his head with a caressing touch.

"Tiger, Tiger," she said, "be thankful that you are a dog, and don't have to study moral philosophy."

She had been sitting there a long time, when she heard a sound that startled her—a carriage was coming. It was useless to try to hide from sight, so she sat very still and waited. Soon the vehicle approached near enough for her to see a pair of handsome gray horses through the trees. Yes, it was the Judge. How strange! She was just thinking about him, and longing for his return. He saw her and lifted his hat. On reaching the bridge, the carriage stopped and the gentleman got out; he walked hurriedly to the spot where she was sitting. "How are you? And what are you doing in this lonely place?" he asked, extending both hands.

"How surprised I am to see you! I thought you were a thousand miles away," she exclaimed.

"I only reached home a few days ago. But come, get into the carriage, and I will give you the ride that I promised you once upon a time. I am on my way to Redbank, and I have a thousand things to tell you. Jim," he continued, addressing the driver, "I will take the reins. You can get out and walk the rest of the way—it is not far."

CHAPTER X.

When they were both seated in the carriage, he turned the horses sharply around, touched them with the whip, and they dashed rapidly down the road over which they had just travelled.

"Where are you going?" she asked.

"Not to Redbank yet awhile," he answered with a smile; "I am not in such a hurry to get there now that you are sitting beside me. We still have at least an hour and a half before sunset, and it will do you good to spend it out-of-doors."

While he spoke he was looking at her very intently. She wore a simple white dress, cut away from the throat, and belted at the waist with a white ribbon. She carried her hat in her hand; she had taken it off on account of the heat. Her beautiful brown hair was loosely and carelessly knotted, but this suited her pure pale face better than the most elaborate coiffure would have done. She felt a little unnatural and constrained under his intense gaze. She knew that he was noting the changes in her, and the thought made her somewhat uncomfortable.

At length he said, as if half to himself, "More than ever like the statue of a goddess."

The words aroused the playfulness of her nature, and

she quickly replied, "More than ever like an Athenian Sage, until he opens his mouth—and then——"

"What then?" he asked.

"Why, then, one sees that he is only an American gentleman of the nineteenth century."

"Evidently a creature to be despised!" he said with a smile.

"By the statue of a goddess—yes; by a young lady of the nineteenth century—no."

"Why, what a sharp wit she hath! What has she been feeding on?" he asked.

"The bitter berries that grow in these swamps," she answered, laughing, "and they have puckered up my mouth."

"I do not see it," he said.

"Well, I feel the bitter taste," she replied.

"That will never do; a bitter taste in the mouth shows that there is something wrong about the system," he said; "we must find an antidote right away. What shall it be? that's the question."

"How do I know!" she exclaimed; "a patient cannot prescribe for herself; that's the business of the physician."

"You are right. Well, I will undertake to play the part of physician. I will not prescribe either pills or powders, but a change of climate immediately."

"What a charming prescription!" she said. "Where shall I go? Quick, I'm dying to hear."

"With me," he answered, looking at her with a kind smile. "Come, fill the aching void in my heart."

She broke into a merry laugh. "The void alone is yours—the aching is mine. Why, I've been aching all the summer. I've made the awful discovery that I have bones and joints."

"Impossible!" he exclaimed; "you cannot convince me of that. You are chiseled out of Parian marble by some unknown Phidias. All you need is a pedestal and a temple."

"You absurd man!" she said; "don't you know you are too old to talk such nonsense?"

"Please, don't remind me of my age," he answered; "I'm getting to be very much ashamed of it. No old maid can be more sensitive than I am on that point. Ah! would I were a boy again!"

"You must start off and try to find the fountain of youth," she said lightly.

"I have already found it, but I'm not permitted to bathe in it," he answered.

"Where is it?" she asked.

"I don't remember the exact latitude and longitude; I only know the name of the country."

"Then tell me that."

"The land of Love," he replied.

"There! that will do," she said, breaking into a light laugh; "give your attention now to the horses, or they will run away, and we will both find ourselves in a land of stones and underbrush."

He seemed inclined to obey her, for he gathered up the reins more tightly and touched the horses with the whip.

Presently he again looked at her and said, very seriously, as if tired of the levity in which they had been indulging, "Jessie, have you really been ill this summer? You look so pale that I would hardly know you."

"Do I? Why, I'm quite well," she replied; "you know it has been very warm ever since the first of June, and I confess I have felt the heat more than ever before. Then Lilian has been very ill, and I have grown somewhat tired trying to help Eleanor take care of her. But I assure you I am perfectly well."

He shook his head as if he doubted her words. "Jessie, I wish you would give me the right to love you and take care of you. There are some women who are strong enough to struggle alone. You are not one of them. You will have to yield after awhile—why not now?"

She was both vexed and touched by his words, and the warm color came into her pale cheeks. She was beginning to realize that he knew her better than she knew herself. Somehow to-day she did not feel equal to renewing the battle with him—she was too weak and tired—she feared defeat; so she only said in a pleading tone, "Hush, please, you must not talk so now. Tell me all about your summer—where you have been, and what you have been doing; and about Alice. How is she?"

"She does not look much better than you do," he answered; "Jessie, I don't know what is the matter with Alice. She is not at all like her old self. Sometimes she is unnaturally gay and excited; at other times she looks tired and listless. She is growing very capricious and hard to please. It grieves me to see the change in her. I'm beginning to feel that all women are alike, and they are all very much like the moon—they exhibit a new phase every night."

Jessie laughed and asked, "Where is Alice now? Did she return with you?"

"No, she is in Virginia, at the White Sulphur Springs, with her mother and Waverley. I do not wish her to return south until October; but she seems quite determined to come, and I'm afraid she will have her way. Jessie," he continued, "she looks so fragile that it almost frightens me."

"I am very, very sorry to hear it," was the reply. "Perhaps she is tired of all the travelling and gayety. I know she does not care for such things. She told me before she left that she would much prefer to stay at home with her books."

"Did she?" he asked, "I wish I had known it. I see now that it was a mistake to travel so much. It has tired her. But I thought she would like it. However, Waverley may be able to set things right." In spite of these reassuring words, it was evident that he was anxious and troubled about his niece. Jessie had not often seen such a shadow on his face. He fell into a long silence.

The gray horses trotted swifty over the smooth white road. The cool air and the delightful motion brought a brilliant glow into the eyes of the young girl. After her long and wearisome bondage in the sick room, she keenly felt the pleasure of lying back in this luxurious carriage, and dashing rapidly along without any effort on her part. Moreover, she was conscious, as never before, of the agreeable presence beside her. Hungry in every fibre of her rich womanly nature, she had never so keenly felt the charm of perfect companionship. The Judge was quietly reading all these emotions in her tell-tale face. "The drive is doing you good," he said ; "how much better you look than when I found you sitting like 'a maid forlorn' upon that old stone. I wonder what you were thinking about."

She smiled and held her peace. "Come, tell me, please," he continued. She shook her head. "Well, I can guess. You were thinking about me, and wishing that I would hurry up and come and give you that ride I promised you long ago. Wasn't that it?"

"Clever as you are, you have not yet learned to read a young girl's thoughts," she said, evasively.

"Jessie, if you would only listen to me, child," he exclaimed after a while; "I know that I could make you very happy."

She drew farther back into the corner of the carriage, and put up her little hand with an imploring gesture.

"Please do not tempt me," she cried; "I cannot, I must not. If I were to yield, it would not be for love of you, but for love of all the beautiful things that you could give me."

"I accept your consent, even on those terms," he answered in a low tone.

"But it would be wrong!" she exclaimed; "I know it would, and only trouble could come from it. If I once fell, who knows what might happen?—No, no, you must not tempt me. I cannot bear it to-day—I feel so weak and helpless. You must have pity on me!"

He said nothing more; soon he again touched the horses with the whip, as if impatient and desirous of going faster. He looked so sad and stern, and held the horses with so firm a grasp, that she was afraid she had wounded him, and asked, almost in a whisper—

"You are not angry with me, are you?"

"No, my darling," he answered; "how could I be angry with you! You have restored to me my boyish faith in angels, and all other good and beautiful things."

She was glad that it was not necessary to make any reply, and gave her attention to watching the trees as they swept by her. Suddenly they reached a spot where the road broadened, and the Judge turned the horses around. "The sun is getting low," he said, "perhaps we had better be thinking of Redbank."

On they dashed again. They had travelled over several miles before she found it in her heart to speak again; then she said, somewhat timidly, "If you do not find your horses too absorbing, do tell me some news. How is everybody I know in the city?"

"Everybody is growing older every day; that is all I know," he answered.

"Is Nettie Hunter married?"

"No, only engaged to a new fellow who has recently come to town."

"What is his name?"

"Mr. Clarence Sage. Let us hope he will have the wisdom requisite for his new position. Can you ever think of Miss Nettie as turning into Mrs. Sage?" he asked with a smile.

"Never!" exclaimed Jessie, "she must not marry him. It would be too ridiculous—too paradoxical. You must resort to some method of preventing it."

"I will try, if you wish me," the Judge said, playfully; "I think, myself, that something ought to be done, but my mind is not quite clear on the subject of who should do it. The truth is, I am rather afraid of Miss Nettie. She is a very clever girl. She has ways of entangling a fellow in his own words and convincing him that he has said what he knows he has never said, and making him declare what he does not wish to declare. I had rather not meddle with her affairs. She is too smart for me. I confess I like simpler girls."

"And yet the gentlemen all find her perfectly irresistible," said Jessie.

"That's a serious fault in a girl," he replied; "to be irresistible is to be dangerous, like a quicksand, or a whirlpool, or a sunken rock. A wise man instinctively avoids such women, and chooses the quiet and unconscious ones."

"You make me think that there are very few wise men in the world," exclaimed Jessie. "I once heard Nettie say that she had had a hundred and fifty offers, and never intended to marry until she had received two hundred. That's a goodly number of men who are *not* wise—according to your notion."

"You surprise me by your knowledge of arithmetic, and you make me ashamed of my sex," he answered, laughing heartily.

"And Belle Duval?—tell me something about her," asked the young girl, eagerly.

"She's engaged too," he answered, "they are all engaged, my dear—every single one of them. You are the only one who is left out in the cold. You will be awfully lonesome before the winter is over."

"When I am lonesome, I will let you know," she said, with a faint glow of color on her cheeks—"until then, you must leave me in peace."

He was touched by her pleading tone. "I will," he replied; "only don't forget the promise."

They were now entering the avenue that led up to Redbank. "You have given me a delightful ride," said the girl, "and I thank you more than I know how to express."

"It is *I* who am the debtor," was the answer.

There was no time for further conversation. The horses soon stopped at the front door, and Jessie and the judge alighted from the carriage.

It was a merry party that gathered around the supper table that evening. Judge Brooks was pelted with questions from every one, to which he replied in his own graceful style, provoking bright retorts, and exciting an unusual amount of laughter. There is nothing on earth quite equal to the companionship of a genial friend: we never realize what fountains of humor and pathos are sealed up in our own souls until he comes with his magic wand,—his witch-hazel,—and touches the spot where the springs lie, waiting to bubble up.

CHAPTER XI.

"Hear the mellow wedding bells—
Golden bells!"

JUDGE BROOKS had come to the country to see how affairs were progressing on the plantation of his sister-in-law, and to make arrangements for her return home early in October, perhaps sooner. The house was to be put in order, some needful repairs attended to, and some refurnishing done on quite an extensive scale. It was the expectation of the Judge, as well as of the general public, that, before the winter was over, a brilliant wedding would be celebrated at the Grove. Almost from infancy, Alice Brooks had been the destined bride of her cousin Waverley, and now that he had returned from Europe to claim her, there was no need of delay in celebrating the happy event.

The next morning, the family at Redbank gathered on the piazza to take leave of their guest. His visit had refreshed each one of them, and they were reluctant to see him depart, but he declared himself too overwhelmed with the business that had accumulated during his long absence from home to remain another day. His last adieus were spoken to Jessie, and she felt the tenderness of his manner as he stooped and kissed her hand. She watched the beautiful gray horses as they trotted off down the long avenue. With his own inimitable grace, the Judge lifted his hat and waved his friends a final good-bye. The girl stood there a long time after the carriage was out of sight. It would have been difficult to analyze her complex emotions. Her respect and admiration for Judge Brooks were very great. He was by far the most attractive man that she had ever met; and, though nearly fifty years old, he was so full of vigor and youthful freshness of manner and soul that one never thought of his age. His social position and great wealth formed a handsome frame for so noble a man. His strong intellect, and his broad and enlightened views on all subjects, gave him great influence not only in the affairs of his native city but also throughout the whole state. Jessie Holcombe realized all this; she felt a longing for the sheltering love of such a man, and the worldly delights of the home in which he would place her. As she watched him drive away, a keen pang of regret seized upon her, a feeling of weariness and depression, as if it were all over, and no further interest were left to life. If he could have stood beside her at that moment, perhaps she would have relented and consented to become his wife. And yet, even now, there was a strange, inexplicable something within her that restrained and subdued the longings of her heart.

While the girl was standing there, lost in thought, the Colonel came across the yard with the mail-bag in his hand. The arrival of the mail was always an exciting event at Redbank. It was necessary to send to the city for it, and sometimes several days passed without any news of the outside world. The Colonel ascended the steps, and took his seat on the piazza; then he opened the bag and assorted the letters and papers. There were none for Jessie, and she felt but little interest in those received by the other members of the family. She was about to go to her room, when she heard an exclamation of surprise from the Colonel. He raised his eyes from the letter that he was reading, and said in a loud tone—" Bless my heart! Well, this is news!"—and he called to Mrs. Winston, who was swinging Lilian in the hammock at the other end of the piazza,—" Come here, Eleanor; I've some astounding news for you."

She came slowly forward, holding the child in her arms. " I hope it is good news," she said, " for I am limp enough now; I don't think I could stand much more."

" You can judge for yourself whether it is good or not. Listen,—the letter is from Philip. Would you believe it?—he is going to be married. He writes that the lady —Miss Percy Lester—is young, beautiful, and very rich. Her father is a prominent business man, well-known throughout the North-West. Her own mother has been dead a great many years, but there is a step-mother, also young and handsome. Philip puts it all in a very brief way, as if anxious to get through with the announcement. There is to be a large wedding, and then he is going to bring his bride East. He intends to spend several weeks in visiting the large cities—New York, Boston, Philadelphia, Washington, and then he is coming South. He wants his wife to see his native state. You can guess the rest. If we feel in a hospitable mood, he will make us a visit. What do you say to it? Here, you may read the letter."

She reached out her hand for it, and read it through in her usual deliberate way, without betraying any emotion. When she had finished it, she returned it to her husband. " Well, how shall I answer it? what shall I say to him? You see the wedding is to take place very soon—the middle of next month. I must write immediately."

"You know perfectly well," she said, "that there is but one answer to be made. Of course, we must send them an invitation to come."

"Do you think you can manage it in proper style?" he asked, as if doubtful of the present resources of the plantation.

"It will not be easy," she answered; "I am rather worn-out with all the sickness in the family, and my corps of servants is not very large nor very efficient. It is more difficult to entertain guests than it used to be in the old days. I'm afraid Southern hospitality is on the decline. However, I'll manage it; I'm generally equal to such emergencies."

"Well, I leave it all in your hands," he said. And that was the end of the matter, so far as he was concerned.

The letter to Mr. Philip Winston, containing an invitation to himself and bride to visit Redbank was immediately written and sent. It was sufficiently cordial in tone to satisfy the most exacting. It left the time of coming and the length of stay entirely to the disposition of the guests. The Colonel would have felt it beneath his dignity to place restrictions upon any one who honored him with a visit.

During the next few weeks there was an unusual amount of commotion in the old plantation home. There was some house cleaning, some hanging of fresh muslin curtins, some unfolding of dainty bed and table linen, some polishing of old silver. Lilian was in a kind of ecstasy, and under this delightful excitement she rapidly recovered her strength. She never wearied of listening to the story of her new uncle and aunt. They seemed to her like a prince and princess from some unknown land, and she endowed them with all the virtues and accomplishments of royalty. Nothing so beautiful had ever happened to her before, and her imagination was filled with pictures as gorgeous as the scenes of a Christmas pantomime. This coming event vaguely satisfied that deep yearning after the far-away, the romantic, the splendid, which lies in the heart of every child.

At length the day, so long anticipated, arrived. It was in the early part of October, and the weather was perfect. During the long summer the heat seemed to have expended itself, and now there was a delightful freshness to the air, rather unusual in that southern climate. The horses and carriage had been sent to the city for the expected guests. The house had been decorated with plants and flowers, which were still plentiful; Lilian and the baby had been dressed in their best clothes, and were playing on the piazza; dinner was in process of preparation. Mrs. Winston had arrayed herself in a soft gray silk, which revealed the perfect lady in every fold.

Jessie Holcombe was one of those girls who never give very much thought to the outward adornment. She possessed that unconsciousness of dress which is so rare in these latter days; but she realized the importance of the present occasion, and wished to show honor to the strangers who were coming from afar. She loved white, and knew that it was becoming to her, so she dressed herself in a long princess robe of white cashmere, and fastened a red rose at her throat. She was conscious of a little unnatural excitement, a little flutter of anticipation, which was both new and pleasant. A breeze from the great world was about to ripple the dull surface of her life. Her experiences had been entirely outside of what is called " fashionable society," and she was rather curious to see what manner of woman is developed in that luxurious atmosphere.

About three o'clock in the afternoon, the carriage drove up to the door. All the family were out on the piazza, and a group of colored men and women were crowded in the hall, intent on seeing the pageant.

The Colonel and Mrs. Winston stepped forward to welcome the happy pair, and congratulations and kisses were exchanged. Then introductions to Miss Holcombe and the children were made in proper form.

The bride was a tall, willowy girl, very stylish in appearance. Dressed in a faultless suit of dark brown silk, with hat, veil, and gloves to match, she looked as if she had just stepped out of the last fashion-plate. She was pretty and delicate in appearance; her eyes were brown and bright; her hair was a rich auburn in color, and her complexion was brilliant. She had a high, thin little voice; but it was not really unpleasant to listen to, unless one were very fastidious. As she turned away with Mrs. Winston to mount the stairs to her room, Jessie Holcombe felt a pang of disappointment. She could not explain the feeling even to herself; perhaps it was the voice, which to Jessie's fine ear sounded flat and soulless, wanting the modulations which betray all the delicate shades of emotion.

"Isn't she beautiful!" exclaimed Lilian, quite overwhelmed by the bright vision.

"Beautiful!" echoed the negroes, one after the other.

"Umph!" said Aunt Lucy, from her post in the remote background.

Mr. Philip Winston lingered on the piazza with his brother, and Jessie had an opportunity of scanning him from head to foot. She saw a family resemblance between the two gentlemen, and yet there were many points of difference. Mr. Philip was not so tall as the Colonel, but his form was more compact and his air more business-like. He wore a very heavy mustache and side-whiskers which were reddish-brown in color. His manners were very graceful and polished, and he bore the unmistakable impress of city life. There was a style about him, which is given partly by the fashionable tailor, and partly by intercourse with fashionable society. But in spite of these external attractions, there was something about his face that Jessie did not like, and she shrewdly guessed that at bottom he was hard, cold, calculating, and selfish. Before long she had reason to know that she was not mistaken.

Afternoon tea was carried into the room of the bride, and she rested several hours. Dinner henceforth was to be served at six, in compliment to the city guests.

The table was looking quite splendid when at length the family gathered around it. Every relic of former prosperity had been hunted up and brought into prominent position.

After the others were assembled, the bride came in, leaning on the arm of her husband. She wore an evening-dress of black velvet, cut low, and profusely trimmed with costly lace. Diamonds flashed from her ears and throat and arms. Her abundant auburn hair was massed like a coronet on the top of her heed, making her appear several inches taller. Her cheeks were aglow with rosy color, and she looked dazzling. The Colonel placed her on his right hand, and then turned and gazed at her with undisguised admiration.

"Why, Philip," he exclaimed, "allow me to congratulate you again; you are a lucky fellow—I can scarcely believe my own eyes. My dear," he continued, turning to Mrs. Philip, "what kind of spells has he been using to bewitch a young and beautiful creature like you?"

She smiled, and, lifting her eyes with a pretty consciousness, replied—"I thought it was I who had bewitched him."

"The bewitching was mutual, of course," said Mrs. Winston.

"Such things are always incomprehensible, so we won't discuss them," said Mr. Philip; "I'm unaccountably hungry, so let's discuss the dinner. To my mind, that is a more interesting topic just at present." It was easy to see that he appreciated a good dinner, and perhaps considered it the most important event of the day.

"Do you feel perfectly rested?" asked Mrs. Winston.

"Oh! yes!" replied the bride; "I feel nicely now, thank you."

"Did you find the ride long and tiresome?" asked the Colonel.

"As if she could find any drive long or tiresome with me beside her!" exclaimed Mr. Philip; "I'm sure she found it heavenly."

Mrs. Philip gave a little turn to her head, and a side glance upward into her husband's face,—it was a pretty trick of hers,—when she said, "He will not allow me to answer for myself. He has me in perfect subjection already. I am very fond of driving, so I did not in the least mind the distance."

"You see, she ignores your presence altogether," said the Colonel to his brother. They both laughed.

"Yes, it is very pleasant to see somebody else," replied Mrs. Philip; "I have grown fearfully tired of sitting down to a hotel-table with only him to talk to."

"Now, I'm fairly extinguished," exclaimed the husband; "and I assure you I have been trying my very best to be agreeable, and to talk about balls and operas and dresses, and all the other feminine topics of conversation. My failure overwhelms me with mortification. My dear," turning to his wife, " I shall never again try to please you. My mind is quite made up on that point." Every one laughed.

"And my mind is quite made up in the contrary direction," she answered, with an emphatic little nod and a coquettish smile.

"We'll see who will pull the hardest," said Mr. Philip, reflecting her smile. " Miss Holcombe, you are a disinterested party; what is your opinion ? Who will win in the pull ?"

"The woman, of course," said Jessie.

" Ah! I might have known that would be your decision. But why do you think the woman will win?"

" Because, in such a struggle, the man never pulls with all his might, and the woman does," answered Jessie.

" Ah! I see you have a judicial mind," Mr. Philip said ; " I fear I'm doomed. What a sad state of affairs after only two weeks of married life."

" Yes," exclaimed Miss Holcombe, " it is an awful warning to the unmarried."

Mrs. Philip looked at the young lady across the table; it was but a glance, and yet somehow Jessie felt that it took in every item of her make-up, even to the cost of the lace at her throat. She did not like that cold, curious stare, and returned it with a haughty flash of her fine eyes. It annoyed her more than she could have explained, even to herself, to be measured by this rich city girl, and she resented it as a rudeness. There was a quick spark of intelligence between the two. Mrs.

Philip was not wanting in sense, and she realized in a moment that there was something more to this girl than her clothes. There was a short silence, and then the conversation turned upon the late wedding, and the tour through the Eastern States. The bride had never been East before, and she had fresh impressions to express, which she did very prettily. With New York she was perfectly fascinated, but Washington was a great disappointment. " After a few handsome public buildings, there is nothing to see," she said; " New York is ever so much nicer. I would really like to go there to live."

" My dear," said the Colonel, " you must not take New York for your standard. If you do, you will be disappointed with everything else. Washington has a character of its own, so has Philadelphia, so has Baltimore, and so has Redbank." and he laughed heartily at this anti-climax. .

" She is perfectly enchanted with Redbank," exclaimed Mr. Philip; " I had somewhat prepared her for its splendors, but, like the Queen of Sheba, she is compelled to confess that the half was not told her." She looked at him steadily for a few moments, and then laughed. " I undertake to interpret your emotions for you, and to put their vague confusion into words," said the husband.

" Thank you," was her reply, and again she laughed.

Colonel Winston was very sensitive about any allusion to the South, and imagined a concealed sting in this little laugh. He keenly felt the contrast between the prosperity of the North and the poverty of the South. He knew that this girl had just come from a luxurious home, and would perhaps despise the simple comforts of Redbank. " My dear," he said, " we are all poor at the South now; we are, as you know, quite broken down in the world. We are sorry to have nothing better to offer you; but what we have is offered with cordial hospitality." He spoke these words with his grandest manner.

"Pray, don't apologize," she said, quickly; "you misunderstand me altogether. I like Redbank and everything about it exceedingly, and I am sure I shall have a perfectly lovely time with you all. I could not help laughing, a little while ago—please excuse me; but Philip has been entertaining me with the most absurd stories about your way of living. One day he would picture something quite palatial, and the next he would describe something so shabby as to excite my disgust. I think he takes pleasure in teasing me."

"I must put a stop to that right away," said Mrs. Winston, with decided emphasis; "I cannot allow you to be teased under my roof. Do you hear, Philip?"

"Her accusation against me is entirely without foundation," replied the gentleman, looking up from his plate with the blank stare of perfect innocence. "She is the tease. She has teased me almost to death to learn the minutest incident in the past life of every one of you. She would have made a good inquisitor, I assure you. Of course, I was obliged sometimes to draw on my imagination in order to satisfy this morbid curiosity."

"You shall not misrepresent me so!" she cried, a flush mounting to her forehead. "You are the most provoking man I ever saw."

The arch smile with which this was spoken extracted the sting from the charge.

"And you are the most provoking woman that I ever saw," he answered back, also reflecting her smile.

"We give our sympathy to the lady," said Mrs. Winston; "here, on the spot, we form an alliance against tyranny and oppression."

"Why, this is dreadful! I'm afraid my happiness is at an end!" cried Mr. Philip, laying down his knife and fork. "Miss Holcombe, can I not at least rely upon your assistance in this unnatural alliance against me?"

"I am afraid not; I have been told that it is very unsafe to mix oneself up in conjugal quarrels, so I shall remain neutral."

"And lose your reputation for valor?" he asked. "You know neutrals are often considered cowards."

"Sometimes 'discretion is the better part of valor,'" Jessie answered.

Again, Mrs. Philip fixed her eyes upon the young girl with a cold, curious stare. Her husband observed it. "Well, what are you thinking about?" he asked, while an amused expression flitted over his face.

She bent her head a little and half-whispered: "I'm afraid of her—her eyes are dangerous."

A faint flush spread over Jessie's face, but the remark was made with such a pretty, arch, innocent air, that she could not find it in her heart to take offence.

"After all, it is not worth while to be vexed with this bewitching creature," thought Jessie; "but she is very different from the girls that I have been used to."

"My dear," said Colonel Winston, turning to Mrs. Philip, "I do not think that you ought to complain of anybody's eyes. I'm sure there is mischief enough in your two."

She smiled and answered, "Oh! no, you are altogether mistaken; mine are very harmless orbs—they are only useful to see with."

"I don't like to begin our acquaintance by declining to believe what you say," he replied; "but in this case I cannot reject the evidence of my own senses."

"She is not referring to the past; she is making

promises for the future," said Mr. Philip. " She means they are going to be very harmless hereafter," and he looked at his wife as if challenging her to contradict his assertion.

" Again you undertake to give expression to the vague confusion of my thoughts," she said, laughing ; " this time I think you have gotten my meaning a little mixed. I promise nothing for the future—nothing whatever." Her manner was very pretty and positive.

" But you have already made a promise which covers the whole ground," he answered.

" Have I ? " she asked, with charming innocence. " When ? where ? "

He put the tip of his finger on the ring that she had given him, and pointed to the one that he had given her.

" By that promise, you annihilated self, your will is now merged in mine."

" I thought it was your will that was merged in mine," she cried gayly, and every one laughed at her saucy way of disputing him.

" I am willing to acknowledge that there is sometimes more than one interpretation to a contract," Mr. Philip answered, " but the reading established by custom is the one that holds good in our law courts. Is it not so, Miss Holcombe ? "

" I am not learned in the law, like Portia," replied the young lady thus appealed to, " but I have heard an old adage which says, ' Man has his will, but woman has her way.' Let me advise you as a friend to avoid contention with a woman, lest you come to grief."

" That is wise advice, Miss Holcombe ; I will try to follow it," he said.

There was a brief pause in the conversation, and then Mr. Philip again looked at Jessie and said, " Miss Holcombe, will you allow me to place my wife in your charge for a brief season ? Will you become her guide, and show her the sights of Redbank ? "

" It would be better for you to act as her guide," replied the girl, feeling that his politeness prompted him to address an occasional remark to her, and that his request was not made with the desire to promote an acquaintance between his young wife and herself.

" But I am sick of sight-seeing," he said ; " Washington has exhausted me, both physically and mentally. I have come to this place for a little rest. It would be a great favor, if you would consent to relieve me of this duty."

" Perhaps the lady may object to having you relieved ? " said Jessie, looking at Mrs. Philip.

" Not at all," was the reply ; " he is a very disagreeable guide, I assure you. He never wants me to ask a single question. He expects me to march around perfectly dumb."

Her husband again laid down his knife and fork, and gazed at her fixedly for a few moments. " A single question ! " he exclaimed ; " why, she will ask more in a minute than one can answer in a month."

" Well, for my part, I like an inquiring mind," said Miss Holcombe ; " it promotes conversation. I am flattered by the compliment you pay me in selecting me as the guide of your wife, Mr. Winston, and I will begin my duties to-morrow. Let me consider what there is to see : The cotton fields, the gin-house, the screw, the quarter, the mill, and the pine wood. Prepare yourself for great physical effort," she continued, turning to Mrs. Philip ; " it will be far more exhausting than the public buildings of Washington."

" Thanks ! You are very kind," replied the bride, in rather a dry tone. " I am full of curiosity to see a southern plantation; I have heard so much about the easy, delightful life that is led upon them. It is Philip's ideal of existence—he sometimes threatens to go upon one himself. Is it really pleasant? I confess it looks rather lonely to me not to have a single neighbor within five miles. How do you manage to endure it all the year round? I'm sure I should die."

"You must have resources of entertainment within yourself," said Mrs. Winston.

"But I have none whatever," she exclaimed, with a little yawn; "I have no talents—I have no accomplishments."

"Yes, you have a wonderful talent for yawning, my dear," said her husband, who had noted the little lapse from good form.

"I never yawn unless I'm dull," she replied, unmindful that she was confessing herself a little tired of the present company; "it is nature's relief for dulness."

"Is that true, Miss Holcombe? Is it not rather a small vice that one can correct?" asked Mr. Philip.

"Is it becoming in you to question a statement made by your wife?" replied the young lady with a smile.

"Yes; married life would be very dull without questions to enliven it, and it is dulness we wish to escape from," he answered.

"Then you must give yourself plenty to do," said Mrs. Winston; "when one is busy all the time, one is never dull."

"Then this little lady must learn how to be busy," he said with playful emphasis.

The young wife looked up at her husband with a little flash of impatience in her eyes. "Was that in the contract, too?" she asked; "I did not see it."

"You know, my dear," he answered, quietly, " that some of these days I am going on a southern plantation to live. I am on the look-out for one now—perhaps I shall find it very soon. Now, since one can only be happy on a plantation by being busy all the time, you must begin right away to learn how to be busy and interested in cows and pigs and chickens."

Again there was a little flash of the brown eyes. "If you go on a southern plantation to live, do you expect me to go with you?" she asked.

"Of course, I do. You don't expect me to go to the expense of hiring a housekeeper, when I have you on my hands—do you?"—and he laughed heartily at her dismayed expression.

She turned to Mrs. Winston and exclaimed helplessly —" Only see how he teases me!"

"Philip, you must not," said Eleanor ; " I shall have to lecture you in private,"—and she shook her head at him, though she could not help joining in the laughter.

When the dinner was ended, they all went into the parlor. The gentlemen approached an open window, threw themselves down in two convenient easy-chairs, lighted their cigars, and began to smoke.

Soon they fell to recalling old times, and their laughter was loud and long.

Mrs. Philip stood a while and watched them ; then she shrugged her shoulders, and said to Jessie—" Come, let's go into the next room. I can't endure tobacco smoke. When I return home, I shall make Philip go to his club to smoke."

He overheard the remark, and called out—" No, you won't."

"Yes, I will," she answered, as she moved away. Soon she laid her jewelled hand on the arm of her companion, and said—" Please tell me what I am to call you."

"My name is Jessica Holcombe," was the reply. "I would like to have you call me Jessie, as everybody else does."

"Then you must call me Percy."

"Very well; we would find it stiff and unpleasant to be formal."

After a short pause, Jessie asked Mrs. Philip if she played on the piano.

"Only a very, very little," the lady answered; "but I see such piles of music that I am sure you do. Will you not play for me? I am rather tired, and will curl up on this sofa and listen."

"What kind of music do you like?" asked Jessie.

"All kinds; I shall be satisfied with your selections."

Soon she had snuggled down on one end of the sofa, spreading out her elegant train on the floor in front of her. Jessie found a pile of operatic music, and began to play some airs from *Il Trovatore*.

"I like that very much," said the lady.

The young girl played on and on, piece after piece. Presently she heard a little snore. Mrs. Philip was asleep.

CHAPTER XII.

"Leaves are light and idle, and wavering and changeable; they even dance. Yet God in his wisdom has made them part of the oak. In so doing, he has given us a lesson not to doubt the stout-heartedness within because we see the lightsomeness without."

Mrs. Philip Winston seemed strangely out of place on a southern plantation. How she came to be there was a mystery to herself as well as to others. Born in one of those great cities of the West whose increase in wealth has astonished the world; accustomed from infancy to almost oriental luxury; unacquainted with any side of life but the sunny side; by what freak of fate had she wandered from her sphere to touch these other lives so full of sharp realities? She was unable to understand her new surroundings, and floated in the midst of these quiet country scenes, perfectly unconscious of the under-currents, bobbing here and there like a bright buoy. She was indeed a rare bit of color in the dull picture. Morning and evening she arrayed herself in something new and beautiful. These exquisite clothes did not seem to be accidental accessories of existence but an integral part of her very being. She spent many hours in the elaborate processes of the toilette, and seemed to derive a refined enjoyment from the exercise. With so small a public to appreciate, it was surely a waste of human energy, to put on and pull off so many dresses, but, like a devotee at some shrine, she appeared to find a spiritual comfort from the mysterious rites. When not actually dressing, or undressing she was arranging the trays of her trunks, unfolding and refolding her costly laces, opening and shutting her boxes of jewels, shaking out her rich scarfs and sashes, or spreading her elegant dresses on the bed or chairs of her room, in order to air or sun them. She seemed to be entirely without other resources of entertainment.

She never opened a book, she did not know how to draw or paint, and she possessed only the most superficial knowledge of music. Her time was wholly taken up in lounging on the bed, or rummaging in her trunks, or arranging the hundreds of exquisite articles, that she had heaped on the bureau, the mantel-piece and the tables of her room. In a pretty, restless fashion, like some bright butterfly or humming bird, she flitted hither and thither over these little tasks, singing snatches of fashionable operas, and seeming as happy as if absorbed in the most exalted duties.

Sometimes she settled down for a few hours and wrote letters; but this appeared to tax her energies *fearfully*, to use her own favorite adverb. She would arise from the task looking worn and collapsed. During the morning hours, she was left much to herself; this was unavoidable in a well-regulated home like Redbank, where each member of the family had clearly defined duties. Jessie's hours were spent in reading and teaching Lilian. Mrs. Winston was occupied in household tasks. The Colonel usually went off immediately after breakfast for a ride over his cotton-fields. Mr. Philip always accompanied him, quietly ignoring the claims of his young wife.

After luncheon, Jessie and Lilian were free to visit

Percy in her room. She was always sweet and charming with them, exhibiting the choice bric-à-brac scattered around, showing them photographs of her friends, and telling them about the splendors of her city home. Sometimes she would consent to take a short walk, but there was nothing to see—no shops—no people, and she was soon tired, and desirous of returning to the house. She did not know much about riding; having once been thrown at the riding-school, her lessons had ended then and there. Occasionally, her husband would propose a drive, and to this she eagerly assented, and always returned much refreshed, even though there was no fashionable park in which to show off her toilette and equipage.

Only a few of the neighbors had yet returned from their summer excursions, so Mrs. Winston did not dare to venture upon a dinner-party, or any other form of entertainment for her guests, fearing lest her effort might, in their eyes, prove a failure. In truth, both Eleanor and Jessie were sorely taxed to furnish some amusement for this bright young creature thrown upon their hands. They were thankful to find that she was fond of cards; a card-table became an established custom in the evening. But Mr. Philip hated cards, and would never join in the game. Night after night, the Colonel, Mrs. Winston, and Jessie sat around the table until nearly twelve o'clock, playing whist with the exacting little lady, who had a most charming way of pleading for another and yet another rubber. If she were losing, she was always eager to retrieve her reputation; if she were winning, she was too excited to stop. This passion for play seemed to annoy Mr. Philip very much; sometimes he frowned, sometimes he reproved, and sometimes he scolded; but it was all of no avail. "You will smoke your horrid cigars, when you know I hate them; so I'm going to play cards, even if you don't like it," she would say with saucy determination. It was evident that she had no more idea of yielding to his wishes than he had of yielding to hers. Jessie Holcombe looked on at this playful warfare, and wondered if it would long continue to be waged without arousing strong passions on both sides. More than ever she realized the meaning of marriage, and felt a vague dread of the life that follows, when there is no spiritual affinity to make the union complete.

Jessie was thrown continually with Mrs. Philip, and under the influence of this familiar intercourse, something akin to intimacy had sprung up between the two. They were both young, lively, and full of girlish chatter. They talked much with each other, and discussed all kinds of questions with the abandon of youth. On almost every point they differed, nor was this strange. They stood on different points of observation, and were themselves different in character—as different as the field flower and the rare production of the hot-house. Percy was thoroughly worldly and conventional, loving society and admiration, and passionately fond of dress and display of every kind. Her whole life had been passed in an artificial atmosphere. She measured everything by the money standard; she had no conception of anything better than a handsome house, a large income, and an unlimited expenditure. Yet she was naturally frank, generous, and affectionate. Her manners were caressing and charming; she understood the potency of winning tones, arch glances, and coquettish smiles. She was such a gay, winsome creature that you could not find it in your heart to disapprove of anything she did; and yet you could not help feeling that her brain was a sad muddle of false ideas and opinions. She was poorly equipped for the battle of life, and you found yourself wondering what she would make of actual trouble, if it ever came to her. It is a pity that young ladies so reared should not be able to command all the favors of fortune, until death comes to transfer them to a world less uncertain than our own.

It would have been difficult to find a girl more opposite in character than Jessie Holcombe. She had grown up in one of those Virginia homes, so simple, and yet so full of comfort and true refinement. She loved the country with its broad fields and forests; she loved her horses, her dogs, her books. Her father had not been a rich man, but he had occupied a high social position and had been widely known and honored in his native state. He had possessed much learning of an old-fashioned kind; this had been joined to a rare simplicity and strength of character. Jessie had been his companion and pupil almost from infancy, and he had instilled into her a love for the best and highest things. Now that she had grown to womanhood, she was full of vague but lofty ideals. She often longed for something more than she possessed—for greater variety, larger means, a broader field of action; but these restless feelings were held in check by a pure heart and a strong will. Jessie Holcombe and Mrs. Philip Winston could never have been very warm friends; the soil of their natures was as unlike as sand and loam; but thrown together, as they now were, in this old plantation house, their companionship was not without its pleasures.

One evening after a chilly, rainy day, Percy came into Jessie's room. "I'm tired to death," she said, wearily; "Philip is off, smoking and talking with the Colonel in that horrid, stuffy, old library; Eleanor is reading in her own room, and Lilian has gone to bed. May I sit with you a while?"

"Of course you may," replied Jessie; "here, take this chair beside the fire."

"No," said Percy, "you may sit there—I prefer this seat by the table. I hate open fires—they burn my face up while my back is freezing. The furnaces and registers we have at home are ever so much nicer."

"I don't know anything about furnaces," answered Jessie, "but I am sure nothing could be more cheerful and beautiful than a wood-fire. At night before I go to bed, I love to sit and watch it die out. The red-hot coals grow fainter and fainter, until they fade away entirely under the white ashes. I don't wonder that people used to think there were spirits in the fire. I think so myself, sometimes."

"What a funny girl you are," said Percy. "I never think about the fire unless I'm cold. Do let's talk about something else. I'm fearfully blue to-night. I've a great mind to go to my room, and lock my door, and have a good cry all by myself. Wouldn't Philip be mad, if I did? there is nothing in the world he hates so much as a woman's tears. I have never had but one cry since I was married. That was in New York, because he would not take me to drive in the park one afternoon. He declared that he was tired to death, trotting around with me—wasn't that a fine expression for him to use? Besides, he insisted that it was too late to go, though that wasn't true a bit. Well, I was foolish enough to cry. Gracious! wasn't he mad! For a while he raged up and down the room, and expressed his opinion very freely about women. I asked him why he had married one, then? That question cooled him a little, and he said very sweetly, because he loved her. But he gave me to understand that I could never carry my point over him by crying." Percy laughed a little at the remembrance; Jessie said nothing. The unsolicited confidence surprised her. The lady was vexed with her husband to-night, and quite inclined to expose his shortcomings.

Jessie's room was above the library, and the two girls could plainly hear the voices of the gentlemen as they laughed and chatted together over their cigars.

"What are they talking about, do you suppose?" asked the young wife, feeling herself somewhat aggrieved to be excluded from this jovial company.

"Old times, of course; you know it has been a great many years since they have met, and they enjoy talking about what happened when they were boys."

"But they couldn't have been boys together," said Percy,—"there is a great difference in their ages."

"Only about ten years," said Jessie; "I believe the Colonel prolonged his boyhood into the twenties. He was very wild in his youth."

"So was Philip, I'm sure," Percy replied; "I would like to know all about it, but he is as close as an oyster with me. I don't even know his age."

Jessie did not know how to answer this remark, so she was silent. Soon her companion exclaimed—

"Jessica Holcombe, how can you endure to stay down here on this lonely plantation! And yet you look as serene as if you enjoyed it. For my part, I had rather be a toad shut up in a mountain."

The young girl laughed, and said, "You know we do not always fashion our own lives; sometimes we must make the best of circumstances that we cannot control."

"Nonsense," said Percy; "you could get away from Redbank if you made up your mind to do it. Why, you could get married—most girls can, especially if they are as handsome as you are. Why don't you marry some rich fellow, and go to the city to live."

"That looks very easy, but I'm afraid I shall never acquire a fortune in that way."

"Why not?"

"Well," said Jessie, "in the first place, I am not likely to meet any rich fellows—we are all poor at the South now. In the second place, I would not marry for money."

"Why, if the fellow was nice, and rich fellows usually are, of course you would love him."

"I don't know about that; but I'm sure I shall never marry unless I truly love, and I shall never love any man unless he is noble and good—splendidly good. Then, I sha'n't care a farthing whether he is rich or not!"

"What a funny girl you are," said Mrs. Philip; "wouldn't you really like to have a beautiful house in a large city?"

"Perhaps; that would depend on a great many other things; but, even if I were rich, I think I would prefer to have a home in the country."

"Well, wouldn't you like beautiful dresses and jewels like mine?"

"I have never cared much about such things. I suppose I might learn after a while to love them and want them as other women do. But I hope not."

"Why?"—and Mrs. Philip looked at her companion intently, as if she were some new specimen of girlhood.

"Percy," said Jessie, "I think it is wrong for women to care so much for dress and style. It makes men sordid and eager to make money."

" How? " asked Mrs. Philip, " I don't understand."

" Dresses often cost a great deal of money; men wish to give their wives and daughters the things they want —the things that make them happy—and so their lives are spent in toiling to make money."

" Well," answered Percy, " what else is there to toil for? Every man wants to have some kind of business, and of course he wants to succeed in it, and success means making money."

" No, no," exclaimed Jessie, flushed and excited, " success doesn't mean making money."

" Then what does it mean ? "

" A thousand other things, far better. I could not tell you—you would not understand."

" I'm not so stupid as you imagine," said Mrs. Philip, somewhat piqued ; " I can understand most things quite well: tell me what you mean."

" To make millions of dollars is not always to succeed in life," said Jessie, very quietly. "The best men that have ever lived—the men who have done the most for the world—did not care for money at all. They worked for something far better. St. Paul did not care for money ; nor Luther."

" I am not talking about those people who lived ever so long ago," replied Mrs. Philip; " the world has changed since then ; nowadays every man wants to make a fortune. If he dies poor, he is considered a failure."

" Well, I don't know much about it," said Jessie, feeling how hopeless it was to try to express what she really meant, " but I believe there are many noble men in the world now, who are doing all the good they can without any thought of leaving a fortune behind them. I know money is a good thing to have—no one can live without at least a small amount of it. The poor man works for it, that he may buy bread for his family. It is the consuming desire to make millions that seems so awful to me. It seems to destroy a man's soul.—But, dear, we will not talk about it any more.—Tell me something about yourself—your life at home." She knew that Mrs. Philip enjoyed nothing so much as the story of her past triumphs. Jessie had heard it all often before; but to-night she felt content to listen again, rather than talk with one whose thoughts and feelings were not in harmony with her own. Percy immediately threw off all listlessness, and became the animated, brilliant woman of the world. She began to recount her delightful experience at balls, masquerades, and operas. She described with minutest details the grand receptions, the magnificent dresses, the costly flowers. On her pretty jeweled fingers she counted up the number of admirers that she had had, and was proud to declare that more than one had been quite desperate and threatened to commit suicide when his suit had been rejected. Finally, she wound up by rehearsing the scenes of her wedding. There had never been anything quite equal to it in her native city—two thousand guests at the church where the ceremony had taken place, and five hundred at the reception at the house, which had lasted three or four hours, until she could scarcely stand for fatigue. The banks of flowers were so fragrant, the lights were so dazzling, and the moving crowd produced such confusion in her tired brain, that at last she almost fainted on her husband's arms. Here she always paused,—that sensation of faintness on the arm of her husband in her bridal toilette, in the full blaze of chandeliers and the fragrant atmosphere of flowers, with the brilliant, buzzing, fashionable world around, was just too delicious.

"It must have been very brilliant," said Jessie, "but I do not think I would care for such a wedding myself."

"Why not?" asked Mrs. Philip.

"Well, a wedding is a very solemn event, like a religious service, and I am afraid I would have my thoughts dreadfully distracted by the presence of so many people. I would like to be a little bit conscious of what I was saying and doing."

"Oh; I wasn't frightened in the least—I'm not one of that kind. I've been in society ever since I was in long clothes. I knew perfectly well what I was saying and doing. I even remembered in kneeling not to crush the orange-blossoms that caught up the lace on the front of my dress."

"You must have been self-possessed; I'm afraid I should forget all about the orange-blossoms and the dress too," said Jessie, laughing.

"Well, I didn't, I knew perfectly well that I was going to wear that same dress at my reception when I returned home, and I didn't want to muss it in the least. It is a lovely dress. I wish you could see it. It is of cream white satin almost covered with white Spanish lace, caught up here and there with sprays of orange-blossom. The train is over two yards long."

"You must have looked beautiful," said Jessie; "you have so much color that even white satin would be becoming. I have heard that it is a very trying dress."

"Yes, it was very becoming to me; the papers next day were quite absurd. They said that I was the most beautiful bride that had ever been seen in the city. I cut out the pieces; I will show them to you some day."

"I would like to see them," the young girl answered.

After a pause, Percy turned and said, sharply:

"Do you really mean to say that you would not like a splendid wedding? I cannot believe you."

"Nevertheless, it is true," replied Jessie.

"Why?" demanded Percy.

"I have already told you why."

"But that is no reason at all."

"Well," said Jessie, after a few moments' thought, "it is not easy to explain my feelings—but it seems to me that everything about a marriage is uncertain; you never know how it is going to turn out, so I should prefer to be very quiet about it."

"I don't see how a brilliant wedding could make a marriage turn out badly," said Percy.

"I didn't say that—but, if it did happen to turn out unhappily, everybody would recall the great display."

"Why, Jessie Holcombe, you are a regular raven," exclaimed Percy.

Jessie laughed. "I only mean that I should feel so about my own wedding—of course, not about other people's."

"You must be very superstitious, then," said Mrs. Philip, with a touch of contempt in her tone. "Well, I always wanted a stunning affair when I got married, and I have had it. Papa gratified every wish that I expressed. I would not feel married at all, if it had been done in a quiet, pokey way. I shall always recall it with pleasure. Besides, when I go back, I shall be inundated with calls. That will be ever so nice."

Just then Mr. Philip rapped at the door. "I have lost my little wife," he said; "is she in here? Come, my darling, it is time to go to bed."

So the good-nights were exchanged.

CHAPTER XIII.

About ten days after the arrival of Mr. and Mrs. Philip Winston at Redbank, Harry Holcombe made his appearance upon the scene. One morning when the family assembled in the dining-room for breakfast, they found him standing with his back to the fire, and his hands crossed behind him.

He was looking splendidly—as if he had come fresh from a bath in the fountain of eternal youth. His thick curling hair was tossed up carelessly, and his heavy black mustache had an additional and most fascinating twirl. He was dressed in a new suit of dark-gray, which recalled his military days, and with the clothes he seemed to have put on the old dashing manner.

" Why, Harry ! " exclaimed Mrs. Winston, who was the first to see him ; " when did you come ? "

" On the midnight train," he replied.

" But the midnight train certainly does not come as far as Redbank," she said, a little mystified.

" This one was an extra—a special—a chartered car that brought me to the very door," he answered, with a laugh.

" Ah ! " she said, and then was silent. She did not like the mysterious air with which Harry surrounded all his actions.

Lilian was overjoyed to see him, and hung about him in her accustomed affectionate manner, to which he warmly responded, pinching her ears, kissing her cheeks and calling her " sweet bird " and " dear little pig."

Presently he caught her up in his arms for a long hug. "Sweeter than all the sugar plums in the world!" he said, biting her rosy cheeks.

"Where have you been, Uncle Hal?" she asked.

"Everywhere, Pet, even to the moon and the evening star."

"I don't believe that," she cried, "you are an old humbug." She always called him by this name, when she was clever enough to discover he was jesting.

Soon Jessie appeared, and gave him a very kind greeting.

"How well you are looking," she said.

"Am I?" he answered, and he seemed much pleased to receive so cordial a welcome from her. "Well, I've been having a splendid time. I have been among a set who appreciate my fine qualities, and they have petted and spoiled me to my heart's content. It does a fellow good sometimes to get a little petting."

Before Jessie could reply, Mr. Philip Winston entered with Percy, the beautiful, radiant Percy, upon his arm. They were much surprised to see their new addition to the household. The introductions were made in proper form, and both the lady and the gentleman surveyed the guest with curiosity and interest. Mrs. Philip eyed him with her well-bred stare. She was evidently impressed with his appearance, and gave him her hand with a gracious smile. Last of all, the Colonel came in; he, too, was very cordial, and complimented Harry on his good looks. These kind greetings were very gratifying to the young man, and he expanded into his best and most genial self. When they were all seated at the table, the Colonel turned to him and said,

"Well, now, give a report of yourself. Where have you been? Whence do you come?"

"From going to and fro on the earth, and from walking up and down in it," was the ready response.

"That answer won't do," said the Colonel, laughing; "it is altogether too suggestive of a certain evil-minded personage whom we are forbidden to mention in good society."

"Well," answered Harry, "I've been to visit my old Colonel—Colonel Beaufort. You know him, I reckon; he lives in North Carolina. I've had an invitation of long standing to make him a visit, and I concluded to go in the summer. When I once got there, he would not let me leave."

"Why, yes," exclaimed the Colonel, "I know Stuart Beaufort better than I know myself. How is he?"

"Just as jolly as ever," the young man answered.

"What is he doing in North Carolina?" was the next question.

"His wife is a North Carolinian, and she owns a large plantation near Charlotte. He is living in capital style—entertains the whole United States."

"Just like him," said the Colonel, "he always did have the biggest heart in the world. But that kind of hospitality won't do for these days. He'll come to grief, certain, if he keeps it up."

"I reckon not," Harry replied; "his wife is very rich—has no end of stocks at the North. She was a great heiress. I think it's a clever trick for a fellow to marry an heiress. I shall try it myself some of these days, when my wild oats are all sown."

Mr. Philip winced a little, as if aware that some members of the family might make a personal application of the innocent remark to himself. Harry went on eating his breakfast, perfectly unconscious that he had touched a weak point in the gentleman's armor.

"By that time," said the Colonel, dryly, "I'm afraid there won't be enough of you left for any girl to marry."

Harry looked up at him, and smiled—"That's one of your mistakes. My heart is so perfectly immense that no prodigality can exhaust its power of loving."

This gay badinage was just the kind of talk that Mrs. Philip liked, and her brown eyes expressed a lively interest in the young man who was evidently a master of the tongue. He caught her looking at him, and dared address a question to her.

"How do you like the Sunny South, Mrs. Winston? It is easy to see that you are not a native."

"I am perfectly in love with it," she exclaimed with pretty enthusiasm, "only I'm not quite sure that it deserves its name. We have had two days of rain since our arrival. But how can you tell that I'm not a native?"

"It wouldn't answer for me to say," he replied, with a laugh. "My acquaintance with you is altogether too short for such confidences."

Of course something complimentary was meant; she smiled consciously.

"Which means you may possibly tell me some time in the future?" she asked.

"Perhaps," he answered; "but I'm sure your curiosity is only a transient emotion."

"No, it isn't. My curiosity is a very permanent emotion. Isn't it, Philip?"

"Indeed it is," answered that gentleman. "Sometimes I think it is the only thing that holds you together—the centre of gravity, you know."

She laughed gayly and said, "I'm learning to bear disparagement from you very bravely."

"Disparagement!" he cried; "I'm as innocent as a lamb of any intention to disparage. I am only stating a plain fact."

"With great exaggeration," she said, emphatically: "you are entirely too old to exaggerate as you do—that is the fault of children."

Mr. Philip flushed slightly; he did not like to be reminded that he was no longer young. She saw the heightened color, and was glad to tease him a little.

"How absurdly sensitive you are about your age. It is simply ridiculous in a man. Now I like your mature beauty. I never could have married a very young man."

"Do all the ladies where you came from feel the same way?" asked Harry.

"Yes," she said; "why?"

"Because I'm thinking of going there to settle."

"Do!" she exclaimed; "I'm sure you will like it. It is a wonderful city, and growing so fast it almost takes away your breath."

"But first I must find out some way of imparting a touch of maturity to my charms."

"Ah, that's easy enough!"

"How?"

"Buy a gray wig. It will be awfully becoming." They both laughed.

The Colonel was getting tired of this dialogue; he put an end to it by saying, "Philip, I want you to ride with me this morning. I am going over the creek to see those fields where the negroes have just finished picking cotton. The yield has disappointed me. I want to see if I can find out what's the matter."

"The negroes have probably been stealing it," said Mr. Philip; "I'll be very glad to go with you. What time will you start?"

"Directly we are through breakfast."

"Colonel," said Percy, "you are very cruel to carry him off somewhere every day. I scarcely ever see him from breakfast till lunch."

"Well, my dear, are you not glad to have him out of the house?" replied the Colonel. "You would not like to see him sitting around all the time admiring you, would you?"

"Decidedly not," she answered, quickly; "but——" she hesitated a moment.

"But what, my dear?" asked Mr. Philip.

She looked into his face, smiled and said, "Sometimes I'm just a little lonely; everybody else, you know, is busy."

"Then you must learn to be busy, too," the husband replied.

"About what?" she asked, innocently.

"I don't know—make me a pair of pants," he said, breaking into a laugh.

"You dreadful man!" she cried; "I would not make you a pair of pants—I would not even try to make you a pair, if you had nothing to wear, and there was not a single tailor in the world." Everybody joined in the laughter.

"Then, my dear, I would petition the courts for an immediate divorce," said Mr. Philip. "Well, accept another suggestion," he continued; "sew on some buttons for me, mend my gloves, darn my stockings. There's lots to be done, if you will only look into my trunk."

"I don't know how to do such things," she answered, carelessly; "I don't believe I have a needle in the world."

"Miss Holcombe will lend you one, I'm sure," said the husband.

"Perhaps she will sew on the buttons, also, and mend the gloves?" the young wife ventured to say, looking at Jessie.

"No, thank you," replied Miss Holcombe; "my services are not for hire; not even when the cause is that of neglected husbands."

"There, my dear," said Mr. Philip, nodding significantly at his wife, "it won't do to jest with Miss Holcombe."

"Jessie is like a flash of lightning," exclaimed Harry. "You must look out or you will be struck dead."

"At home that's the popular impression of all Southerners," the lady answered.

"Yes, we are kegs of powder; a spark of fire will set us off in a minute. I wonder you ventured to come among us. It shows that you have a very brave heart."

"Perhaps it only shows that I do not share the popular impression. For my part, I like Southerners immensely."

Harry Holcombe bowed:—"Allow me to return a vote of thanks for the whole company here assembled. It is very gratifying to see that you appreciate our good qualities. It fills my bosom with patriotic pride." He laid his hand impressively upon his heart.

"What an orator you are!" cried Mrs. Philip.

"Do you think so? I have sometimes suspected as much myself, but Redbank is a very bad place for developing latent talents. Occasionally one is sat down upon. The truth is there are several wits in our family. Have you discovered the fact?"

"I should think I have. If you were all to go to Boston, you would be famous in a week."

"That's just my opinion," returned Harry. "I'm thinking a little of leading the way. Won't you give me a letter of introduction to somebody of note at the 'Hub.' Some literary character you know?"

The lady laughed. "I'm not from Boston; even if I were, I'm afraid I would not be acquainted in that set."

"I'm awfully sorry, because that's the set most to my taste—any success I achieve in life must be made in that line of work. I'm great on an after-dinner speech, especially if champagne has flowed freely."

This was a little too near the mark to suit either Eleanor or Jessie. "Harry," said the latter, "do stop your nonsense. What will Mrs. Winston think of Southern gentlemen? She will be making contrasts and reaching dreadful conclusions."

"Don't be alarmed about her conclusions," said Mr. Philip, dryly. "She has a very illogical mind."

"All women have," Percy replied; "that's what makes them so charming—they cannot argue."

"You are mistaken, there," said her husband. "I think most of them can argue *ad infinitum*."

"I mean they do not argue logically, they only jump at conclusions, and I believe that men generally consider their conclusions very absurd."

"Yes," her husband answered quickly. "I know one whose conclusions are almost always very absurd."

"Which, according to her statement, is the secret of her being so charming," said the Colonel; "but we have had nonsense enough now."

He pushed his chair back from the table, and they all got up. Eleanor turned to Harry, as he was about to leave the dining-room, and said:

"I wish you would go out this morning and kill some partridges for us; we have not had any this fall and

Peyton says the fields and woods are swarming with them."

"All right; I will go immediately and hunt up the dogs. I'm afraid my gun needs cleaning, but I reckon I can manage with it this morning."

"Well, I rely upon you for a game-course at dinner."

"All right," he again replied.

When they found themselves upon the piazza, they paused a moment, and then paired off. The Colonel and Mr. Philip lighted their cigars, and strolled down to the stables. Jessie and Lilian went to the hammock, and the child was soon laughing merrily as she swung back and forth. Mrs. Philip Winston and Harry Holcombe by some subtle attraction moved off together, and sought a distant corner where the sunshine fell warm and bright. Here they stood, leaning on the balustrade, chatting and jesting and dallying for more than an hour. Percy was in her element, she had at length found an admirer, for the gentleman's gaze was full of admiration, and his tongue only too ready to fashion the delicate compliments that she loved. She was certainly a charming creature to look at as she stood there in the sunlight, turning her pretty head from side to side, and smiling her arch little smiles. She was dressed in a *negligé* costume of pale blue cashmere with puffings of silk and jabots of white lace. Nothing could have been more becoming.

Harry had never seen a creature quite so bewitching, and, minute by minute, was falling more hopelessly under the spell of her fascination. He felt almost powerless to break away. At last, Eleanor came out of the dining-room, where she had been reading the newspapers, and joined them.

"What, Harry! not gone yet?" she exclaimed; "I'm

afraid the game-course will be wanting on our bill of fare this evening."

"Not if I can help it," he answered, "there's time enough. Where are all the dogs?"—and he strolled down the front steps, and began to whistle. Soon Beppo, his favorite pointer, answered to the call, and then the gentleman went off to hunt up his gun and game-bag and to change his clothes for high boots and a shooting jacket. Presently, he was equipped, and waving a graceful adieu to the ladies, he started off towards the woods. Mrs. Winston and Percy stood on the piazza and watched him until he disappeared from sight.

"Your brother is perfectly splendid," said the latter; "I've lost my heart."

"I didn't know you had any of your own to lose," replied Eleanor; "Harry's a sad flirt—you must look out for him."

"Oh! I'm up to all that," said Percy; "don't be afraid for me—I've flirted ever since I was out of baby-clothes."

"But now you are married, it is time to stop," returned the elder lady.

"Why?—It is perfectly harmless, isn't it?—and it's such fun."

"It is not always perfectly harmless, my dear; and your husband may not like it. I am afraid you have not yet realized what a very serious thing it is to be married."

Percy was quiet for a few moments, as if she were busy thinking, then she said: "You are right. It seemed perfectly splendid to buy a magnificent *trousseau*, and to have a stunning wedding; but it has been rather dull ever since."

" You ought to have something to do, Percy," said Mrs. Winston; "I hope when you return home you will not board. Philip must take a house, and then you will find plenty to occupy your time."

" I would like that exceedingly; I have so many lovely friends, and could give charming entertainments." Percy paused a while, and then continued: " But do you know, I don't believe that Philip cares for society. If he does not, it will break my heart."

Eleanor laughed. " Don't talk about broken hearts; I hope, dear, that yours may never have even a little ache."

" I hope so too," said the young creature. " Mamma, my step-mother, I mean, used to say, that I did not have enough of a heart to break or even to ache; but she is a horrid, spiteful thing, and wanted me married, dreadfully. How she does manage papa! It's a perfect shame."

No more was said, but Eleanor went off to her morning duties with a new thought. This, then, was the secret of the marriage, hitherto so inexplicable to her. The clever step-mother had married off the pretty step-daughter who was in her way. Philip, old and wary as he was, had allowed himself to be fascinated by youth, beauty and wealth, and Percy had been captivated by the fine manners of a thorough man of the world. Eleanor felt a vague apprehension about the future of this newly-wedded pair.

Marriage is not altogether clear sailing, even when the sea is calm, the ship sea-worthy; and the crew loyal and well-trained. Sudden gales will spring up in the most unexpected manner. But when the ship has a leak at the start, and the crew cannot be trusted, there is indeed danger of a wreck before the voyage is over.

CHAPTER XIV.

THE acquaintance between Mrs. Philip Winston and Harry Holcombe advanced with rapid strides. Morning after morning, they lounged for hours on the piazza in the warm sunshine, and chatted in that familiar fashion which indicates perfect understanding and sympathy. Mr. Philip Winston quietly ignored the growing intimacy. He had that grand manner that always seems to look over the heads of others. He appeared scarcely to see either Harry or Percy. Ever since his arrival at Redbank he had treated his beautiful bride with the well-bred indifference which is considered good form in fashionable society. He seemed to find all the entertainment and happiness his soul desired in the companionship of his brother. Together, they rode, walked, talked, and smoked; the affairs of the plantation apparently absorbed them both. Percy, poor child, had been left to her own devices to find amusement in some shape for herself. Unfortunately, her resources were meagre, and, during the long days, she had suffered much from *ennui*, but she had borne it without complaint. Now, at length, there was some one else, idle as herself—some one who was willing to give her a little attention, and assist her in killing time. Can we wonder that she welcomed this knight?—that she had a smile and a beckoning gesture for him whenever he appeared in sight?

When the Colonel and his brother had ridden off

after breakfast, and all the other members of the family were busy with the tasks of the day, these two idlers would resume the thread of their flirtation.

One morning, sweet and summery as June, Mrs. Philip was sitting on the piazza in an easy-chair, looking delightfully comfortable and happy. Lilian and the baby were at play in a distant corner of the yard, and she was getting an insipid kind of entertainment from watching them. Mr. Holcombe had not made his appearance at the breakfast table, and she was wondering what was the matter. No one had seemed to notice his absence, and she had wisely decided to ask no questions. Suddenly she gave a little start, and adjusted her dress in more graceful folds. There he was!—coming up the avenue with two or three dogs behind him, and his gun carelessly slung over his shoulder. He had been out hunting then; he had not gone off to parts unknown. As he approached the house, he called a little negro boy to come and carry his well-filled game-bag to the kitchen. Then he lounged up the steps of the piazza, and threw himself lazily down in a chair near her.

"Where have you been?" asked Mrs. Philip—"you look tired."

"Out hunting," he replied; "I like to go out early in the morning, when everything is fresh."

"Where did you get your breakfast?" asked the lady, —"you were not at the table this morning."

"Thank you for missing me. I did not get any breakfast. I did not want any. I have been feeding on the nectar and ambrosia of my thoughts,"—he said, looking at her, and smiling.

"Then you must be awfully hungry now; do go and get something to eat."

"Don't trouble your tender little heart about me," he answered; "I'm so comfortable that I could not be hired to stir. The thought of bread and meat does not tempt me. Man does not live by bread alone."

"Hush!" she said, with a little laugh; "you must not be so wicked as to quote Scripture."

"I thought that it was written especially for the wicked," he replied, joining in her laugh.

"Well, we won't argue about it now. Tell me what success you have had. How many birds did you kill?"

"Twenty-five and two rabbits; the game is amazingly plentiful, but it is rather tiresome to go hunting all alone. I'm a confounded sociable fellow, and am always longing for companionship."

"Why don't you invite the Colonel or Philip to accompany you on your hunts?"

"Because they would be far more likely to shoot themselves or me than to shoot anything else. Whew! they look down upon sport from an Olympian height."

"I observe that they are very willing to eat the game when it comes on the table."

"Yes, that's human nature; but their time is far too valuable to be spent in killing it."

"Do tell me," she inquired, "what is it that they do, day after day? They ride off, or walk off, and talk, and talk, as if very important business was on hand, but one can't make out what it's all about."

"That's the sacred truth," he answered, "they both consider me a good-for-nothing fellow, hardly worth the powder and shot it would take to shoot me, and yet when I go off I do bring home a bag full of game. I truly believe, if I were married I could support myself and my wife with that old shot gun. Wouldn't it be jolly, living down here in these swamps in a little log cabin, and eating nothing but game?"

"Awfully jolly!" she answered.

"Do you think there is a woman in the world who would share such a lot?" he asked.

"I'm afraid not," she said, shaking her head.

"Not if I allowed her to accompany me on the hunts?"

"Well, that might furnish a little excitement, but scarcely enough to satisfy any woman that I know. They may be different down here. Do tell me," she asked, after a little pause, "why you find hunting so fascinating? It seems very cruel to me."

"Yes, it is perhaps, when one stops to think about it," he answered. "I suppose it must be because we all have some of the blood of that old savage ourang-outang ancestor still flowing in our veins, and now and then the impulse to kill seizes us. I frankly acknowledge that I'm a savage—just about as hopeless a specimen as can be found anywhere, whether it's in Africa, or New Guinea, or the South Sea Islands. The truth is, there are lots of heathen down here, Mrs. Winston. There's plenty of room for missionary work. Don't you want to embark in it?"

Percy smiled and said, "I'm afraid it is not my vocation."

"Suppose you try and see," he replied; "you may stumble upon an unknown talent. I'm an excellent subject for beginning your experiments on. Shall I give you a list of my vices in order to prove how great is my need of missionary effort?"

"Do!" she exclaimed; "it will be very amusing."

"Well, first of all, I'm dreadfully idle."

"So am I—I'm afraid I could not undertake to cure you of that fault."

"Without first curing yourself," he said, with a laugh.

"That would be impossible," she replied, "it is inborn, engrained, a part of my very self. It would be necessary to annihilate me before you could get rid of it. But what's next on the list?"

"Then I'm extravagant; the very worst sin in the world to be joined with laziness."

"Why, that's another of my faults," she said, breaking into a merry laugh. "What next?"

"Thirdly, I'm puffed up with vanity and conceit—so some people think."

"Well, so am I," exclaimed Percy, with another peal of laughter; "I cannot attempt to cure you of that either."

"Fourthly,"—and here Harry paused a moment, "I'm an awful flirt."

"And so am I."

He looked at her intently.

"It seems to me we are very much alike; I have never before met a person so completely the counterpart of myself. But let me go on with the faults. I was at fifthly, wasn't I?" She laughed and nodded her head. He was really a very entertaining fellow.

"Well, fifthly, I am very fond of my own way. When I make up my mind to do a thing, there's no power under heaven that can turn me."

"Just the same with me."

"Then, sixthly," continued Harry, "I'm awfully fond of display and style and all kinds of fiddlesticks."

"So am I!" she again exclaimed.

"Seventhly, I'm fond of filthy lucre—I would like a purse so long that there was no bottom to it."

"So would I!"

They both laughed heartily as if they found the recital very amusing. Soon she said, "There, I think the catalogue is long enough now; you may stop."

"I am glad you permit me to pause, for it is somewhat fatiguing; but I assure you that I could go on forever, like Tennyson's brook."

"Please don't," she entreated, "I am convinced of your benighted condition, and my own too."

"I hope you are also convinced that our souls are cast in somewhat the same noble mould. We ought to be good friends."

"I'm not so sure of that," was her reply; "it is said that opposites attract."

"Opposition of character, but similarity of taste."

"Well, is it the characters or the tastes that are alike here?" she asked; "I confess I can't make it out."

"I must get a slate and pencil to find that out," he said, with a light laugh. "Whenever I'm in doubt about a thing, I go to algebra, and say, let x represent the unknown quantity. One can find out anything that way."

"Except a woman's meaning," she said.

"Except a woman's meaning!" he echoed, and then they were both silent.

"How delicious this sunshine is!" she exclaimed after a while; "I would like to bottle some of it up, and send it to my friends at home. People rave over Italy, but I'm sure it is no better than this."

"Have you been there?" he asked.

"Yes, twice. The first time, I did not like it at all. It was in winter, and the weather was very wet and cold. We spent most of the time in Florence and Rome, and I assure you we came near freezing. The last time, it was spring, and we went through Southern Italy and down to Sicily. That was delicious. Mamma—step-mamma, I mean,"—and she laughed, " said I liked it because there were several young gentlemen in our party. She even accused me of flirting in the streets of Pompeii, but I assure you it was a libellous attack on my character. You would not believe such a thing of me, would you?"

" By no means!" he replied, " I hope you prosecuted her, and recovered damages."

" No, I'm not vindictive," she laughingly answered. " I left her to be punished by her own conscience."

" Tell me something more about Italy," he said.

" There is nothing to tell," she replied—" I hate travelling and sight-seeing. One has to tramp around until one is tired to death, and poke into old holes and cellars, and keep up a perpetual scream—'Oh! how beautiful!' I cannot tell you how glad I was to get back to Paris!"

" And what did you enjoy so much in Paris?"

" Everything; but especially the shops and the drives in the Bois. You ought to go there. I know you would like it."

He smiled, and said, " I don't doubt it in the least; perhaps, I will go, when I marry my heiress."

" You had better go there to find her. The city is perfectly infested with wealthy foreigners. Everybody goes there who wants to have a good time. One sees swarms of American girls, and many of them are beautiful! Do you know that the American girls are now considered the most beautiful in the world?"

" That is just my opinion," said the gentleman. " The most beautiful woman I ever saw is an American."

"Who is she?" asked Mrs. Philip. "Where does she live? How I would like to see her!"

"Well, at present, she is not very far from an old plantation house in the State of Georgia."

"You are a dreadful flatterer," exclaimed the lady, with a conscious blush.

"Why, I have not spoken one word of flattery," replied the gentleman, very innocently.

"But your meaning was evident enough."

"I am glad you can read my meaning so well," he said, looking at her fixedly from under his half-closed lids.

"Do you know you have a real military air," she said to him, after quite a long break in the conversation. "To look at you, I would think that you were an officer in the army."

"I was once," he replied, "but that was long ago—in the hoary past."

"Did you like it?" she asked.

"Immensely; it is the only profession that I would care to follow. It suits me exactly, for my temperament is spasmodic. The truth is, I'm seriously thinking of offering my valuable military services to one of the despots of the Old World—the Czar or the Sultan, for instance; only I would want a staff appointment, and that might be a little hard to get. I'm beginning to doubt my capacity for active service—I fear I'm rather played out, and will have to take things easy for the brief remainder of life. Nothing now suits me so well as a hammock in the sunshine. I'm afraid that the most eventful period of existence is past for me. If I were a Frenchman, I would try to get a snug little corner in the *Hotel des Invalides*."

"What an absurd fellow you are!" cried Mrs.

Philip, laughing at his soliloquy. "You are not much over twenty, I'm sure, and yet, to hear you talk, one would imagine you were in the nineties."

"True," he said; "but my years have been long. That makes the difference between you and me. Your years have been all summers, and mine all winters, and I suppose fate has just the same in store for me in the future." He lay back in the easy-chair, and twirled his mustache as if it did not much matter—the sunshine just then was so warm, and the lady opposite so confoundedly pretty!

"I hope not," she answered, putting a little tenderness into her tone.

"If my hard lot excites your pity, I am content to bear it," he said, with a mock-heroic air.

"Now, don't begin to talk nonsense!" the lady exclaimed; "you know perfectly well that you don't care a fig for ladies; they have never entered at all into your thoughts."

"Not until recently," he remarked; "I confess they have always floated before my eyes like airy nothings; but now I am beginning to look at them a little more seriously—at least one of them. You know I am still very young."

"How perfectly inconsistent you are!" she said; "a moment ago, you were very old—at least ninety-nine, and now you are in your teens, and as innocent as a school-girl. Really, you amuse me very much. I have never seen anybody like you, before!"

"And are you fond of novelties?" he asked.

"Why do you wish to know?"

"Because then I might be able to guess your opinion of a certain poor fellow in whom I'm a little interested."

"I'm afraid he would not care for my opinion, so I will leave both you and him in the dark."

"There you are mistaken," he answered; "your opinion would weigh against that of the whole round world."

"You can talk more nonsense than any fellow I ever met," she exclaimed, with a laugh.

"And do you like nonsense?" he asked.

"It is the only kind of sense I do like," was the reply.

"Then I shall talk it forever and ever," he said, sinking his voice almost to a whisper.

Before she could reply to this remark, Mrs. Winston stepped out on the piazza and joined them. Harry arose and handed her a chair, but in his heart he felt that she was *de trop*. Of late, she had often appeared suddenly, and interrupted his charming conversations with Mrs. Philip. Was it by chance, or by design? He could not tell, but he had a vague suspicion that it was by design.

CHAPTER XV.

THAT afternoon, Harry Holcombe went out in the back-yard to clean his gun. This was a performance which always gave Lilian great delight; she seated herself on the steps to watch him. Before he had finished his task, Percy and Jessie came out on the back piazza; in the afternoon it was the sunny side of the house, and, at this season of the year, when the weather was warm and fine, it was often selected as the sitting-room of the family. The ladies soon found themselves almost as much interested as was Lilian in the work of the young man. Mrs. Philip was particularly amused by his costume. He had on a butler's apron and looked very funny, Lilian thought.

"Uncle Hal," she cried, "you look exactly like Uncle Oliver."

"You saucy puss!" he said, "you shall answer for that disrespectful remark." He put down his gun and ran towards her, but she eluded him by rushing down the steps into the yard; there they had a long chase, for the little maiden was fleet of foot, and it was some time before the gentleman caught her. When she was at length a captive in his arms he kissed her, and tickled her, and tossed her up and down, until she cried loudly for mercy. Soon he brought her on the piazza, and seating himself on an old joggling-board in a corner, he began to joggle her furiously, indulging in all kinds of boyish capers himself.

"What *is* the matter with you, Uncle Hal?" she cried out more than once. "You are too funny for anything to-day."

"I've been sipping the elixir," he whispered.

"What is the elixir?" she asked, much mystified.

"Why, it's something that makes grown people little children again. I've found a bottle of it," and he gave her a sly wink, "and now I'm a little boy again. Isn't it jolly? Whenever I feel grown-up hereafter, I'm going to take a drop or two, and become little again, like Alice in Wonderland, you know.

"Sweet bird," he continued, solemnly, "never, never consent to grow up to be a young lady, do you hear?"

"But how can I help it? you know I have to grow."

"You mustn't eat," he whispered, mysteriously.

"Not even when I'm hungry?" she asked opening her eyes wide with astonishment.

"Not even when you are hungry," he echoed in a sepulchral tone.

"Why I must—I cannot help it."

"Anyhow, you must manage not to grow up; ladies are not half as sweet as little girls—they are always doing some mischief and getting other people into trouble."

"Are they?" asked the child with innocent surprise.

"Yes," he whispered. "Let me tell you a dreadful secret which I have just found out. Little girls when they grow up turn into witches!"

"Why, Uncle Hal, what do you mean? now I *know* you are an old humbug."

"No, I'm not," he said, shaking his head.

"Aunt Percy isn't a witch, I'm perfectly sure."

"Yes, she is," was the awful reply; "she mounts her broom-stick every night after we have all gone to bed, and rides through the air with all the rest of them. Aunt Jessie goes along too. They are both awfully sly about it, but I have seen them lots of times."

The little girl broke into a peal of laughter to signify her incredulity; Percy and Jessie joined in the mirth, for they had heard every word of the conversation.

"You need not laugh," he said; " it is just as true as preserved ginger and orange marmalade. And, sweet bird, I'm awfully afraid for you; I'm sure you will grow up into a perfectly dreadful witch, and bewitch all the poor foolish young men in the country; I see it in your eyes this very minute."

"I won't do any such thing!" she cried, indignantly.

"We'll see," he replied, solemnly, beginning to joggle her again.

After a while he released her, and then came and sat down quietly near the ladies.

"Well," said Mrs. Philip, who had never before seen him in such a mood, "are you ready to subside now?"

"Yes," he answered, "I think I've had enough to last me six months. I must have a frolic every now and then, or I feel as if I had a bone in my back."

"What do you mean, you absurd fellow?" she exclaimed, laughing. "I thought you had several bones in your back."

"No," he answered, "my anatomy is very defective; I haven't got my full share of either bones or brains."

"Harry," exclaimed Jessie, joining in the laughter, "pray don't talk so much nonsense. Percy will really think that you are demented."

"No, she won't," he said, very soberly; "don't you suppose I know an angel when I see one? I often see them in my dreams."

"Percy would not feel complimented if she knew the

kind of angels you are accustomed to see in your dreams," replied Jessie, and she indulged in so violent a fit of laughter, that Mrs. Philip entreated the gentleman to explain what his sister meant.

"Do tell me what kind of angels you see," she begged; "favor me with a description of one, please."

"What are you laughing at, Jessica?" he asked.

"Don't you remember the peculiar variety you saw at Culpeper C. H.?" she replied.

"Give us the anecdote by all means," exclaimed Mrs. Philip.

"Well," he said, "it was a long time ago, when I was a young thing, and couldn't leave my mother, or at least ought not to have left her. This is a war tale, you know."

"Charming!" she cried, "go on!"

"One night after being relieved from very fatiguing vidette duty, I found an old deserted house, and thought I would enter and take a little nap before returning to camp. Luckily I found a bed in one of the rooms on the ground floor, for the family had refugeed and left everything. I was very tired, and threw myself down on it to rest awhile. The night was very hot, and the moon was shining, so I left my window wide open. It was so near the ground that a child could have climbed in. There was not a soul within miles, and everything was as still as death. I fell asleep almost immediately. About midnight, I was awakened by awful sounds— cries, groans, screams. I started up in bed, and rubbed my eyes. There in the window, right in the moonlight, was the most dreadful, the most unearthly being that I had ever beheld—gray-headed, gray-bearded, flaming eyes, and, worst of all, hoofs and horns. I thought surely that my time had come; my sins flashed through my mind like forked lightning, and I was preparing to surrender without a struggle, when the awful silence was again broken by a loud ba-a-a-a-ah! At first, I thought it was the language of the lower regions, but soon I saw my mistake. It was only a goat—a pet goat of the family to whom the house belonged. It had been left behind in the general stampede, and I suppose was almost dead from hunger. It was standing outside on the ground, with its fore-feet on the window-sill. I flung my pillow at it, and then lay down and went to sleep again."

"Which anecdote proves your liability to mistake goats for angels," said Percy; "I shall remember that."

"Nothing of the kind," replied the young man; "it only proves that it is not healthy to sleep on the ground floor."

Before Percy could answer this remark, the Colonel and Mr. Philip, who had been smoking in the library, came out on the piazza and joined the ladies. The latter drew a chair up close to his wife, and said:

"Well, my dear, aren't you enjoying this?"

"Enjoying what?" she asked.

"Why, everything; the sunshine, the blue sky, this beautiful veranda, this quiet country scene, and last but not least, this pleasant company."

"Of course, I'm enjoying the pleasant company, but I'm afraid that I prefer Art to Nature," she replied, "and the city to the country."

"Now, that seems perfectly incomprehensible to me!" exclaimed Mr. Philip. "My dear, I call Redbank a terrestrial paradise. I like everything about the delightful old place. It is a real haven of rest. But especially do I enjoy this hour near sunset, when the cows and the horses, and the mules, and the dogs, and the cats, and the pigs, and the ducks, and the chickens, are all let loose in that lot," and he pointed to a large enclosure in the rear of the stables and plainly visible from the piazza where they were sitting. Here the stock were all fed late in the afternoon. "It makes me feel young again," he continued, "to hear the lowing and the neighing, the barking and the cackling, the quacking and the grunting."

"And this from our elegant, fastidious brother, who has for years lived in a great city, and delighted in fashionable society!" said the Colonel. "Really, I'm amazed, Philip."

"Allow me to assure you that I mean what I say," the gentleman replied. "I have lived in the city until I hate it. The glare and style and artificial atmosphere sickens and disgusts me. A breath of pure country air is worth more than all the cities in America. I believe that it was intended by the Creator that man should live in the country, and cultivate the ground. In these latter days, he has become entirely perverted, and the millennium will never come until there is a change. We must become quieter in our manners, simpler in our tastes, and purer in our morals, and the country is the place for this reformation." As he spoke, there was a half smile upon his face; it was not easy to know whether he meant what he said or not. His young wife looked at him with a well-feigned expression of dismay in her brown eyes.

"How long have you been holding these new doctrines?" she asked.

"For a long time, but I have not dared to express them."

"I suppose you selected me as the proper help-meet in carrying them out."

"Of course I did," he answered, still smiling.

"I am afraid that some day your sins will overtake you and great will be your repentance." She laughed as she uttered these words; then, rising from her seat, she said, "Come, Jessie, let's go for a walk, before the sun sets." Harry also arose, and strolled off with them down the avenue. He was soon chatting with Percy, in his usual light manner. Jessie did not like to see them so free and easy with each other; she did not like the unconstrained personal allusions and compliments which were tossed to and fro between them, like bonbons at a carnival. She wondered how Percy could forget her dignity as a wife; she wondered how Harry could keep up such senseless badinage from noon till night. To her it seemed that the two were drifting into a dangerous intimacy.

Percy was young, vain, and thoughtless; and Harry was very sincere in his admiration for her. He had never before seen quite such a woman; she was so bright, so stylish, so ready, so fascinating, so exquisitely artificial, so profoundly trained in all the subtle ways of society. The daintiness of everything about her was a perpetual delight to him. The jewelled hands with the costly laces falling over them; the white throat with its band of black velvet on which shone a blazing diamond; the little feet encased in silk stockings and high-heeled slippers; the sweep of her velvet trains; the perfume that hung around her; he felt it all, and thrilled to its inexplicable charm, as a musician to the harmony of deep chords.

Percy, on her side, had never met just such a man as Harry Holcombe. He was brilliant, dashing, reckless, with no taint of business about him, and no studied, drawing-room polish. He was utterly unconscious, and the grace of nature was in all that he said and did. Is it a wonder, then, that each felt the attraction of the other? Is it strange that both Eleanor and Jessie realized that there might be danger ahead? At length, these two had a talk over it. "I'm vexed beyond measure at the thoughtlessness of Harry," said the former; "he ought to know better than to carry on in that way with a married woman. Philip's of a very jealous disposition, and just as soon as he sees it, you may be sure there will be a scene. I cannot forgive him for marrying that young creature; at his age, he ought have known better. They do not care at all for the same things, and there will be perpetual collisions; I'm afraid her money was the great attraction in his eyes."

"Don't say that, Eleanor, she is certainly pretty and fascinating enough to attract any man. I have fallen completely under her spells myself. If I were a man I know I would be bewitched too."

"Well, Philip has seen too many beautiful women to be captivated by a mere Paris doll."

"She is more than that," said Jessie. "She seems very giddy, but she is not soulless. She possesses both mind and character."

"A new edition of Nettie Hunter, bound in velvet with gold clasps," replied Mrs. Winston.

"That type of woman is becoming very common, North, South, East and West, one finds pretty coquettes in flocks, like sparrows. Don't be too full of contempt, Nell; after all, they are very charming, and they do get much more out of life than the sober ones. Sometimes I envy them and long to be like them."

"I don't believe you, Jessica Holcombe."

"It is nevertheless true. Nettie Hunter has always fascinated me and so does Percy."

"There is a difference between them after all," said Mrs. Winston; "Nettie is more restless and full of chatter, but she has at bottom a very warm and loving heart, and some sense of right and wrong. Percy has the self-possession and repose of the fashionable woman and the hardness of one of her diamonds. She enjoys playing with Harry—there is no other amusement within reach, but she will never care a fig for any one but herself."

"You are too severe, Eleanor."

"No, I'm not, and, Jessie, I do wish you would speak to Harry and advise him to let her alone."

"It would do no good. I have no influence over him. He would laugh at me, and call me a pious little prude; besides, he is not always amiable when one gives him advice."

"I did hope that Alice Brooks would accept him," said Eleanor. "She is just the wife for him, and would make a man of him. With all his faults, he has good stuff in him."

"I hoped so too," said Jessie; "I think she liked him very much, and I believe he really loved her, but there was interference from some quarter."

"It is a great pity that people will interfere in such matters," Mrs. Winston replied.

"I'm not surprised in this case, for Harry is hardly worthy of such a splendid girl as Alice." The conversation ended here.

One evening, a week later, when Jessie went into the parlor, she found Mrs. Philip and Harry playing backgammon together. They seemed to be in the wildest spirits, and, as the game progressed, they grew loud and familiar in tone and manner. Jessie seated herself at the piano and began to play, hoping that her presence might impose some restraint upon them, but she was disappointed. When, at bed-time, Mr. Philip came in search of his lost bride, as he called her, he paused a moment at the open door, and surveyed the excited gamblers. From her post at the piano, Jessie caught a glimpse of him. His brows were unpleasantly knit and a dark shadow swept over his face. She had seen that expression more than once of late.

When the husband and wife had left the room, Jessie arose from the piano-stool, and approached the table, near which her brother was sitting. He had closed the backgammon board, and was looking into the fire. His hair was tossed up rather wildly, and a strange light was burning in his eyes. The young girl sat down, took up a newspaper, and tried to interest herself in the items of the day, but she could not read, her thoughts were far away. She wanted to talk with her brother, and yet she hardly knew how to begin. He appeared to be utterly unconscious of her presence. Presently he got up and put two or three sticks of wood on the fire, for the evening was cool. Still he showed no signs of speaking, and evidently his mood was not a pleasant one.

"Harry," said the sister, after a prolonged silence. He looked up at her with his cold black eyes, but made no response. She was too frank and ingenuous to begin with a roundabout introduction; she continued very simply, "Do you think that it is quite right for you to carry on as you are doing with Mrs. Philip Winston?"

"Confound it!" he exclaimed; "a fellow cannot make himself agreeable even to a married woman, without raising a cry from all the other females in the world. I've no patience with it."

"Would you like a fellow to make himself agreeable to your wife in just that way?" she asked.

"I never expect to have a wife, so I cannot imagine anything about it."

"Well, reckless as you are, I believe you have some sense of right and wrong, and from the very expression of your face at this moment, I know that your conscience is troubling you. You are treading on dangerous ground."

"Explain yourself," he said, coldly. "What do you mean?"

"You know without asking. You are carrying on a silly flirtation with a married woman, and some disagreeable consequences may follow. I have seen Mr. Philip Winston's face more than once, when he has found you and his wife together, and the expression was not pleasant."

"He is a jealous, suspicious old fool."

"Hush, Harry; I'm sure he has not paid much attention to either you or Percy. He has not watched you in the least. He has given you perfect liberty to make yourself agreeable to her. He would be blind, indeed, not to see that you are going a little too far. It has evidently surprised him, for he imagined himself in the midst of an honorable household."

"And who dares to say to the contrary?" he exclaimed, "he pays no attention to his wife himself, and then he is angry if any one else looks at her."

"That is nonsense," she said; "I have seen you and Percy together, and you are more like lovers than many a man and woman who are engaged. You look at each other, and talk to each other, in an unbecoming fashion. I make the assertion and I defy you to contradict me."

"How can I help admiring her?" he asked.

"You can help showing it quite so plainly."

"She wouldn't be satisfied if I did. She is as pretty as a picture, and she knows it, and she wants everybody else to tell her so."

"Then, if her demands are such, I would get out of her way immediately."

He laughed a light mocking laugh, and said, "I'll be darned if I ever run away from a pretty woman."

"Don't grow profane, please, let me remind you that you are in the presence of a lady."

"Well, it's enough to make a fellow profane to talk with such a little goose as you are. You don't know anything about the world. In society, married men and women occasionally notice each other without exciting scandal."

"Occasionally they excite scandal by noticing each other too much. I know that I'm not in society, and I don't care to be, but sometimes I take up a newspaper and read it. I observe that divorces are very common."

"Jessie, you have a rare faculty of making mountains out of mole-hills," he said in a light tone.

"I know that very serious consequences often follow thoughtless acts. I believe that both you and Percy are innocent of any intention of doing wrong, but you are drifting toward the breakers."

"How poetical you are!" he said.

"Harry, that kind of exclamation is lost on me now. I am talking seriously. I entreat you to be more careful in your manner towards Percy. You have grown familiar, and familiarity is vulgar. Treat her as a lady should be treated."

"By heavens, you sha'n't say that I don't treat her as a lady should be treated."

"You did not to-night. I saw you lay your hand on her more than once, and you even pulled her hair."

"Well, she's to blame as much as I am. She would inveigle a saint into admiring her and complimenting her."

"Just like Adam—always throwing the blame on Eve. 'The woman tempted me.'" He laughed.

"When a fellow is cornered, he must throw the blame on somebody."

"There," she said, "I hope you have recovered your sanity, that laugh sounds natural." Soon she added, "Harry, please promise me that you will be more careful. Nobody loves you better than I do, and it grieves me to see you go wrong. Remember our mother, Harry!"

"There, that will do," he replied, raising his hand as if to ward off a blow. He had loved his gentle mother with passionate devotion, and could not bear to hear her name mentioned.

After his sister had said good-night and closed the door behind her, the young man sat a long time looking into the fire. He could not shake off the uncomfortable feeling that had taken possession of him. A strange warfare of emotions was going on within him. He knew very well that he had been doing wrong in a great many different ways. He did not approve of himself, and yet he was ready to undertake his own defence against all the powers, within or without, that dared to condemn him. His admiration for Mrs. Philip Winston was very genuine. She was a fascinating woman, and in her presence he often felt himself a captive hopelessly bound, but he had never mistaken her for a divinity. He knew that she was mortal, and made of very common clay. He had been foolish to go so far with her. Then came thoughts of another woman, sweeter and gentler, but lost to him forever, because he was not worthy of her. In a vague, wretched way, he realized what *her* love would have been to him—a power to uplift—a star to guide.

It was long after midnight, when at last he arose from his seat. The fire had died entirely out, and the desolation of ashes was over the hearth and over his own heart. His face was pallid and gray, but there was a fixed look about the mouth which betokened a strong purpose.

CHAPTER XVI.

Mrs. Philip Winston had more than once expressed a desire to ride. She waylaid the Colonel, one morning, as he was leaving the house, and said, " Brother, haven't you any good riding-horses in your stables? Jessie, Mr. Holcombe, and I, want to go out for a ride this afternoon. Mr. Holcombe has his own horse, of course, so you have only to find a steed for Jessie, and one for me." The Colonel hesitated. " Now, do be nice and find something for us to mount," she pleaded, laying her beautiful hand caressingly upon his sleeve. He could not resist that argument.

" Yes," he answered, slowly, " I reckon I can manage it. You may have my horse—he's safe enough, and Jessie is not afraid to ride the colt."

" Gracious heavens!" she exclaimed, " we don't want an accident. Don't give Jessie a colt, I beseech you."

He smiled and said, " You needn't be alarmed about Jessie; she could ride a mustang at a circus; she was raised in a saddle. The colt is good enough—he is very well broken, only he has a few ugly tricks. I would not like to see you on his back, my dear."

" Thank you," she replied, with a light laugh, " I can realize that my life is rather more valuable than hers. I have a husband to grieve over me, and she hasn't."

This gay city girl completely bewitched the Colonel by her airs and grace, and he was willing to take any amount of trouble to gratify her. He abandoned his own plan for the afternoon, and even sent over to a neighbor's house to borrow a side-saddle of a newer and better fashion than any that were hanging in his stables.

Before three o'clock, the horses were at the door. The Colonel himself lifted his sister-in-law into the saddle, tightened the girth, and arranged her skirt in the most approved fashion. Mr. Philip looked at the riders from his comfortable post on the piazza, and called to Mr. Holcombe to take good care of his wife, and bring her back all right.

Harry expressed his determination to do that, whatever might happen.

"I will bring her back, if I don't come myself," he said, laughing. He soon saw that she would require a good deal of his attention, for she did not know much about managing a horse, and did not appear to advantage when mounted. Her self-confidence was somewhat diminished, and the graceful ease of her manner was entirely gone. Her riding habit was elegant and fitted faultlessly, yet she did not give the impression of an Amazon, as Jessie Holcombe did.

The three cantered slowly down the avenue. The afternoon was beautiful, with some of the chill of coming winter already in the air. Jessie felt ready for a gallop, but she restrained herself, and walked quietly beside the others.

"I was thrown by a horse at the riding-school a few years ago," said Mrs. Philip, "and I have been rather timid about riding ever since."

"You need not be afraid of that old cob," Harry replied; "he has jogged over the plantation for so many years with our venerable brother upon his back, that he would not know how to run away, even if he wanted to—he has forgotten how to use his legs."

"Stop making fun of him this minute," said Mrs. Philip; "I think he is very nice; he has a very easy gait."

"Yes, like a rocking-chair," the gentleman answered. "I had rather sit on the piazza and rock backwards and forwards all day than ride him."

"I will turn round and go home, if you say another word," said Percy, laughing.

"Heaven forbid! I'll be as mum as a cotton-stalk," he said, looking at her with a merry twinkle in his eye.

"I know a part of your ridicule is meant for the rider," Mrs. Philip ventured to assert.

"Now, I call that a cruel charge. Here I've been admiring you until I've hardly got any eyesight left, and that's the way you repay me. I don't think any weapon was ever invented quite equal to a woman's tongue. It runs you through the ribs, breaks all your bones, and takes off your head at the same time."

This smoothed down the ruffled self-love of the lady.

"Good-bye!" exclaimed Jessie, "I'm off for a gallop. I can't hold in this restless creature any longer." And away she dashed.

"How beautifully your sister rides," said Mrs. Philip; "she sits so firmly in the saddle that she seems to be a part of the horse."

"Yes, few ladies ride better than Jessie," the young man replied; "she has been in the saddle ever since she was a baby. She used to ride over the plantation with my father when she was too small to be seen without a microscope. She is very fond of it." They watched her as she disappeared from sight; soon she came galloping back, her fiery little steed occasionally indulging in a side plunge.

"Look out," called Harry; "he's a vicious thing, and would enjoy throwing you."

"I'm not in the least afraid of him, and he knows it well," she answered back. Soon she quieted down her horse, and cantered along beside them.

They had passed the mill, and were in the midst of the pine grove beyond it, when through the trees they saw two other riders approaching from the opposite direction.

"Gracious goodness!" said Harry, and his face flushed somewhat, as if the sight were not pleasant.

"Who are they?" asked Percy.

"Miss Brooks and that conceited puppy of a cousin," he returned.

"Hush!" said Jessie, "you must not speak so; you do not even know him."

"I've no desire to know him," was the reply; "he has the air of the Grand Turk. If she marries him, I know he will murder her in less than a year."

"What tragical predictions!" exclaimed Percy; "you must be interested in her fate to judge by your looks."

"I am," he said; "I'm interested in the fate of every pretty woman."

"Harry dear, do be polite to them," his sister entreated in a low tone.

"Of course I shall; I should like to kill them both with politeness,"—and he laughed unpleasantly.

The two parties were now in front of each other, and greetings were exchanged, and introductions made.

"Why haven't you been to see me, Jessie?" Alice asked immediately.

"I only heard that you were back at The Grove, a few days ago. How glad I am to see you!" She could not add, "How well you are looking."

Alice Brooks was indeed changed. The bloom was gone from her cheeks, and her slender form appeared too fragile for perfect health. The impression of ethereal delicacy was farther increased by her blue eyes and blonde hair. She was dressed in a habit of dark green cloth with facings of a lighter shade. Instead of the conventional beaver, she wore a little three-cornered hat ornamented with ostrich tips. Jessie thought she had never seen her friend look so lovely. Alice was not beautiful, but there was something so refined, and sweet and spiritual about her face and manner, that one could not help admiring her.

"We were just going over to call on you," she said; "but it is still so early in the afternoon, that we will turn and ride awhile with you. Then we will go to Redbank and make our call, for we want to see Mrs. Winston and the Colonel, as well as the present party."

"That's a charming arrangement," said Jessie.

The riders now fell into order, and Miss Holcombe found herself in front with Mr. Waverley Brooks, while the others fell behind. Alice managed to place Mrs. Philip between herself and Harry, but she did not appear to avoid conversation with him. She began to talk about the places that she had visited during the summer, and Mrs. Philip was glad to know something about them herself. The two enjoyed comparing notes, while Harry threw in an occasional question.

At a single glance, Jessie Holcombe took in the person of her companion. In a moment, she decided that he was not at all like his father. Soon, however, she changed her mind; yes, there was a great resemblance between father and son, though it eluded one at first. Both had the same clear gray eyes, the same finely chiselled mouth and chin, and the same playful smile, hiding under the heavy mustache.

"Miss Holcombe," said the gentleman, "I've heard my cousin talk so much about you that I seem to know you already."

"I'm very sorry indeed," the young girl replied, looking into his face to catch the expression of his father's eyes which she was anxious to see again.

"You must tell me why?" he asked, somewhat surprised at her words.

"Because it is always better to begin an acquaintance without expectations. Now, I'm sure you will be disappointed in me."

"Indeed I'm not," he answered, emphatically.

"But you don't know me yet," she said, "you are over-bold to speak so confidently."

"I deny that also," he replied, his whole face lighting up with his father's smile. "But, Miss Holcombe, I hope I am not exposed to the same disadvantage with you. I would be sorry if anybody had been talking to you about me."

"Oh, no," she said, very simply, "I was quite determined to be without prejudices, so I have never asked a single question about you."

"I'm afraid that argues great indifference."

"By no means; only a man would misunderstand my remark."

"And is that your opinion of men?" he asked. "Do you always find them obtuse?"

"Not always, but sometimes," she answered, reflecting his smile; "but on the whole I like them very well, especially when I'm on horseback."

"I shall remember that statement, but I do not at all understand what you mean by it. Perhaps you will pity my obtuseness and explain."

"Well, Mr. Brooks, I have never, never in my long and eventful life, been allowed to ride unless accompanied by a man. Now, when I tell you that I like nothing on earth so well as a gallop or a trot on the back of a good horse, you may be able to realize my appreciation of men."

"You acknowledge, then, that there are emergencies in which they are indispensable?" he said.

She assented with a smile. The gentleman looked at her with curiosity and admiration. Her conversation amused him. She was not at all like his cousin Alice, whose words, with all their gracious charm, were never sparkling or piquant.

"I find that our tastes are alike, Miss Holcombe; I am very fond of riding, too. I had rather live without a house than without a horse."

"I can't go so far as that. I do appreciate a house very much, especially when it rains, as it sometimes does in Georgia."

"But a tent would answer instead, even in rainy weather. But what could ever take the place of a horse?"

"Why, steam seems to be pushing him aside everywhere. After a while I suppose we will have wooden horses, filled with machinery and propelled by steam."

"Or ride on wheels, as they do in France," he said.

"Well, those contrivances might be very convenient, but I prefer a living creature which responds with intelligence when I pull the reins, and gives me back a little love for my domination. Come, let's have a gallop; riding is better than talking." They were soon out of sight, lost in the deep woods, nor did they again see the other three riders until they met them in the parlor at Redbank, a few hours later. That October afternoon passed gloriously for Jessie Holcombe. Her companion was a dashing horseman, ready to leap a ditch, jump a fence or ride a race, and though he did not indulge in that kind of riding on the present occasion, yet she felt his enthusiasm, and responded to it. The acquaintance between the two advanced rapidly under the stimulus of this exhilarating exercise. When they at length fell into a walk, he entertained her with reminiscences of his travels. As she listened to his conversation, her cheeks, already flushed, became more brilliant, and her fine eyes gave expression to every shade of her pleasurable emotion.

She soon found that his tastes, as well as his looks and manners, were very English. Everything about him proclaimed a healthy, wholesome nature; the clear gray eyes, the florid complexion, the hearty laugh, the frank, unaffected way of talking. You felt that he possessed an unlimited capacity for enjoyment.

The afternoon was almost over and the sun was dropping low, when the two riders came within sight of Redbank. As they were entering the long avenue, Jessie turned to her companion and said, "I do not think that Alice is looking at all strong. She seems tired and worn."

"Yes, it grieves us all to see her," he replied, "but she never complains, and declares that there's nothing the matter with her. We have been trying to build her up, as the doctors say, but she is just a little obstinate, and does not assist us in our efforts. I think we travelled too much in the summer, and she got tired. I hope she will improve now that she is at home again."

"It would be strange if she did not," said Jessie. and she looked at the gentleman as if she expected him to understand her meaning, but he did not—he was obtuse again.

When Jessie and her companion entered the parlor at Redbank, they were greeted by a volley of questions. "Where have you been?" "Why did you go so far?" "Did you get lost?" They only laughed, and refused to satisfy public curiosity.

"Why, we have been home an hour," said Mrs. Philip; "and, Jessie, I have been half dead with anxiety about you. I was sure that wicked colt had thrown you over his head, and broken your neck."

"And what did you think I was doing in the meantime?" asked Mr. Brooks.

"Looking on!" replied Mrs. Philip; "I thought you would allow it to be done for the pleasure of picking her up."

"Thanks for your good opinion of me!" he said; then turning to his cousin, "Alice, I hope you are not tired waiting."

"Oh, no—not at all," she answered; "but I think it

is time now for us to start home." And she arose from her seat, and the good-byes were spoken.

That evening around the dinner-table, Miss Brooks and her cousin were thoroughly discussed. Mrs. Philip began by saying, " Do tell me something about Mr. and Miss Brooks. Who are they? "

" They are neighbors of ours," the Colonel replied.

" That is not sufficient," Percy said, " your account is too general; I want to know something more."

" Well, they are friends of ours. Is not that enough to give them the stamp of respectability?" he asked, laughing at her.

" Yes, of course; but they interest me, and I want to know who they are."

" Are you sure it is interest, and not curiosity?" inquired her husband.

" I will not answer such a question," she replied; " you are always ready to suspect me of bad motives."

" Well, Percy," said Mrs. Winston, " I will give you a history of the lady and gentleman so far as I know it. Miss Alice Brooks is the only daughter of Mrs. Eustace Brooks, who is a widow and owns a plantation called The Grove, about five miles from here. Mr. Brooks is her first cousin. He is the son of Judge Brooks who lives in the city."

" Are they lovers?" asked Percy.

" I suppose they are," Mrs. Winston replied. " It is said that they are going to be married soon. They have been engaged ever since they were children."

" She is very sweet-looking," said Percy, " but she lacks color and animation. Her riding habit was beautiful, but hardly the thing for the country."

" She has been at Long Branch and Newport, most of the summer, and I suppose she bought it to wear there. She is fond of riding," Mrs. Winston said, very quietly.

" Are they rich ? " asked Percy.

Harry looked up with a flash of annoyance in his eyes, which did not escape the notice of the lady.

" Yes," he exclaimed, " they own half the State of Georgia."

" They are among the few rich people at the South now," said Colonel Winston. " The mother of Mr. Waverley Brooks was an heiress from New York, and he inherits a large property through her."

" Then they have connections at the North ? " asked Mrs. Philip, whose curiosity was not yet satisfied.

" No end of them," said Harry; " they are kin to all the big-bugs in the United States."

" Miss Brooks is quite pretty, but she lacks style," remarked the lady.

" Of course she does. That's a plant that doesn't grow down here," said Harry; " wire grass and poke weed have rooted it out."

Percy laughed and said, " Mr. Holcombe, if you are so tart, I shall suspect that you are more interested in Miss Brooks than you are willing to confess."

" I have told you already that I am interested in every pretty woman," he replied ; " Miss Brooks comes in for her share."

" But there is something more than that, I am sure," she insisted.

" Do you think so ? " he asked ; " well, I would not be so rude as to contradict a lady."

" Mr. Brooks looks like an Englishman," Percy continued ; " he has a *distingué* air."

" He is like his mother," said the Colonel ; " she was a large, handsome woman, with a fresh complexion and yellow hair. I remember her well. She did not live long; she died of some kind of fever. That was at least twenty years ago, and the Judge has never married again."

"What beautiful devotion!" exclaimed Mrs. Philip. Then turning to her husband, "I hope you will show your love for me in that way."

He only laughed and said, "There, now, I hope you have finished with the Brookses; your curiosity must certainly be satisfied by this time. I think you know everything about them except their ages. Miss Holcombe, how old do you think Miss Brooks is?"

Jessie laughed.

"Ought I to tell? She might object. Ladies are said to be sensitive on that point."

"Well, the gentleman, then; how old do you think he is? Percy will never be content until she knows."

"Anywhere from twenty to twenty-five," Jessie answered, much amused at the husband's manner. Mrs. Philip did not seem to share in this feeling, for she looked up at him with a very severe expression. Afterwards she continued her dinner in silence.

Just before bedtime that same evening, Jessie went into the dining-room in search of a newspaper which the Colonel had mislaid. On her entrance she was surprised to find Harry, sitting all alone, his head bent down on both arms which were crossed upon the table. At first she thought him asleep, and, not wishing to disturb him, she turned quietly to leave the room. Suddenly he lifted his head, and said, "Jessie, is that you?"

"Yes," she answered, approaching him. She was frightened when she saw how ghastly his face looked in the dim firelight. "What's the matter, Harry?" she asked. "You look ill?"

"Nothing," he replied. "I'm only a little out of sorts."

"But you are very pale; I am sure you are suffering. Do tell me if anything has happened." And she laid her hand tenderly upon his head, running her fingers through his soft hair.

"Nothing new—nothing but what you know well enough already."

"What do you mean?" she exclaimed, rather aghast at his manner.

He laughed a hollow kind of a laugh, and answered with a curl of the lip:—"I'm only feeling the weight of my numerous sins. They are rather heavy, you know, and sometimes threaten to crush a fellow to the earth."

"You are joking, now, I'm sure," she said, with a sense of relief.

"No, I'm not," was the reply. "I'm a poor devil, and to-night I feel it more than usual. You think that I'm perfectly indifferent to everything, Jessica; but there you make a mistake. I do have a twinge of conscience now and then. I'd give a good deal to be a better fellow than I am."

"Oh! Harry," exclaimed the girl, the tears springing to her eyes. She knew well enough now, what was the matter with him, and her heart was full of pity. "Oh, Harry, if you only would try to make something of yourself. Just make one honest effort, and the next will be easier, and the next easier still. It is the first step that costs."

"Yes, I know it," he said, burying his face in his hands. Soon he looked up and continued, "Jessie, I would be strong enough for any effort, if I had the hope of winning her in the end, but it maddens me to feel that she belongs to another."

"Harry, you are not worthy of the love of any woman now; make yourself worthy, and then, though she is lost to you, there are other noble women in the world to whom you may aspire."

"What do I care for all the rest!" he exclaimed; "they might sink together in a wrecked ship if only she were saved."

"Harry, she will soon belong to another, and it will be a sin for you to love her then."

"There is no sin in a pure love," he cried, "even though the woman who inspires it is a thousand times married. I shall love her as long as there is life in my body. When I'm dead, it will be the only part of me that will be immortal. And I believe she loves me too. I could see that she was suffering to-day, just as well as I was."

"You are mistaken, I'm sure, Harry. She is not the kind of girl to marry unless she loves very deeply, and she is certainly going to marry her cousin."

"Well, I only know that she doesn't look now as she did last winter. I've seen a light in her eyes that's not there now. I've seen her flush and flutter; and I've felt her little hand tremble in mine. Confound that cousin of hers! I'd-like to kick him back to Europe. I believe that I could have won her, if it had not been for the whole lot of them. Jessie," he exclaimed, wildly, "the thought of her pursues me like a fiend, I cannot get rid of it. If I go to perdition, it will be her fault. She could have saved me easy enough."

"You ought not to blame her, Harry. She must have felt that it would be unsafe to marry you, or she would not have rejected you."

"I know I could make her happy, even if I'm not as

pious and proper as a parson. I would love her as a woman was never loved before."

"That would not make her happy, Harry, if she felt all the time that you were below her standard of manhood. I know her well, and her ideals are high."

"I know it," he said; "but I could have reached even up to her standard, if she had only consented to be my wife."

As he spoke, there was a look in his eyes that Jessie had never seen there before—that she never saw again. He run his fingers through his hair in an absent-minded way, as if trying to relieve the restlessness and wretchedness of his soul.

"Jessie," he continued after a few moments, "I do believe I will try to make something of myself. I would like to have her feel that she has made a mistake, that there is something in me after all; that I'm not absolutely and entirely good-for-nothing."

"Oh! Harry, if you only would. Do not drink any more. Do not gamble any more. Find some honest work to do, and do it with all your might. You are still so young—the future is all yours."

He looked at her steadily for a minute, and then said, "Jessie, you are a good little thing; you ought to enter the ministry. You have a real talent for preaching."

The color rushed to her face, but she said nothing. It was like Harry to disappoint expectation by such tricks of speech. She could not continue the conversation any longer, and arose to leave the room. He saw that he had hurt her, and had the grace to say, "I wasn't making fun, Jessie; I was really in earnest. It does me more good to have a talk with you, than to go to church. I think you understand me better than anybody else does. Only you were mistaken when you thought I was in love with Mrs. Philip Winston. I've got more sense than to commit such a folly as that. But one must have a little fun sometimes. Even then the world is dull enough." He sighed and began to rap on the table with his fingers. Soon he turned abruptly to his sister and said:

"Don't despair of me altogether, Jessie; perhaps even yet, I may be 'plucked as a brand from the burning.' Isn't that the way the preachers put it? You mustn't give me up, dear; if you do, I'm afraid I shall travel downhill pretty fast."

"Harry, dear, I would die to save you," she said, in earnest, solemn tones.

"That would be very silly," he answered; "it would be like giving a million of dollars for a pop-gun. I'm not worth any such price. Don't think about me any more. Go to bed, and sleep like a good girl."

"Good-night," she said, and in a few moments she was gone.

Again Harry Holcombe crossed his arms upon the table and bent down his head. Why should we try to guess the thoughts and feelings that were struggling within him? Let us rather leave him to the silence of that lonely room.

CHAPTER XVII.

THE next morning, Mrs. Philip Winston did not appear at the breakfast-table. Her husband, whose manner was silent and sullen, explained her absence by saying that she had sprained her ankle slightly the evening before, and found herself unable to walk without pain. She had caught the heel of her slipper in the loose braid of her skirt, and had fallen headlong on the floor. At the time she had laughed, for the injury appeared to be very slight; but in the morning she had found her ankle much swollen and very painful. Mr. Philip seemed to be angry with her, angry with the high heels, angry with the loose braid, angry with everything. The mood was a new phase of character. What had happened between himself and wife, no one knew, but evidently his temper was seriously ruffled. Every one was silent and constrained. At last the meal was over, and the family arose and left the table.

For almost a week Percy was compelled to keep her room. Everybody was full of sympathy for her, and each one made some contribution to her entertainment.

Harry alone was excluded from the sick-room. For a few days he wandered around aimlessly, looking rather disconsolate. At length one morning he went off to the city with a wagon-load of cotton. He did not return in the evening, and no message came to tell where he had gone, how long he intended to stay, or when he expected to return. From the bottom of her soul Jessie pitied him.

When Percy's ankle was well and she was able to leave her room, she looked pale and subdued. Even the Colonel, who was usually too much absorbed in his own affairs to be very observant, remarked the change, and expressed his regret anew for an accident which must have cost her much pain. She smiled and thanked him, but declared herself all right again, and happy to join the family gatherings.

"Well," said Mr. Philip, "I am sincerely glad that the injury was no more serious. Those high heels are very dangerous, but women will wear them, even at the risk of falling and laming themselves for life."

"I have always worn them," replied Percy, very coldly and quietly, "and I have never before fallen. I think people are liable to fall, heels or no heels; only it is a great satisfaction to be able to lay the blame on somebody or something."

"You are right," said Mrs. Winston, smiling; "we get rid of half our annoyance over a mishap, if we can only find somebody to put the blame on.

"That's very true," replied Mr. Philip; "but, in this case, I insist upon the actual guilt of those high heels. I hate them. I have a great mind to cut them all off."

"I guess you won't," said his wife, in the same cool, quiet tone. Every one felt that a dangerous point had been reached in the controversy, and the subject was dropped. Nothing is so indescribable, and yet so quickly felt, as the want of sympathy and harmony in the members of a family. This indefinable something was now present at Redbank. Mrs. Philip Winston was changed. Day after day this fact became more apparent. Jessie's keen eye noted a new expression in her face, a listless, unhappy expression, very different from the bright, self-satisfied consciousness of a few weeks ago. She was no longer restless. She no longer appeared to find real enjoyment in anything; she seemed all the time to be looking, waiting, listening for some one. Yet she never once mentioned Harry's name, nor asked what had become of him. This reticence was unnatural in one so full of curiosity. There was but one explanation for it; she must have divined the truth—she must have analyzed her own feelings as well as fathomed his. In the meantime, her manner towards her husband was still cold and distant. He had, without doubt, done or said something that had deeply offended her, and she was slow to forgive. Nor did he show any sign of relenting. There was no expression of a desire for reconciliation in his manner or face. Mrs. Winston looked upon this drama of married life with sad interest. She saw the danger for both in this hard, cold attitude, and she determined to talk with Percy and try to influence her for good. One rainy afternoon, she went to the young wife's room with a tray of fruit. She rapped several times at the door without receiving a response; then, thinking that Percy might be out or asleep, and that it would be well to leave the fruit as a surprise for her, she softly turned the knob. When the door opened, she saw a white figure lying in a heap at the foot of the bed, the face buried deep in a pillow. A faint sob reached her ear. In a moment, she was beside the prostrate form.

"What is it, dear?" she whispered tenderly, "are you ill? Why did you not call for some one? Cannot I do something for you?"

Percy raised a pale and tear-stained face. "No, I am not ill—I am only tired, fearfully tired."

"Will you not let me get you a glass of wine?" said Mrs. Winston, "I'm afraid you have taken cold."

"No, no," was the answer, "I do not want anything, and I have not taken cold. I shall feel better presently. Sit down beside me. I think your presence will do me good."

Eleanor seated herself on the edge of the bed, and began to stroke the soft tangled hair that fell loosely over the pillow. She had no great love or admiration for her young sister-in-law, but remembering the many sorrows of her own married life, she pitied her, and sincerely desired to help her.

In a short time, Percy said, softly, "I am better now. I like the touch of your fingers on my head—it feels so soft and nice. I don't really know why I was crying, but I feel very sad and lonely to-day."

"It must be the monotony of the place that oppresses you," said Mrs. Winston. "I wish we knew how to entertain you better, but indeed our resources are very limited, dear. It must be hard for you, and different from anything you have ever known."

"Yes," she answered, very simply, "it is; but please don't think that I fail to appreciate the kindness of every one. You have all been so good and nice to me, but somehow I long for a change. I have been so used to gayety that I'm afraid I cannot live without it."

"I understand the feeling," said Mrs. Winston; "It is perfectly natural for young people to love gayety. I used to love it once myself, but I've learned to find enjoyment in other things. Redbank is a dull place for a pretty creature like you."

"Why does Philip like it so much?" she asked; "I cannot make it out. Sometimes he talks of buying a plantation. I believe that I would go insane, if I were compelled to lead such a lonely life. The very thought of it is terrible to me. You don't think he will?"

"Oh! no, I don't believe he really likes it himself; he only feels refreshed by the quiet. Besides, dear, all plantations are not like this. You must not make up your mind too hastily. And then you are rich, and could have all the company you want. You could keep your house filled with pleasant guests."

"Where would I find them?" she asked, helplessly; "All the people I know in the world are far away from here. Besides, I love all the diversions of the city too well to be contented in the country. It would kill me—indeed it would; and I don't believe Philip would even grieve over me, if I died. Do you know I'm beginning to feel that I shall not make him happy. He is so much older than I am, and so unlike me in every respect, and somehow I seem so little to him. He is quite content to be with the Colonel—he forgets me entirely."

"But, my dear, that will not be the case when you leave here," said Mrs. Winston; "Philip is very fond of his brother, and very interested in all the affairs of the plantation. Remember he spent his boyhood here, and likes to visit every familiar spot."

"I'm afraid that's not the whole truth," Percy answered, sadly; "I do not seem to be at all necessary to his happiness."

"Well, you must learn to make yourself necessary," said Mrs. Winston; "that will be an easy task for one so charming as yourself."

"How?" she asked, in a listless way.

"I cannot tell you, dear; I wish I could. I suppose you must find out what he likes, and do, or be that."

"I cannot," she said, wearily. "Oh! I wish I were at home again, in my father's house."

"Well, my dear child, you are going to return in a few weeks. When you are back again, you will have so many interests and occupations that I am sure you will be happy. This is only a rainy day,—

'Into each heart some rain must fall,
Some days must be dark and dreary.'"

There was a long silence. Finally, the young wife said—"And do you think that Philip really cares for me? He has been so cold of late. He treats me as if I were a naughty child. It is not right for him to act so—it makes me angry."

"How can he help loving you, my dear," said Mrs. Winston. "You must not indulge in such suspicions. You are his wife, and you must take it for granted that he loves you. To doubt is treason. Don't begin your married life by expecting too much from your husband. Give liberally yourself, and try to be satisfied with what you get in return."

"But he is so different from what I used to think he was. He seemed to worship me before we were married; he was always paying me the most extravagant compliments, and was ready to gratify every wish that I could express. I thought him absolutely perfect."

"No human being is perfect, Percy," said Mrs. Winston. "You must not be disappointed, if you find that your husband has faults as well as others. Remember that you are not perfect yourself. Perhaps he finds a difference in you also."

She looked up and laughed. "I daresay he does. Indeed he tells me so half a dozen times every day.

Do you wonder that I get vexed with him? I'm sure I don't know what I do that he should talk to me so."

Mrs. Winston could not help smiling. It was useless to give advice to this pretty self-centred creature. "Well, you must not cry any more," she said; "I know it would vex Philip to see you in tears—he would not understand it."

"Of course, he wouldn't," Percy exclaimed, with a curl of the lip; "he always gets angry when I cry—as if I did not miss many things that I used to have, and feel the dreadful change. I assure you there's enough to make me cry. I have given up a great deal for his sake."

"My dear, every woman gives up a great deal when she marries," said Mrs. Winston; "but there are compensations. The man thinks that he gives up a great deal too."

"I should like to know what!" she cried impatiently. "Philip will not even give up smoking for my sake, though he knows that I detest it. I don't believe he would change the style of his necktie or the cut of his coat, to save my life."

"Oh, yes, he would, if your life were at stake, dear; perhaps he might not be willing to do it merely to gratify a whim on your part."

"Well, I always wear just what he likes; he has only to express a preference, and I am ready to please him. I don't see why he can't do as much for me, without feeling that he is making a terrible sacrifice. Whenever I ask him to do or not to do any little thing, he simply ignores me."

Eleanor Winston listened to all these grievances of the spoiled child with a sad heart. Her own married life had been wretchedly poor in the love and sympathy

that every woman craves. Here was another life which was threatened with the same cruel privation. She could only hope that Percy's heart would be less keenly alive to the sorrow and bitterness of this destitution than her own had been. Soon the young wife exclaimed—
"For my part, I think marriage is a very one-sided affair. The woman is altogether married, and the man not at all."

Again she laughed.

"And sometimes it is just the other way," said Mrs. Winston; "don't be too hard on the men, my dear; sometimes I feel very sorry for them. They have their burdens too. But one thing is very true, after a man and woman are married, they must both make the best of it. They cannot get out of it without losing much more than they gain. Percy, dear, when you are once more at home, you will not feel all these little frictions that vex you so much now. There will be many new occupations to fill up your time. You have everything to make you happy, dear; you have only to mix the materials aright, and the result will be beautiful. There, cheer up, my child, and give your husband a sweet kiss of welcome, when he comes. I must go now. I shall expect to see you perfectly radiant at dinner. Put on that black velvet dress which makes you look so queenly. Good-bye." And Mrs. Winston left the room, and closed the door softly behind her.

For a long time Percy lay quietly on the bed, thinking in her fragmentary way. She was inclined to believe that her sister-in-law was right. There was no use in sulking and crying and getting up scenes. She was married now; she had decided the matter for herself; from her numerous suitors, she had chosen the most distinguished-looking man; she had had a magnificent *trousseau* and a grand wedding. If every single day since that happy event had not been filled with sunshine, she must not fall into complaints and spoil her eyes by weeping—there was no use in it. She did admire her husband very much. In his own particular sphere at home he was splendid. When he returned to the city with her, she knew she would be proud of him—he was so greatly superior to the husbands of her various schoolmates and friends, then she thought of the entertainments she would give, and those to which she would be invited, of the concerts and theatre parties to which she would lend her charming presence. Gradually the unpleasant experiences of the past few weeks faded from her mind, and she arose from the bed and began the mysteries of her elaborate toilette. When at length her husband entered he was delighted to find her resplendent in velvet and diamonds. He approached her with the old-time admiration and compliments. She smiled and put up her lips to be kissed.

"We won't quarrel any more, will we?" she said.

"I hope not," he replied; "it's awfully uncomfortable, and does no good."

"Then, you mustn't be cross to me," she said.

"And don't be cross yourself, my dear," he answered. They both laughed. He sat down in a large arm-chair, and she seated herself on his lap.

At dinner, Percy satisfied the expectations of her sister-in-law. She was herself again. After all, the little heart was not broken. Perhaps it had felt a pang or two, but that kind of suffering does not merit pity; it is only an antidote to vanity.

A week later, Mr. and Mrs. Philip Winston left Redbank. Thanks were most graciously expressed for the kind entertainment they had received, and regrets that so delightful a visit had at length come to an end. They continued their wedding-journey to Florida and New Orleans, and by the beginning of the New Year were at home again.

After their departure, a change came over the Colonel. His late genial mood gave place to gloom and ill-temper.

Again he went through the house, slamming the doors, scolding the servants, and kicking the dogs. Jessie was glad that Harry was out of the way, and that the shower of epithets usually lavished on him now fell on the head of Peyton. The negro only grinned, and bore it with amiable resignation.

After a few days, the young girl heard with astonishment that the plantation of Redbank had been mortgaged to the Colonel's brother.

"This, then, was why he brought his bride to see us— this is the southern plantation over which some day she is to preside as mistress," said Eleanor, in a tone of bitterness. "I never thought much of Philip, but I confess I did not believe him quite so selfish and mean. It has wounded the Colonel terribly; his whole aim now will be to pay back the money which he owes Philip, and redeem Redbank. He loves this old plantation with a proud and foolish affection. It would break his heart to part with it; it is his title-deed to nobility." She sighed as she spoke, for no one realized so well as herself the hopeless entanglement into which her husband's affairs were slowly drifting.

CHAPTER XVIII.

ALICE had sent Jessie an invitation to visit her. She had written a pleading little note which it was impossible to resist, and the two friends were again together. The affection between them had been strengthened rather than weakened by absence. In her own home, Alice was like her former self. The effort to entertain her guest effaced even the slight traces of a change in character. She had always been gentle, silent, and reserved—she was scarcely more so now. Mr. Waverley Brooks was a visitor at The Grove, and Jessie daily saw the cousins together. She was puzzled to understand them. The manner of each to the other was frank, familiar, and delicately polite, but it was difficult to believe that they were lovers. No tender little glances ever passed between them—no softly-whispered words. Jessie had had but little experience in love affairs, but she knew that there were endless varieties of the disease. She made up her mind that this was a very mild form. Having been engaged from childhood, they had probably passed the violent crisis, and were now on the road to recovery. It was almost the same as being married—they had grown so used to each other. Alice was a charming little hostess; she was always thinking of something pleasant for Jessie to do. She showed a great desire to promote the acquaintance between her friend and her cousin, and threw them much together. She insisted that Waverley should tell Jessie and herself all about his life in Europe. With eager interest the two girls looked over the piles of photographs which illustrated his journey from country to country. They had both read and studied enough to be familiar with much that he told them; it was just that kind of familiarity which asks intelligent questions.

"It is better than going to Europe oneself," exclaimed Alice, " for we can have it all without stirring from this dear, comfortable old room."

" I don't know about that," said Jessie ; " there must be great enjoyment in travelling. The continual movement and excitement and variety must be delightful ! "

" Waverley, what country did you enjoy most ? " asked his cousin.

" In a way, I enjoyed all," he answered. " I liked England because it was somewhat like home, and yet full of all kinds of interesting objects that one does not find in America—ruins, cathedrals, castles, and quaint old towns and villages. I tramped over it from one end to the other, and it all seemed beautiful to me, the quiet lake scenery, the cliffs of Cornwall, the moors of Yorkshire, and the downs of Sussex. Then I liked France immensely; the country is picturesque, and the people gay and charming. I spent the best part of a summer with a party of artists, going through Normandy and Brittany, and we had a glorious time. Then Switzerland is grand beyond description. To climb its mountains tones one up to a pitch of sublimity. Its air is so exhilarating that it makes one feel heroic. But Italy is the country that best satisfies the artist. Its wonderful sky gives a charm to everything—lakes, rivers, mountains, and plains, all seem a part of dreamland. Its beautiful old cities are filled with the richest and rarest treasures of art. It is almost impossible to exhaust them. Oh, it is a wonderful land! I often felt that I would like to linger there forever, going from town to town, and studying history, art, and music side by side. I want to go there to live some day."

"And what city would you select for your home?" asked Alice.

"I would go from one to another. I would choose Venice and the Lakes for spring, some villa in the high Apennines for summer, Florence and Rome in the autumn, and Naples in winter. With some sweet, congenial spirit to enjoy it with me, the existence would be simply divine."

"Well, I know I would not like it," said Mrs. Brooks; "I had rather be in my own home, and have things exactly as I want them. It was bad enough last summer—it would be worse still in Europe. So you need not invite me to go with you, Waverley," and the old lady smiled.

"And what do you say, Alice?" he asked.

She flushed slightly, and then said, "You know I am not fond of travelling, and I would be dreadfully confused by so many things to see all the time. I would soon grow tired and long for The Grove and my books."

"But you could take the books along with you, or buy some more there," he replied.

"But I like to read them in some bright, particular spot, some cosy rocking-chair in a certain corner—some cushioned window-sill, from which I can look out upon a familiar view."

"I'm afraid you have grown too foreign, Mr. Brooks, to deserve an American wife," said Jessie; "you will have to choose a dreamy Italian girl."

"Did you fall in love with any of them, Waverley?" asked Alice. "Now, speak the truth—honor bright."

"Of course, I did," he replied, laughing gayly; "I was always falling in love, wherever I went; superficially, you know, for I had a well-rooted attachment before I left home," and he looked up at his cousin. Again a delicate color came into her cheeks.

"Do tell us about your various love affairs," she exclaimed, "it will be very amusing."

"Are you perfectly sure you will like to hear about them?" he asked.

"Indeed I am!—perfectly sure!" she answered emphatically.

"Well," he said, "I met my first love in England. One day, while in London, I went to the Royal Academy to see the pictures. Soon after entering, I saw a tall, elegant creature—a perfect vision of loveliness, moving slowly around from canvas to canvas, and studying her catalogue very devoutly. I took my seat in a comfortable corner, and gave up my time entirely to looking at her. Afterwards I found out that she was an Earl's daughter, and quite beyond my reach. Seeing that those grapes were sour, I turned away and left them."

"Describe her to us, Mr. Brooks," said Jessie; "I am curious to know what an Earl's daughter looks like. There must be a halo around her head."

"She was very fair and tall—a kind of Scandinavian goddess, with great liquid blue eyes, and such a maze of gold-colored hair around her face as I had never before seen. Yes, she did seem to wear a halo about her head. I followed her when she left the gallery, and saw her drive away in a handsome carriage with a coronet upon the panels, and a coachman and footman in livery. I was curious to know who she was, so I went to the custodian and found out. Lady Geraldine

Stacy was her name. Well, I got over that hopeless passion after a while. I saw from the papers that she was going to marry a duke, so I knew there was no chance for me." Here he paused.

"Do go on!" said Alice; "it is like a charming romance."

"Let me see—I was in Paris, I believe, when my next grand passion seized me. I was sauntering around the *Madeleine* one afternoon, looking at the flower-show in a listless way, when I saw the daintiest, most distracting little creature come up, and begin to bargain for some roses. She had lovely dark eyes and lips like cherries. It was perfectly intoxicating to watch her; she moved in a fairy, floating way as if she were swimming in the air. I followed her for quite a distance, and saw her finally disappear in the *Magasin du Louvre*. I went to the *Madeleine* every day for a week, hoping to get another glimpse of her, but all in vain. One night, I was at the theatre, and recognized her on the stage—she was a ballet-girl. Her dancing was supernatural. Isn't that enough?" he asked, looking at Alice and smiling.

"Oh! no!" she said, "do go on. I cannot tell you how interested I am."

"Must I, Miss Holcombe? Are you not tired of listening to me?"

"By no means; go on and give us the whole story," replied Jessie.

"My next love-affair came on in Venice. I had just taken an apartment in an old palace on the Grand Canal. It was a lovely evening in June. A party of friends had dined with me, and after leaving the table, we went out on the balcony for a smoke. We were laughing and talking rather noisily, when we saw a gondola approaching; a lady was reclining on the cushions under a handsome awning. She had some kind of lace affair over her head, so we could not see her face very well. Soon the gondola stopped at the door of the palace next to our own, and the lady got out. By this time our curiosity was excited—we were all waiting for something to happen. About ten minutes passed, and then a perfectly divine creature came out on the adjoining balcony. A servant in livery brought her a crimson cushion, and she leaned over the balustrade and smoked her cigarette in full view, eyeing us with the most delightful *nonchalance* imaginable. She was a Venus of Milo with all the rich coloring of the South in her face. We were charmed to see the grace with which she handled that cigarette, and how she puffed out the cloud of smoke from her lovely lips. I used to watch her every evening for weeks, and she watched me with the same coolness. I found out all about her, and I'm sorry to say that the record was not altogether good. She was a *Signora Marchesa*, and accounted the most beautiful woman in Venice. She was married to a little homely fellow at least twice as old as herself, but immensely rich. I used to see him sometimes passing in and out of the palace, but never with her. You see there are pretty women all over the world. How can a man help seeing and admiring them? Is there any harm in it, Aunt Kate?"

"I'm afraid there is," she said, shaking her head and smiling.

"Well, Alice will absolve me, I know," he replied. "I'm not sure but she has been using her time by falling in love too."

Again the girl blushed slightly, but made no reply.

"Nonsense, Waverley," said his aunt; "Alice is not

the kind of girl to fall in love with every man she meets, even if he does happen to be handsome."

"Are you sure you have reached the end of your romances, Waverley?" asked his cousin.

"I think I have—I can't remember any more." He paused a moment, and then exclaimed, "Oh! yes, I did fall in love with a voice once—it haunts me even now. Late one winter afternoon, I was walking down an obscure street in London, when I passed a little church and heard the tones of an organ. I thought I would drop in for the service. When I entered, I saw no one but the sexton, who was walking slowly up and down the aisles; but somebody was playing on the organ. I am fond of music, so I entered one of the pews and sat down. Soon, above the organ, floating upward and filling the whole church, I heard a rich contralto voice, the strongest, the purest, the sweetest that I had ever listened to in all my life. Hymn after hymn was sung, and chant after chant. My curiosity was so excited that I called the sexton, gave him a sovereign, and asked him who the singer was. He told me that she was the daughter of the rector of the church, and that she came every afternoon to practice on the organ. I used to go to the church continually just to hear her sing. I tried very hard to see her, for I had drawn a picture of her in my mind, and was curious to know if there was any resemblance, but she always left the organ-loft by a back stairway which communicated with the rectory. At last, I got a glimpse of her; she was very small, no longer young, and not at all beautiful. She looked old and sad and over-worked. It was a dreadful disappointment to me."

"Well, I must say that you have been a very faithless fellow," said Alice, shaking her head at him.

"Now, that's not fair, when I've made you my confessor; is it, Miss Holcombe?"

"Hardly," said Jessie; "that is, if you have told the truth, the whole truth, and nothing but the truth."

"Indeed I have—those were my very worst offences. I did carry on a harmless flirtation on the steamer with a pretty little American girl, but it was entirely her fault, I assure you. She flirted with every man on board, from the steward to the captain."

"How do your country-women compare with European ladies, Mr. Brooks?" asked Jessie.

"In good looks, style and cleverness, American girls cannot be beaten the world over; but their manners are sometimes too free and easy. Occasionally I used to feel sorry to see them flirt so promiscuously."

"Waverley," said Alice, looking at him very intently, "I want to know one thing. Has life in America lost its attractions for you?"

"By no means," he exclaimed, emphatically; "it is full of charm and freshness. I am proud to be an American. I am proud to have a share in such a grand country, and to have a voice in such a noble government. A man gets tired of tramping around Europe forever; he wants a country of his own and a part to play in it. In order to get real enjoyment out of life, a man wants constant occupation of a very earnest kind. I don't think I should be satisfied with patchwork for a profession, Aunt Kate,"—and he looked at her and smiled. "It seems a dreadful waste of time to cut pieces of silk into little bits, and then sew them together again. Why don't you sew the big pieces at once, and then you will finish much sooner?"

"You must not ask questions about what you cannot understand," his aunt replied.

"How do you know I cannot understand?" he asked; "I'm sure there's no great mystery about it. I could easily do it myself—only it is not worth while."

"Let me see you do it," said Alice, laughing. "Do give him some scraps, mother; let's make him prove his rash assertion."

"No," said the lady, very decidedly, "I shall not spoil my silk by letting him handle it; of course, he believes himself capable of doing anything and everything."

"Please don't be so sarcastic," replied the young man. "It makes me feel like shrivelling up and sinking out of sight."

"Well, Waverley, what is your opinion of my knitting?" asked Alice, holding up for exhibition the long stripe of an afghan.

"I don't think much of that either as a continual occupation, though when one has such pretty hands as yours and uses such bright yarns, the picture is very charming. But knitting is altogether too slow; one does not merely want to work—one wants to see some satisfactory result."

"As if this beautiful stripe were not a satisfactory result!" exclaimed Alice; "you deserve to be pinched."

The gentleman laughed and said, "When one considers that you have been at work on it all the summer and half the winter, the result is wholly insignificant. Now, it seems to me that knitting is only meant to fill up a void; the German market-woman knits while she sells her vegetables; the nursery-maid knits while she watches the children play in the park; the shop-woman knits while she is waiting for a customer. You take the work too seriously."

"Waverley, your head is entirely filled up with foreign ideas," said Alice; "you don't deserve to live in

America any longer—you ought to be ostracized and banished to Europe."

"And how about my crochet work, Mr. Brooks?" asked Jessie, exhibiting a dainty shawl which she was making for Eleanor's birthday present.

"I'm sorry to say that it is open to the same objection as the knitting," he answered again, indulging in a laugh.

"Well, what kind of work would you recommend for us? You condemn idleness, and you condemn our fancy-work. What shall we do?" asked Jessie.

"Ah! that's altogether another thing, Miss Holcombe. I will think about it. Perhaps, in the course of time, I may evolve an answer out of the inner folds of my brain."

"Well, in the meantime, go to the piano and give us some music."

Like an obedient servant, he went to the instrument, opened it, and began to play. Jessie Holcombe had never before heard anyone touch the keys with so masterly a hand. She laid down her work and listened with delight. As the shadows of evening came on, the musician seemed to be more and more inspired. His fingers lingered lovingly on the keys, making the piano sing with almost human tones. When at last, he paused and arose from the stool, she entreated him not to stop. "This is just the hour for music," she said; "it is like a vesper service."

"I feel that way myself," he answered; "I always practice at this time. There is a mystery about music in the dark that makes it more satisfactory as the language of the soul. Sometimes I seem to be talking to the great masters, or rather listening to their divine talk. I feel their sorrows as if they were my own. I know just how Beethoven felt shut up in a prison-house that no sound could penetrate. I can understand Chopin's refined wretchedness and Schuman's incipient madness." And once more he began to play. After a while, Mrs. Brooks went softly out of the room to attend to some household duties. Alice moved noiselessly to the west window, and seated herself behind the curtain. She was fond of looking at the evening sky, and watching the stars come out. Jessie lay back in a large arm-chair near the fire, closed her eyes, and listened to the music with a feeling of happy restfulness. An hour passed, and still the gentleman continued to play, forgetful of all around him.

Suddenly he struck a few deep chords, and left the piano. He came and sat down near Jessie.

"What are you thinking of, Miss Holcombe?" he asked, after a short silence.

"I can hardly tell," she answered; "I have been dreaming, rather than thinking. I have had visions of far-away, unattainable things. I've dipt into the future far as human eye can see."

"Ah! you have been reading *Locksley Hall*," he said. "I wonder if you like that poem as well as I do."

"How can I tell? I only know that it is a great favorite of mine. There are some very fine lines in it."

"Yes," he said, "from beginning to end, it has a splendid ring. When you read it, you feel as if the world were spinning on to some grand consummation— the poor old world, with its burden of sin and sorrow."

She did not reply. Soon he added,—" Miss Holcombe, I want to help the world along—to be one of those who take part in its progress. It is not enough to live; I want to leave the world better for having lived in it. Can you understand the feeling?"

"Yes," she said, rather sadly; "it is a noble ambition, but we are such atoms. What can we do, except in a small, inappreciable way! Our individual work hardly seems to count. Each one of us is a mere drop in the great ocean."

"Yes, that thought is rather discouraging," he replied, "but, Miss Holcombe, the strong purpose in a man's heart to do something great and good, lifts him above the common herd. He is no longer a mere atom—a mere drop. He becomes a force. I believe in the power of the human will. If a man determines to do a thing, and works steadily towards that end, he succeeds at last. The struggle may be severe, but the success is as certain as anything human can be."

"Yes, I believe you are right," she said, "our wishes and our hopes, if they are earnest enough, become prayers."

"And prayers are not merely words, but acts. That I really pray for, I work for," he added. "The mass of mankind are too feeble in purpose, and too indolent in temperament to accomplish much. And some are too selfish to care for anything but the accumulation of treasures for themselves, and so the world drags on; human progress is so slow that angels as well as men must sometimes feel discouraged. It is a beautiful world, and it ought to be the very brightest planet in the skies."

Here the supper-bell rang and the conversation was interrupted.

After a fortnight spent in this pleasant family circle, each day enlivened by walks and talks, readings and rides, Jessie Holcombe returned to Redbank. Both the Colonel and Mrs. Winston welcomed her back, and she fell once more into the home routine.

"Well, Jessie," said the Colonel, soon after her arrival, "when is the wedding to take place?"

"What wedding?" she asked, for a moment at a loss to know what he meant.

"Why the wedding of Miss Alice Brooks and her cousin, of course. Whom else could I refer to? The whole country, and the city too, as for that, are in a state of expectation, waiting for the cards. · Come, tell us when it is to be."

"That is more than I know," she replied; "I certainly heard no talk of a wedding, and I saw no signs of preparation."

"You surprise me," he said; "I thought that you had been sent for purposely to assist in the mysteries that precede the ceremony."

"You are mistaken," she answered.

"Well, now, that is strange!" exclaimed the Colonel. "I wonder what they are waiting for. I'm sure they have been engaged long enough to know each other pretty well by this time. They will soon be getting old, if they don't look out."

"The period of engagement is so pleasant that they wish to prolong it as much as possible, perhaps," said Mrs. Winston.

"Well, I don't believe in long engagements," the Colonel replied, "it keeps young people restless and unsettled. Let them get married and begin life in earnest."

Soon he turned to Jessie again and said, "I suppose they are very much in love with each other? You must have felt out in the cold."

The girl laughed and replied, "Oh! no, I did not feel at all out in the cold. I suppose they are attached to each other; they seem to enjoy each other's society very much, but I did not see any signs of excessive devotion.

I imagine that they reserve that kind of nonsense for private occasions when there are no guests in the house."

" And how do you like Mr. Waverley Brooks?" asked the Colonel.

" He is more agreeable, perhaps, than most gentlemen, because he is very finely educated, and has travelled, and seen a great deal of the world. He talks well, he reads well, he plays on the piano well, he sings well —indeed I suppose he does everything well, for he has had the best possible advantages in the world."

" Plays on the piano!" exclaimed the Colonel. " I don't see what a man wants to play on the piano for, unless he expects to make a living by giving music-lessons. When I was young that kind of thing wasn't considered manly."

" You see the world is changing," said Jessie, laughing. " It seems to me a very beautiful accomplishment for a man to possess. No man can be tiresome or commonplace who understands and loves music. I have an idea, even, that it improves his temper and makes him easier to live with."

" I don't believe that," said the Colonel; " it is more apt to make him a conceited puppy."

CHAPTER XIX.

It had been raining for several days—a real wintery downpour that kept one helplessly in the house. Jessie was again at The Grove. Mrs. Brooks had sent for her, insisting that her presence cheered Alice, and enlivened the whole family. During the long-continued storm there had been much quiet gayety in the old plantation house. Waverley Brooks was thoroughly accomplished. No one played so well on the piano, no one read with more taste or feeling, no one could give a scene out of Shakespeare with finer effect. He was unconscious and obliging, and threw a good deal of the enthusiasm of his nature into whatever he did. Altogether the days had passed swiftly and delightfully, in spite of the patter of rain against the windows.

At last, one afternoon, a fresh wind sprang up, the clouds broke away, and the sun came out. Waverley, who had been reading to the ladies, soon laid aside his book, and suggested that they should all go out for a walk. Jessie eagerly assented, but Alice declared that it was too damp and cold; her throat was already sore, and she did not dare to leave the house. "But, Jessie dear, you and Waverley must go," she said; "I'm sure you will enjoy it."

"Yes, the air is delightful, I know, and we will have time to go to the mill," he pleaded. "Do come. You will not mind a little mud?"

"Oh, no," Jessie replied, "only I don't want to leave Alice. I wish you could go, too, dear."

"Never mind about me," cried the girl; "I'll go up and take a nap, and be fresh when you return."

"She must not go," said Mrs. Brooks, very decidedly; "she has complained of her throat a great deal for the past few days, and it is time for her to be careful. But you must go, Jessie. You are so fond of walking that you won't mind the mud, and the air will do you good, only do not stay out too late."

Jessie ran upstairs and soon returned equipped for a walk.

"Are you well shod?" asked the gentleman.

"Oh, yes," and she showed him the stout little boots.

"That will do," he said, and off they started.

"I do wish that Alice were stronger," remarked Jessie as they descended the steps.

"Yes, we all feel anxious about her," the young man answered. "It makes my aunt very nervous to see Alice ill. But I think she is getting better; it seems to cheer her up wonderfully to have you in the house, Miss Holcombe."

The remark surprised the girl, but she made no comment, only saying: "How delicious this fresh air is! I am sure it could not have done her any harm to come out. She stays in the house too much. It is not cold in the least, but just keen enough to make one feel thoroughly alive."

"I agree with you," replied the gentleman. "I love a cold day—it tones one up and makes one feel equal to a tough job. I'm afraid our climate has a tendency to make one feel just a little bit indolent."

They went on rapidly over the open road. The white sand had already dried, the walking was good, and the clear sunshine was very pleasant. They moved along side by side, now talking, now falling into silence, as good comrades usually do. Soon they reached the pine-wood, and were obliged to choose their steps with more care. Waverley often found it necessary to give a little assistance, but this only furnished an occasion to laugh and say pleasant things to each other.

"I am very fond of this pine-grove," he remarked, looking up at the stately trees.

"So am I," said the girl, "I wish it were as near Redbank as it is to The Grove—I'm sure I would live in it —it has such a strange fascination for me. But I think it suits a melancholy mood."

"Yes, there's something solemn about it," he replied; "the trunks are so high and massive, and the foliage so dark and heavy that one seems to be in a vast cathedral. I can almost hear the tones of the organ."

"How I wish that I could see a cathedral!" exclaimed Jessie.

"Perhaps you may, some day."

"I'm afraid not. If I were a man, there would be some hope for me; but being only a woman—" she left the sentence unfinished and was silent for a moment, but then continued in her bright, impulsive way, "It must be so nice to be a man, and form plans, and carry them out."

"Has not a woman the same right?" he asked.

"No, she only stands and waits, without any plan in life—only a vague yearning to be useful to somebody, sometime, and somehow." There was a plaintive little undertone to her voice. She was thinking of her own life; her eyes were looking straight ahead to a bright spot where the sun-light fell through the pine trunks. Her large black hat, heavy with plumes, was turned up at the side—the side on which the gentleman was walking. It left her white cheek perfectly revealed, and the little ear gleaming among the stray curls that had escaped from the comb and pins. Waverly Brooks was rather cold in his temperament, but somehow he looked long and often at this girl who was walking beside him. Presently he said, "I think women have their triumphs as well as men. There are always compensations in nature."

"Yes, the triumphs of fortitude, patience, and resignation," she answered sadly—as the position of woman's lot in life arose before her mind.

"Are they to be despised?" he asked.

"No; after all, the spiritual triumphs are the highest and best, but—"

"But what?" he asked, seeing her hesitate.

"How do I know that you care for the end of the sentence," she replied with a faint smile.

"Try me and see. An unfinished sentence always provokes curiosity."

"If it is only curiosity you feel, I will leave it unfinished."

"You do me injustice," he said. "I assure you that I feel something more than curiosity. I think I know what you were going to say."

"Tell me then."

"Something like this: a woman cannot make a career for herself; she is shut in by conventional hedges; she cannot more than half use the force within her; the conditions of society allow her only to develop the passive virtues. Am I right?"

She was surprised that he had understood her so well.

"I think you are in a measure right," he added, "but things are changing. It seems to me, that a woman has the same right to make the most of herself that a man has. If she possesses talent, she ought to use it. If she is, by nature, strong and independent, society should allow her to follow her impulses and choose a profession, and earn an honest living."

"You are more liberal than most men," she said, "they are generally shocked by the independence of a woman. They like her to be timid, and clinging, and a little worshipful of their 'larger bones and stronger sinews.'"

He smiled at her slightly contemptuous tone—

"Yes, I confess we are rather selfish. It is a great comfort to us to know that the sweetest and best women generally find their career in keeping the house of some man. For my part, I'm glad it is so." They both laughed.

"Ah! I see you are just like all the rest of them," she said, "and I was beginning to think you a little better."

"I am miserable to have fallen so soon in your good opinion," he answered; "but don't you remember *Tennyson's Princess?* With all her haughty strength and determination, she yielded when the Prince came."

"A man wrote that!" she exclaimed, a little impatiently. "Now, if I had written it, I would have made that Castle a great social centre, from which an influence would have gone out to convert the world. It spoils the poem to have the great purpose of its heroine fail so soon. Don't you think so?"

"That depends upon the way you look at it," he said, laughing; "now I like that end exceedingly."

"Of course you do. It is always nice for a man to find a good housekeeper. That's the end of every story that's written. There, don't reply to that," she added; "I will not hear any defence. Just look at that glimpse of the pond through the trees; we have almost reached the mill."

"It is rather a picturesque spot," he said; "I used to be very fond of it, when I was a boy, and many a fish I've pulled out of the water. I don't care much for the sport now. How we do out-grow our tastes and affections! I used to feel that Paradise itself would be incomplete without a gun and dog and plenty of partridges to shoot, and now I'm rather indifferent to that, too."

"You have reached a higher plane of civilization," said Jessie; "such signs of growth are very gratifying. I remember that I felt quite glad when I ceased to love my doll. It seemed as if I were at last really a young lady." They both laughed. Soon they came out of the woods in full view of the mill. The pond was very high, the dam was a roaring cataract, the stream a rushing river. They walked around and obtained more than one point from which they could take in the whole scene.

"It would make a beautiful picture," he said, "I would like to paint it."

"Do you paint?" she asked, surprised that he possessed an accomplishment almost unknown at that time among the gentlemen of the South.

"Yes, a little; I've made some very bad pictures in my life; but I like it very much. There is great enjoyment in looking at Nature with the artist's eye—in trying to catch fine effects, and feeling for tone and color."

She told him the tragic story connected with the mill. He had never heard it before, and declared that it lent an additional charm—an air of melancholy sentiment—to the place.

"I suppose you used to spend much of your time at

The Grove, when you were a boy?" she asked, as he pointed out the various spots with which he was familiar.

"Not a great deal—only a part of every vacation," he answered; "the truth is, my father kept me awfully busy from the time I was out of long clothes. He wanted to make an extraordinary man out of me, and made me study everything under the sun. Sometimes I feel dreadfully sorry to see him so disappointed."

"But is he disappointed?" asked the young girl; "I don't see why he should be."

He laughed and said, "A thousand thanks for the compliment. It makes me hope that I am not a total failure." She looked at him with surprise. "I did not mean to shock you," he continued, "but the truth is, my father is disappointed in his son. In educating children, I suppose all parents have their ideals, and they expect the boys and girls to reach them, but human nature is too imperfect for that. It is as difficult for a father to make his son perfect as it is for him to make himself perfect."

"I understand what you mean," she said, simply, "but I am sure your father always speaks of you with the greatest pride. You are his idol. I know you will never disappoint him in one single thing."

"It delights me to have you express so much confidence in me, Miss Holcombe," he replied, "but I cannot allow you to be deceived. I am obliged to confess that I am on the eve of dealing him a very heavy blow."

"Oh! don't, please," she pleaded; "your father is one of the best and wisest men in the world; you must not do anything in opposition to his wishes."

"I cannot help it. If I am true to my own self, I must sometimes disagree with him. No two men, or women either, are made exactly alike."

She thought awhile and then said:

"I believe you are right; sometimes in pleasing others, even those who love us best, and would save us from all harm, we go wrong ourselves. Yes, it is really so Each one must decide the great questions of life for himself."

"I am glad that you understand me, Miss Holcombe; I am not sure that my father will. I have hurt him several times of late without intending it. I will tell you about it, if you care to listen."

"Of course I do. How could you doubt it?"

He was glad that she was so simple and direct and unconscious.

"Well, in the first place, he wants me to begin the practice of law. For years I have been fitting myself for it. I went through the law course at Harvard, and also studied a year at Heidelberg. I like the history of law very much. I enjoy working up a fine case; the whole course of study has been delightful; but I know there are a great many things about the practice of law that would be odious to me, and I have made up my mind upon the subject. I shall never be a lawyer."

"I know your father must feel that very keenly," said Jessie; "he desired you to be associated with him; you could have helped him in so many ways. Are you sure you are right—perfectly sure?"

"Yes; there is a profession that I prefer, and in which I have already had some training. It is journalism. It deals with all the broad public questions of the day—those questions that affect not only men but nations. I could never be content to fight the petty battles of rogues and swindlers. No, I have no taste whatever for the practice of law. I cannot make it my life-work even to please my father. Then, again, I wish to go to New

York to live. My education has been cosmopolitan, and I cannot be happy in our provincial little town. I would feel all the time as if I were panting for breath. I love the South, but I am tired of hearing sectional questions discussed. We have one country now, and it is time to get rid of unreasonable prejudices. This is a great grief to my father, and I am not surprised, but I cannot help it."

"And you are very certain that you are right?" asked the girl, wondering at his boldness and quiet determination.

"Yes, perfectly certain, Miss Holcombe; I cannot follow in my father's footsteps—I must make a path of my own. I don't believe it will be down-hill, either," he added, smiling.

He did not continue the conversation, and she had too much delicacy to solicit his confidence any farther; but she could not help wondering what Alice thought of all these plans and purposes. During this conversation, they had been standing on the old bridge over the mill-stream.

It was fascinating to watch the sweep of the water over all obstruction, and its steadfast flow in one direction. Jessie thought of it and, in a vague way, saw the resemblance between its strong current and the strong will of the young man beside her. She felt that he would as surely reach his goal. Perhaps he was thinking the same thing. She looked at him with some curiosity. He was standing very still, lost in thought. Suddenly he turned his head and their eyes met.

In a moment she felt strangely uncomfortable and moved away from him.

"It is growing late; we must start home," she said, rather faintly. They walked very rapidly through the pine woods, never speaking a single word. She chose her way carefully over the mud without his assistance. When they came out of the woods, the sun was setting, and they paused to see the western sky, which was brilliant beyond description. In silence they watched the colors slowly fade away. Presently, there was a rift in a large cloud, and the new moon was revealed.

"Isn't it beautiful!" she said, her eyes still fixed upon it.

"Yes; I love to see the new moon—it seems like the promise of something better," he answered.

"I feel so too, and ever since I was a little child I have always made a wish when I see it for the first time. I'm going to make one now," she said.

"I am, too," he whispered, as if talking to himself; "there are so many things that I want."

"Are there?" she asked; "why, to me you seem to have everything that a mortal could possibly desire."

"Do I? Then I'm an awfully deceptive fellow—I'm wanting something all the while. Just at this moment, I'm especially hungry for something that hangs up high —out of my reach, I'm afraid. But I intend to get it, —with the help of the moon," he added, breaking into a light laugh.

When they entered the house, she went immediately upstairs to remove her hat and jacket. Everything was very quiet; she wondered where Mrs. Brooks and Alice were—"In the parlor, perhaps," she said to herself, as she arranged her hair in the dim light, and fastened a bow of scarlet ribbon at her throat. She heard the tones of the piano, and knew that Waverley Brooks was playing. When she descended to the parlor, she found the lamps lighted and the fire burning brightly, but the hostess and her daughter were not there. Jessie was moving away to go in search of them when the gentleman at the piano called to her.

"Come here, Miss Holcombe, I have a favor to ask of you. Do you feel like making yourself useful?"

"What can I do for you?" she asked.

"If it is not too much trouble, will you find Chopin's Nocturnes for me? They are over there in that pile of music. I feel just in the mood for playing them, and I am afraid the spell will be broken if I get up and begin the search."

"I know where they are," she said; and soon she had found them and placed them on the music-desk before him.

"Please, don't go away," he pleaded; "stand behind me, and see if I play them right."

"But you know them far better than I do."

"I insist that I don't," he said, running his fingers lightly over the keys.

She was standing beside him; she was a little tired from her long walk; her small white hand was resting on the instrument. He played on and on, as if the very spirit of the dead master had possession of him. She listened like one in a dream; she was floating away from time and space. Finally the last chord was struck. As the tones died away, he lifted one of his hands, and laid it gently on hers. She turned, and again they looked into each other's eyes. What did they see there? If she had been less simple and true-hearted, she could have read his whole soul. For him, there was only an expression of surprise, of anger, melting away at last into sorrow and pity. Slowly she withdrew her hand, and moved away from the piano. Soon she left the room. He heard her ascend the staircase, and a door was softly closed. Then he got up from the piano, and went out of the house.

Jessie Holcombe took her seat by the window, and looked out upon the clear wintry sky. She was trying to take in the meaning of this strange thing that had happened to her. She longed for the shelter of her own room at Redbank, that she might think it all over. She was weary from her long walk, and her brain felt hot and confused. She hardly knew where she was; she had gone astray, and was lost in some wilderness of trouble and despair. Why, oh! why should one look thus disturb this sweetly simple maiden, this perfectly poised nature? Was there truly a deep and passionate meaning in his eyes? She could not tell. Perhaps she had been dreaming. Perhaps the music had affected both the outward and the inward vision. Perhaps the glare of the lamp had given that strange light to his eyes. Perhaps the touch of his hand had been but an accident, after all. She must forget it, she must calm herself; that, at least, she knew was imperative. For a long time she sat there in the darkness. Suddenly she heard the supper-bell ring. It called her back to the world of sense and duty. She knew that she must get up, and go downstairs, and meet Mrs. Brooks and Alice, and the gentleman also. She must sit through a long evening, and laugh and talk as usual. How could she do it! And yet not for the world would she show that her heart was on fire—that her pulse was beating wildly. She was a strong woman; she had been schooled to self-control in the past; she stood up erect and firm in the darkness, and nerved herself for the task. She moved slowly through the long hall and down the stairway. By the time she reached the dining-room, she was herself again; the spell had been cast off, and the blood was once more flowing calmly in her veins. Mrs. Brooks and Alice were standing in front of the fire, waiting for her. She greeted them in her simple, affectionate, playful way; there was no suspicion on the part of either that anything was wrong.

Waverley Brooks lingered outside. He was at the stable, inspecting his horse, for he had made up his mind to start to the city in the morning as soon as it was light. He wished to have an explanation with his father. He came in after the ladies were seated at the table, and played his part in the conversation with his accustomed ease. Alice asked about the walk.

"Yes, the walk was very pleasant," he said; "the ground was a little muddy, and the air a little chilly and damp, but on the whole Miss Holcombe and I enjoyed it," and without lifting his eyes, he appealed to the young lady to confirm his statement.

"Yes, we enjoyed it, but not so much as we would have done, if you had been with us, Alice," Jessie replied. "The mill-pond is very full, and the dam, a perfect Niagara. If possible, you must go and see it to-morrow." Alice thought she might be able to go if the day was fine.

"And if the day is fine, I really must go home," said Jessie. "I had a little note from Eleanor this morning, and I'm afraid she thinks that I have deserted her."

This was scarcely true, for, in the note, Mrs. Winston expressed her delight that her sister was having a pleasant time, and begged her to stay just as long as possible.

"There is nothing to call you back to Redbank, dear, so do not shorten your visit on my account." These were the words; but the conscience of the young girl did not seem to trouble her in the least; so she, perhaps, had read something more between the lines.

"No, you must not go, Jessie," said Mrs. Brooks, "we cannot spare you."

"You are very kind, and I thank you more than I can express, but I really must go. There are some things that I cannot leave undone any longer. You know a visit may be protracted until one becomes demoralized. Too much enjoyment is not good for human nature. Besides, Eleanor misses me."

"I can well believe that," said Alice; "but I shall be dreadfully lonely without you, dear."

"Then you must come and make me a visit. It is scarcely fair to have all the hospitality on your side."

But Alice shook her head. It was impossible for her to make more than a short call at Redbank. Harry Holcombe was there, and she did not wish to meet him. Their friendly relations had been disturbed, and he had been very angry with her. Soon Waverley remarked carelessly:

"What a pity our pleasant party must be broken up! I, too, shall have to leave you for a while. I must go up to the city, Aunt Kate, and see about the sale of that cotton. You know we sent off two or three loads a few days ago. The price is up now, and we must take advantage of it. Always sell on a rising market; isn't that the motto of the planter? However, I shall not be gone long. There is always the pleasant thought of coming back again."

That evening Alice and Jessie played chess. Waverley Brooks seated himself at the piano, and, opening a volume of Beethoven's Sonatas, began a soft *andante* movement, which gradually rose to louder and more impassioned strains, as the musician became wholly possessed by the noble theme of the great master.

"Why, Waverley, how well you play to-night?" exclaimed his cousin more than once. " What is the matter with you? One would think you were inspired."

"So I am; Beethoven always inspires me." And he continued hour after hour without pause. He was playing for relief from consuming thought. Jessie Holcombe vaguely understood that he was giving expression to his own feelings in those deep, wild, heart-breaking chords. Her own soul responded in great waves of strange and conflicting emotion. She was stirred to the very depths of her being. If his heart had indeed wandered from its allegiance to his cousin, what was left to them, or to herself but despair?

" I shall checkmate you now very soon, if you are not careful," exclaimed Alice; " you are not playing well to-night. What is the matter with you, Jessie?"

" My walk has made me stupid and sleepy," the young girl said by way of apology. She was very tired; she lifted her face from the chess-board, whose red and black squares seemed to confuse her. Unconsciously she looked towards the piano. Waverley's eyes were fixed upon her. She felt the burning color come to her cheeks. Yes, she could not help it—she knew that he possessed a strange power over her. Again she was falling under the spell of that mysterious expression in his eyes,—she was slipping down a fearful precipice, enveloped in clouds and darkness, and there was no hand to save!

The next morning when she came to the breakfast-table, the gentleman was not there.

" Waverley started off to the city this morning before sunrise,—so Evans tells me," said Mrs. Brooks. " I'm sorry he did not get something to eat before he left. It's a long ride, and I'm afraid he will be quite faint before he gets there. But young men never know how to take care of themselves. They do all manner of foolish things until they get married,"—and she looked at her daughter and smiled.

"Sometimes that's the most foolish thing of all," said Alice, in her quiet way.

"Not often; a wife usually sobers a man down. Women generally have a great deal of common sense."

Jessie was looking out of the window at the pleasant sunshine. It was a fine day—she must keep her word—she must not linger longer at The Grove. That afternoon she returned to Redbank.

CHAPTER XX.

AFTER taking his breakfast at the hotel, Waverley Brooks went to his father's house; the old butler met him at the door.

"Harris, is my father at home?" the young man asked.

"Yes, sir," the servant replied.

"Where is he?"

"In the library, sir."

"Will you step to the door, Harris, and inquire if I can see him on business for a few moments. Tell him I will not detain him long."

It had always been one of the regulations of the household that the Judge should not be interrupted during the morning hours, which he spent, when at home, shut up in his library at work. Before moving off to obey the command of his young master, the old servant surveyed him quietly, and said, "You looks tired, Marse Waverley. Have you had any breakfast, sir? Can't I get something for you?"

"No, thank you, Harris. I have come from The Grove this morning, and it is a long ride to take before breakfast. I was rather tired when I got to the city, so I went to the hotel and got something to eat, and rested a while. I don't care for anything more."

"I hope everybody's well at The Grove," said the old man, whose curiosity was excited.

"Yes, all are well. Now, go immediately, and ask my father if he can see me."

In spite of the calm exterior of the gentleman, Harris detected the signs of suppressed emotion, and was very sure that something serious had happened. He went softly to the library, and soon returned with the announcement that the Judge could see his son. In a few moments, Waverley was in his father's presence.

The Judge had evidently been at work; papers, letters, all kinds of written documents, together with heavy law books, were scattered over a large desk which stood in the centre of the room. He arose from an easy-chair, in which he had been seated, and came forward to meet the young man.

"Well, Waverley, I'm glad to see you," he said, shaking hands with him. "This is rather an unusual hour for you to make your appearance. I hope you bring good news from The Grove."

"Yes, my aunt and cousin are well. I trust I am not intruding, or taking you from your work," Waverley replied. "I want very much to have a talk with you, father. I have delayed it as long as possible. I cannot really be myself until it is over. The truth is, I've been wretchedly uncomfortable for the last two or three months."

"Well?" said the Judge, looking at him very steadfastly. His manner was a little cold with his son; it had always been. Few signs of affection had ever passed between them, and yet they loved and respected each other very deeply. "Father," said the young man, "I find it impossible to fulfil your wishes in regard to Alice."

The Judge contracted his brows slightly, but only answered, "Well, go on; make a clean breast of it."

"That is what I intend to do," was the quick reply. "I'm awfully sorry to disappoint you in this matter, for I know how near it lies to your heart; but I cannot hold myself to blame. Alice has been perfectly cold and indifferent to me ever since my return, and has told me frankly, whenever I have mentioned the subject, that it is impossible for her to care for me except as a cousin. I have been ready to keep my pledge, but I cannot marry an unwilling bride, even to please my father."

"I have never desired you to marry an unwilling bride," said the Judge, a little severely; "I thought that you had always loved Alice, and that she had always loved you. I am sure, before you went to Europe, there was sentiment enough on both sides—too much I used to think sometimes."

"So there was, but it was only youthful gush; it is over long ago, on both sides," Waverley answered. "When I came back I found her so changed in manner that my own feelings were chilled. I see now that we are not suited to each other, and it is better to end the whole matter, and break at once."

"Do you think she has formed any other attachment?" asked the Judge.

"I'm afraid she has," replied the young man, "though she is too reserved to allow it to be discovered, and I have no right to question her."

"Have you ever met that young Holcombe?"

"Yes, several times, and I have sometimes suspected that Alice likes him."

"What do you think of him?" the Judge inquired.

"Why, he seems to be a fine fellow. He is certainly very handsome, and might prove dangerous as a rival; but I have heard that he is dissipated; I don't know how true it is."

"Yes," said the Judge, shaking his head slowly and solemnly, " I should be very sorry for Alice to care for him. I'm afraid, from all I hear, that he is utterly unworthy of her. Last winter, during that long illness of her mother, he used to go there a good deal—so Evans told me, and I daresay he made love to her. The change in her dates from that time. She has never been the same girl since."

" Well, I don't feel that I can continue to persecute her any longer," said Waverley. " The truth is, my own feelings have undergone a change."

" What!" exclaimed the Judge, " do you mean to say that you have been falling in love, too?" and he laughed as he added—" with Nettie Hunter, I suppose?"

The young man colored, and quietly replied, " You are mistaken. I have met a lady whom I would like to marry, but she does not live in this city."

" I hope to goodness she is not a French woman," said the Judge.

Waverley smiled. " Don't be alarmed, father; my affections have never been very erratic. I think you may trust me to give you a native American girl for a daughter. The young lady to whom I refer is Miss Jessica Holcombe. I suppose you have met her."

Waverley Brooks was entirely ignorant of his father's feelings, and he was too much absorbed in his own thoughts to notice the shadow that spread over the face of the Judge. Several minutes passed before either of them spoke. At length, Waverley continued: " She is a lovely girl. You may be disappointed in my choice, but, unless you are very prejudiced, you cannot have any objection to her, as you have to the brother."

" Have you spoken to her yet?" asked the Judge.

" No; but I have managed to betray myself," he said,

in his simple, manly way. "I did not intend to do it until after I had had this explantion with you, and had also spoken with Alice and received a final rejection; but, somehow, I could not help it. She is the kind of woman to inspire a grand passion. A man is perfectly carried away in her presence, and forgets what he is doing. I intend to marry her." He said this in the tone of determination which was usual with him.

"How did she receive your betrayal, as you call it?" asked the Judge in a husky voice.

"She was angry, I think; her eyes flashed with indignation for a moment, and then they seemed to go out. The lids dropped over them. She believes that I'm engaged to Alice, as everybody else does. She will soon get over her anger, when I tell her the truth. I am determined to marry her. I have your consent, I hope."

"You are a man, and free to pursue your own course; I shall never again attempt to influence you," said the Judge in the same husky tone. His face was dark and stern.

"It is scarcely kind in you to speak to me in that manner," Waverley replied. "I wish always to be influenced by a father whom I love and honor. Up to this time I have been willing to be guided entirely by your judgment. If you had permitted it, I would now be the husband of Alice, but you thought us too young to marry—you sent me away. I do not feel that I am to blame that things were changed when I returned. Father, you know well enough that when a man chooses a wife, he has the right to please himself. There are plenty of risks even then. I cannot believe that you have any serious objection to Miss Holcombe. I know she is without fortune, but there's not a lovelier girl in the world."

Judge Brooks made no reply. He felt only anxious to terminate the interview.

"Well," he remarked at length, "if you have said all that you desire to say, you had better leave me now. I have a great deal of work on my hands and cannot spare you more time at present."

"Father," replied the young man in a very earnest tone, "I wish to go immediately to New York and make arrangements for my future. I cannot waste any more time at The Grove. Aunt Kate does not need me. She is so accustomed to manage her own affairs that she does not require the assistance of any one. Of course, I shall return and have a talk with her and Alice, and, with your permission, I would like to call on Miss Holcombe."

"I would defer that awhile, if I were in your place," said the Judge, his face growing colder and sterner. "At least wait long enough to be sure of your own feelings."

"If I were to wait a century, I could not be more sure of my own feelings than I am now," Waverley replied, very gently, but with a shadow of annoyance on his face. "Besides, I wish to relieve Miss Holcombe's mind of a false impression."

"Well, do as you think best; as I said before, you are old enough to decide for yourself."

Waverley arose and extended his hand to his father. "I see that I have hurt you," he said; "I am very sorry, but, somehow, I cannot help it. I hope you will forgive me."

He always felt like a boy in his father's presence, for the discipline of the Judge had been severe, and was not relaxed until the young man was sent to college. The years spent away from home had strengthened the self-reliance of the son without wholly subduing the domination of the father. The Judge felt the change in his child, but he had been reluctant to adjust himself to the new relation. They shook hands.

"You will come and dine with me, I suppose," said the Judge, as the young man moved away towards the door.

"No, I am going back to The Grove immediately," Waverley answered; "I feel in a perfect fever to get through with this business. I shall be in town again in a few days."

As he was hurrying away, the Judge detained him a moment. "Waverley," he said, "I wish you would allow me to give you some advice in regard to Miss Holcombe. I do not think you have any right to speak to her until your plans are somewhat settled. Just now, you are all at sea. You can go to New York immediately, as you wish, and make the necessary arrangements for the future. When that is done, you can return, and address yourself to her. It would not be well to involve her in all your doubts and uncertainties. She will bear a prolonged absence from you under the present circumstances better than if engaged to you. My son, you must not be too hasty in this matter. Your conduct towards Alice proves that it is possible for your sentiments to undergo a change. I think you should require some test of yourself now, and also give the young lady an opportunity to examine her own feelings. Your acquaintance with her has been very brief. I cannot believe that either of you are yet very deeply in love. If you have betrayed your admiration for her, and she has really understood you, she has too much good sense to suspect you of faithlessness towards Alice. She must perceive that you are a gentleman and incapable of baseness. She will know at once that your relations with your cousin are at an end." He paused and looked at his son.

"Father," said the young man, "I love and honor you too much to decline to accept your advice, but it is terribly hard to leave things as they are—to go off without any explanation and run the risk of having her doubt my honor. I do not think you quite appreciate the delicacy of my position."

"I am sure, Waverley, that I understand your position better than you do yourself; I am not so sure that I can estimate the strength and impetuosity of your passion."

As he stood and pleaded with his son, Judge Brooks looked ill and tired. The young man began to realize how deeply he had wounded his father, and an emotion of mingled remorse and regret swept through his heart.

"Father," he said, in a voice whose every tone vibrated with affection, "I will do anything that I can to atone for the pain and vexation that I have occasioned you. I will follow your advice, whatever it may cost me. It grieves me to feel that I am disappointing you in so many different ways. I hope you may live to see and acknowledge that I am right—that my own growth as a man depends upon my following the deepest convictions of my soul. You have helped largely to make me what I am; I know you would not undo your work by forcing me now into a false environment, and giving me a wife whose companionship could never satisfy me."

"My son," said the Judge, and his voice trembled with emotion, "since you were first placed, a helpless infant, in my arms, and I knew that I was a father, I have had no sincerer wish than to see you a good and happy man. I have tried to train you wisely; I have tried to choose the best things in the world for you. I have always thought that your gentle cousin was suited to you, and would make you a worthy wife. If I have erred, you must forgive me."

"It is I who must ask to be forgiven," exclaimed the young man, approaching his father, and extending his hand in an impulsive fashion. "Nothing could ever make me happy, if I felt that I had forfeited your respect and love. I should be an outcast, in my own eyes, even if the whole world applauded my success."

"Thank you, my son," said the Judge; "it satisfies me to know that you are thoroughly manly and noble, though you may disappoint some plans that I have made for you."

"Father, before I speak another word to the woman whom I love, I would like to have you say that you approve my choice." He looked at the Judge as he spoke, and again noticed the extreme pallor of his face.

"Waverley, I know Miss Holcombe well, and I believe her to be worthy in every respect of the noblest and best man God ever made. If you can win her, I shall not withhold my blessing."

"Thank you, father," said the young man. "I'm afraid that I have tired you. If so, forgive me. Good-bye," and they clasped each other's hands.

When his son was gone, the Judge did not resume his seat at the desk. He went to the door and softly locked it. Then he began to pace slowly up and down the floor. He looked old and worn now that the effort of self-control was relaxed. The blow dealt by his son had been a heavy one, for he had not abandoned the hope of winning Jessie Holcombe for himself. His love for her was the one passion of his life, not the less strong because it had come to him when his hair was gray.

Now, he knew that he must resign this woman to his son. Waverley had always got what he wanted; he would get it now. In the bottom of his heart, the Judge admitted the righteousness of the young man's claim. The best gifts of the world are for the young, not for the old. As a father, it was not in his heart to withhold from his son this crowning glory of manhood—a noble wife; but the situation was unnatural, and he felt it keenly. The fiercest struggle of his life was before him. The battle must be fought, and defeat must be borne. For several hours he paced the floor without once pausing. At length he sank exhausted in a chair. The fire had died out, and the room was cold. A chill seized upon him, and with difficulty he reached the bell and rang it violently. In a few moments Harris entered. The faithful old servant was greatly shocked to see the condition of his master.

"Harris," said the Judge, "bring me a glass of Cognac immediately, and build up the fire. I feel ill—I'm afraid that I have a chill."

The orders were promptly obeyed. As Harris moved off he muttered to himself, "It's Marse Waverley has done it, I knows. Oh! these chillen! these chillen! When they's little, we'se mighty proud of 'em, and thinks they's goin' to turn the world upside down, but when they gits big, they's nothin' but an eternal vexation and trouble." He shook his head more than once, for he was speaking out of the depths of his own heart.

For a few days the Judge was obliged to keep his room, and narrowly escaped a serious illness. Waverley was recalled to the city to assist in transacting some needful business for his father, and several months elapsed before the young man again found himself at The Grove.

CHAPTER XXI.

THE afternoon was cold and dreary. The breath of a coming storm was in the air. Jessie Holcombe was sitting at her window with the dainty heap of crochet work on her lap. Her patient fingers were busy making the endless meshes, but her thoughts were far away. She was thinking in an incoherent, fragmentary way, and trying at the same time to escape from all mental effort; it wearied and tortured her beyond expression. Several weeks had passed since that last visit to The Grove, and she had received no news from Alice during that time; not even a little note had been exchanged between them. She found herself often wondering if Alice had discovered the treason of her lover, and was showing her anger and resentment by silence towards her friend. Jessie was restless and wretched. She felt like a helpless ship which the winds and waves are driving against the rocks. The old peace of mind, the old interest in the homely tasks of daily life, was gone. She longed for some excitement into which she could plunge and forget herself : more than ever before, her desires reached out to the gay world of which she had occasionally caught glimpses. To be left alone day after day with these harassing thoughts, was more than she could endure. To struggle from morning until night for self-control—to shrink from the gaze of loving eyes lest they should note a change in her—this surely was too much for any woman's strength. She lifted her eyes from the heap of delicate wool in her lap and looked down the long avenue. The bare branches moved hither and thither in the rising wind. The lines were hard and black against the steel gray wintry sky. A pang of desolation, such as she had never before felt, pierced her heart. The complications of life were getting stranger and more cruel, year after year. Was there no escape? Would it not be possible to run away from it all? Might she not go to some new place, and work for her daily bread?—work so hard that there would be no time to think, or long, or grieve? She had a great dread of meeting Waverley Brooks again—perhaps she never would!—and her face grew still paler with a sickening sense of loneliness and despair. She knew that he possessed a mysterious power over her which she could never hope to resist. She knew that it would be worse than madness to yield to his mastery, and yet the thought of seeing him no more was intolerable. She laid her head back upon the cushions of the chair, and closed her eyes in weariness and perplexity. She was aroused by a low tap at the door, and Oliver entered with some letters and papers. The mail had arrived, and she was glad to have a share for herself. She took up one envelope and looked at it; the writing was not familiar, and she tore it open with feverish haste—only wedding-cards. Nettie Hunter was really going to be married at last. The next letter was from the young lady herself. It contained an urgent invitation for Jessie to assist at the ceremony as one of the bridesmaids. No refusal would be accepted. Her dress would be ordered immediately with the others, and she must come up by all means the day before the wedding. Jessie Holcombe and Nettie Hunter had been schoolmates years ago in Staunton, Virginia, and the intimacy between them then had been close and warm. When Jessie came South to live with her sister, the friendship had been renewed with enthusiasm on both sides, and occasional visits had been exchanged between the two girls.

Jessie smiled as she laid down the letter of her friend. After all, there were diversions in life; one was not left to brood without a break over annoyances and troubles.

Something was happening continually. Who could guess what the future might contain? It was not reasonable to be oppressed by gloomy thoughts—to yield to despair. "Behind the clouds the sun was still shining."

The girl arose from her seat, folded up the snowy shawl in its protecting napkin, and laid it away in a drawer. Then she shook out her dress, smoothed her hair, and went to find Eleanor.

That evening at the supper-table, the Colonel looked at Jessie, and said, "Well, I hear you are going to a wedding. That sounds very nice. I would like to go myself, if I could find the time. I hope Miss Nettie won't jilt the fellow at the last minute. If I were in his boots, I would feel a little scared."

"She must be in earnest now, since she has sent out the cards," said Mrs. Winston.

"I can never imagine her very much in earnest about anything," said the Colonel. "How many times has she been engaged, Jessie?"

The girl smiled and shook her head.

"I have not kept the account very carefully, but I should think about twenty-five times at least. When I first met her, she had a diamond ring on her third finger, and talked very freely of her *fiancé*. That was a good many years ago. I really believe she was born engaged."

"Well, I do not feel inclined to congratulate the gentleman who has picked up the fragments of her poor little heart," said the Colonel, breaking into a laugh.

"I wonder if he knows how many times the poor little heart has been broken," exclaimed Jessie, reflecting the amusement of her brother-in-law on her own face.

"Jessie, my dear," he said, "it is all nonsense for us to be talking seriously about hearts. Young ladies don't have hearts these days. They have Saratoga trunks instead, and the bigger and fuller the trunk, the happier the girl. Nettie Hunter is a typical girl of the period."

"Not so bad as that," said Mrs. Winston; "it has been her misfortune to be an only child. She has been petted and spoiled to death, and is consequently very selfish; but there is some latent good in her nature. Life has not been earnest enough for her yet awhile. When she has a family and real care falls upon her, she will develop into a good and sensible woman. I'm sure she will. I believe in the laws of heredity, and she has excellent parents."

"I'm very fond of her," said Jessie; "at school everybody liked her; she was so kind-hearted and generous and amusing. One thing is certain, her husband will never suffer from dulness."

"I'm glad fate did not choose me for the place," exclaimed the Colonel, "she is so restless, and such a dreadful chatterbox. It would kill me to live with such a creature. I like a quiet woman, whose voice is low and sweet."

"That is what men always say," remarked Mrs. Winston, a little impatiently; "it is a kind of theory with them; but in practice, they invariably choose the sprightly, saucy, restless, coquettish chatterbox."

Her husband looked at her and said: "I didn't, my dear."

"Your wife wasn't far from it when you chose her," the lady replied; "time has subdued her."

"And the discipline of living with me," he added with perfect good-humor.

"Yes," she assented with a smile.

"Well, you might have got a worse husband, my dear."

"Of course, there are always risks in marrying. Possibly I might have got a better one."

"Very true. It's a pity we cannot go back, and do it over again. Isn't it?"

"Yes," she answered, still smiling.

"Well, my dear, however it may be with you, I can truthfully say that I have never yet repented of my bargain."

"There, Nell," cried Jessie, "after that splendid compliment, I'm sure you cannot continue the controversy. I would ask nothing more of my husband, after fifteen years of married life, than such an acknowledgment. It is almost as good as canonization."

"I think you will get it, my dear," said the Colonel, very soberly.

"Thanks!" exclaimed Jessie, "I'll come round and kiss you for that gracious speech." She arose from her chair and approached the Colonel. He threw back his head and stroked down his long gray beard. "Promise to take me to the city a week from to-day," she said, gayly.

"I promise."

Then she gave him two kisses in quick succession.

"Make it three for good luck," he said. She stooped and kissed him again. The price of cotton was up, and the Colonel's spirits were high.

When the appointed time arrived, Jessie, accompanied by the Colonel, started on the journey to the city. Nettie Hunter welcomed her friend with the most enthusiastic cordiality, and poured out a stream of eager talk, interspersed with laughter. "You dear, darling, delightful girl!" she exclaimed again and again; "I can't begin to tell you how glad I am to see you. I didn't really believe that you were coming, and, if you had disappointed me, I would have refused to be married."

"Why did you think that I would not come?"

"Oh! because—let me see if I can find a reason,—I didn't think you would feel sufficient interest in the sacrifice to care to witness the agonies of the victim."

Jessie laughed and said, "Well, you see that you were mistaken. I assure you I shall find the agonies of the victim very interesting. A wedding is always a spectacle worth seeing. You know it is the central point of life, as birth is the beginning and death the end."

"Please don't moralize," said Nettie; "it makes me feel too solemn. I am nervous, and cannot stand it," and she laughed merrily.

"You nervous, Nettie! I cannot believe it."

"Well, it is the truth nevertheless; and that's really one reason why I wanted you to come so dreadfully. Papa's nervous, mamma's nervous, I'm nervous, and the servants are nervous, and the house itself is getting rather shaky. We wanted you, dear, to steady the whole establishment—you sweet, serene creature! The ceremony would have been a perfect failure, if you had not come; we would all have broken down at the most interesting part, and, probably, floated off on a sea of tears."

"I can't understand how I'm to prevent it."

"Why, you are a bit of *terra firma*, my dear, and we are all going to anchor there. Jessie, darling," said Nettie, after a short pause, "I've got no end of things to tell you. I want your advice and assistance in clearing the atmosphere of my thoughts. Everything within me seems to be dissolving into mist and moonshine."

"That is indeed pathetic; but I'm afraid you are expecting too much of me. I'm a person of very limited capacities. Your boundless vitality and vivacity always makes me feel as if I were not more than half alive."

"Nonsense!" exclaimed Nettie; "you've got enough in you to make half a dozen women like me. Around you there's a calm like the serene heavens!"

"Oh! Nettie, Nettie, don't rave, I beseech you. Too much happiness has affected your brain."

"I am not mad, most noble lady, but speak forth the words of soberness and truth."

"Well, we will not quarrel. I hope, dear, you have not tired yourself to death over the trousseau." The two girls were now upstairs in the bedroom of Miss Hunter, and garments of different kinds lay around in promiscuous heaps.

"Yes, I have," replied Nettie; "I have worn out at least a dozen pairs of shoes, walking the streets, and going to that dreadful dressmaker. I trust I may never be compelled to have another gown, as she calls them, for I've been fitted until my dorsal column is worn out. Jessie, if you are ever silly enough to consent to marry a man, don't, I beseech you, have a *trousseau*. It is by far the most serious part of the whole affair. Without it, things would move on smoothly, but when one is tired to death, what is more natural than to get cross, and quarrel with the guilty man who has brought so much trouble on you?"

"I will be sure to remember," said Jessie, smiling. "But do tell me something, please, about the particular man. I'm full of curiosity. I want a complete account of him from your own lips."

"There is nothing to tell," replied Nettie, shaking her head. "Just at present he seems altogether negative to me."

"But, surely, he has eyes and hair. Tell me the color of them, and whether he is long or short, fair or dark."

"No; I will leave you to see for yourself. I used to think him handsome, but either he has lost his beauty, or I have been disenchanted. I never think of his looks at all now."

"Which proves that you are very much in love."

"Yes, Jessie," and her tones were almost solemn, "I seem to have entered a little world where there are only two people—he and I. Everything is in a kind of beautiful disorder. I feel as if it were to be my task to regulate and arrange and reign over this new sphere. Jessie, Jessie, that thought frightens me!" she exclaimed, with a nervous jump and clutch at her friend. "What kind of a world will it be with such a silly little creature as I am for its queen?"

"A beautiful little world, with everything well arranged and well governed," said Jessie.

"The truth is, I'm getting thoroughly scared at the thought of the future!" and the young lady shivered slightly. "That is what I want to talk to you about to-night. I must make a full confession before my execution, and you have been selected as the confessor."

"How are your mother and father?" asked Jessie, after a short pause.

"Worn to a frazzle, both of them! Mamma is downstairs, attending to something—I don't know what,— and papa is at the vestry."

"Tell me about all the girls. Are they changed?"

"Not in the least. Bess and Clara and Hetty and Sue and Laura are all going to be bridesmaids. They will be round in the morning for a kind of rehearsal, and I know they will be delighted to see you. The dear old Bishop is going to perform the ceremony."

Here Nettie jumped up from her chair, and exclaimed, "Don't you want to see some of my finery, Jessie?" She pushed back the sliding doors of a large room which communicated with her own. "It looks like a big fancy store, doesn't it?" and she broke into a merry laugh.

Dresses, dressing-gowns, breakfast-sacques, sashes, ribbons, stockings, slippers, and every other article of a woman's toilette, were thrown in confusion upon the bed, sofa, tables, and chairs. Drawers and trunks were wide open, and their miscellaneous contents were streaming out upon the floor.

"Did you ever see such a room in all your life, Jessie?" she asked; "it's enough to give one the brain-fever, isn't it? It's a thousand pities that I'm not going to marry a doctor, for I know I shall be desperately ill, when it is all over. Well, it is at least a consolation to know that his name is Sage. I do hope he will have wisdom enough for both of us." Again she broke into a peal of laughter, in which Jessie heartily joined.

"It does seem amusing, Nettie, that you of all persons in the world should be called Mrs. Sage."

"Yes, it's a punishment for my past levity. I accept it as such." She bustled around as she spoke, moving things here and there without much idea of what she was doing. "Only think of it!" she exclaimed suddenly, as if the idea had just that minute occurred to her—"I have got to put up all these things, and know exactly where every article is. Doesn't the task look perfectly hopeless?"

It was still early in the afternoon, and Jessie said, quickly, "Well, begin right away, then; I will help you pack your trunks. I think we can get it done before dinner. Then there will be some comfort in talking. I never have any sense when a room is in disorder, the confusion seems to be communicated to my brain."

"You darling girl! The suggestion is admirable," cried Nettie. "I feel considerably clarified since your arrival. Your very voice helps to settle me. I will go and lock the doors, and we will begin right away."

She went into her own room and locked the door of entrance from the hall. "That's to keep poor mamma out," she said; "the truth is, she is only one remove from a lunatic, and I don't wonder, for I have almost killed her. I have wanted everything under the sun, and she has tried hard to satisfy me. Jessie, it is a great misfortune to be an only child—you never get half whipping enough." Soon she went into a small room beyond the one in which they were sitting. In a moment she called through the open door, "Come here, Jessie; come and see it."

Jessie promptly obeyed the summons. Upon the bed, spread out in all its spotless purity, was the bridal dress and veil.

"Isn't it lovely?" asked the happy little bride, as she raised the corsage to pull out the lace and orange blossoms.

"Yes, it is exquisite, and much more appropriate for a petite creature like you, than white satin would have been."

The dress was of creamy silk, with clouds of illusion falling over it. There was something almost spiritual in its gauzy daintiness. As one looked at it, one thought of fairies and sylphs, and other ethereal creatures.

After contemplating various bits of the wedding finery, the girls went back to the room where the open trunks were standing ready to receive the condensed wardrobe of the bride. Nettie began to turn the contents of the bureau drawers upon the floor.

"There, if you will, Jessie, you may fold up those things and put them into that trunk, while I will undertake this one. You see how selfish I am, for I give you the biggest trunk. I always lay the heavest burdens on others."

"Well, you know I am perfectly fresh, while you are almost tired to death. Besides, I really enjoy handling all these lovely things. How pretty they are!" And she tenderly lifted the linen, so exquisitely embroidered and trimmed with dainty lace. While they folded and laid away the garments, the gay talk went on ceaselessly, interspersed with exclamations and merry peals of laughter. At the end of two hours, the rooms were cleared of confusion, and the trunks were almost packed. Then there was a gentle tap at the door, and when it was unlocked, Mrs. Hunter entered.

"Why, Jessie," she exclaimed, "I did not know you were here, dear. I have been so busy all the morning with caterers and confectioners and florists, and all sorts of people, that I have not once looked out of the windows. How glad I am to see you! And how pleasant it is to find things somewhat in order! I know I'm indebted to you, dear. I just came upstairs to see about the packing. There were so many other things to be done, that I could not get to that, and, as you know, Nettie is very helpless unless she has some one to direct and assist her."

"Yes, mamma, the worst of it is over now. The rest can easily be done to-morrow morning. So you may just seat yourself, and fold your hands on your lap. Poor little tired mother!" she exclaimed, going up to Mrs. Hunter and kissing her.

"Well, dear, I am so glad to have this packing out of the way, that I will sit down a minute. Now we can hope for a quiet evening—our last evening together!" And she sighed. "I know your father will like that, for he has been so disgusted with the flurry and confusion. He said only this morning that he had a great mind to stay at the vestry until it was all over. He is a quiet man and dislikes commotion. Poor papa; what would he have done with a dozen sons, one daughter has almost killed him. I am only thankful that I have but one," said Mrs. Hunter.

She was a sweet, gentle, unobtrusive woman, with a loving heart and a weak will. It was strange that she should have such a daughter as Nettie; and yet the virtues of a mother are sometimes fatal to the growth of a daughter's character. From her cradle, Nettie Hunter had ruled both father and mother with pretty imperiousness; she had grown up so frivolous and self-willed as greatly to endanger her own happiness. Within the shelter of home, her thoughtless and undutiful conduct had reduced her mother to a mere cipher; and, outside, it had reflected upon her father, and lessened his influence as a clergyman. Yet, excuses were always made for her; she was an only child, and her selfishness was overlooked on this plea. She was pretty and bright and overflowing with animal spirits, and these attractions covered up a multitude of minor transgressions. She was also very good-natured and free from envy, or malice, or uncharitableness, and so made many friends and few enemies. On the whole, she was very popular in her native town, and her marriage was an event which interested every one.

In the evening, Mr. Sage called, and Jessie looked at him with a great deal of curiosity. He was a handsome man, with a slight tendency to stoutness; his manners were very easy and natural, and it was evident that his temperament was phlegmatic. There was something exceedingly frank and pleasing about his face, and, at the same time, a certain clearness of gaze which convinced you of his shrewdness and business ability. It was easy to see that he was very much in love with his fiancée; he was amused at her chatter, and watched her graceful motions with quiet contentment. It was also probable that he would know how to manage her when she belonged to him, for he looked both patient and determined. He had recently come to the city to establish a branch firm of a banking-house in New York, and immediately, on his arrival, he had become the big fish for which all the pretty girls began to angle. Miss Hunter had been the successful one. It now remained to be seen what he would do with this spoiled child, this flippant belle.

When Nettie marched Mr. Sage up and presented him to her friend, she exclaimed in her clear, ringing voice, "Now, Jessie, do tell me what you think of him. I have left you unprejudiced on purpose. Come, out with it."

The gentleman laughed, and so did the young lady, but Miss Hunter was very sober.

"So you think you have left me unprejudiced?" said Jessie; "that's a mistake. To be your choice is a decided prejudice in his favor. Have I not always considered your taste faultless?"

Mr. Sage bowed his thanks, but Nettie was not satisfied.

"That won't do," she said; "I want him judged on his own merits. Look at him well, and tell me honestly and truly what you think of him."

As she spoke she touched the gentleman under the chin to make him hold up his head.

"Now turn out your toes, throw back your shoulders, and prepare for regular military inspection!" she exclaimed.

All three were now laughing, and Jessie's face was brilliant with color, as she said—"The modern gentleman appreciates his own merits so highly, that he can dispense with praise from others."

"And is that really your opinion of the modern gentleman?" asked Mr. Sage. "To look at your face one would not suspect you of such harsh judgments.

"I only speak of them as a class; there are always exceptions—possibly your case may be one. About that I cannot yet decide. Five minutes is too short a time for making up one's mind on such a subject."

"Don't feel badly, Clarence," said Nettie in a caressing tone; "before she is twenty-four hours older, I'll get at the very bottom of her heart, and then I'll tell you exactly what she thinks of you, provided you'll promise to be a good boy and mind me always." And she laughed lightly.

"I'm surprised that you should care for my opinion, Nettie," said Jessie; "since you are satisfied with him, you can afford to be indifferent to what other people think."

"By no means," replied the gentleman; "we always wish our choice to be approved by our friends. It is like putting a seal upon an important document."

"Well, I think you will answer, Mr. Sage," said Jessie, smiling, "and I give you both my blessing. If good wishes were favorable winds, mine would waft your ship safely into port."

"Thanks, Miss Holcombe; I think good wishes are very much like favorable winds. They fill one's sails with hope and encouragement."

"Yes, the crises of life—such as violent illness, or matrimony, are not without their pleasant side, Mr. Sage. So many people gather around you with spoken or unspoken kindness that you feel wonderfully strengthened."

"The crises of life, such as violent illness or matrimony!" he repeated, while a smile lighted up his face. "That's a strange sentence. Why do you couple illness and matrimony?"

"How stupid you are, Clarence!—for the sake of contrast, of course," exclaimed Miss Hunter. "Because they both excite attention in a community; they both appeal to the multitude for sympathy, and the multitude usually respond with a generous outpour. To-morrow the whole city will be excited, and stirred up by the thought that a beautiful girl is going to be married.

"It is awfully jolly to be the centre of such excitement, isn't it?" asked Nettie, looking up at the gentleman, and laughing; "only think of being the centre of gravity of the Universe!"

"You irreverent creature!" he said, joining in her laughter.

"No, I'm not. The universe to me is that part of creation which comes within my own feeble powers of observation—a small section of this city, for instance. What's all the outside to me? Only infinite, unpeopled space."

"The most interesting part of creation to me is that which is outside," said Jessie. "The unknown possesses more awful fascination than the known."

"Ah! that shows the difference between my personality and yours!" cried Miss Hunter.

"You have imagination, and she has none," said Mr. Sage, looking first at one, then at the other.

"That's a very perplexing statement," Miss Hunter replied; "who is the *you*, and who is the *she*. Tell me instantly, sir."

"No," he answered, reflecting her playfulness, "I'll leave you to find out. Behold a problem for your clever little brain to solve."

"I know perfectly well," she said, nodding her small head in a threatening manner; "the complimentary part of that sentence was meant for Miss Jessie Holcombe, and I have a great mind to pull your hair."

"Please do; it will be a foretaste of the delights in store for me. I shall enjoy it very much."

"Yes, it will indeed be a foretaste," she replied, laughing as merrily as a little child; "I always pull the Rev. Mr. Hunter's hair when he vexes me, and you see the result."

Her father entered the room at that moment, and the slight baldness to which she had referred was plainly visible. She arched her brows, and glanced at it.

"I heard my name spoken. Who was talking about me?" he asked. He was a small, meek-looking man, very noiseless in all his movements; he had glided into their midst like a phantom which appears at the utterance of a name.

"Who but your graceless daughter?" she said in a playful tone; "no one else would dare to take your name in vain."

He rolled an easy-chair near the fire and sat down. Presently, he held out his hand and said, "Come and sit beside me, Jessie." The girl promptly obeyed and he took her hand in both of his, stroking it softly, while he looked into the glowing coals. "Tell me about the Colonel and Mrs. Winston. How are they both? I have been wanting to go down to Redbank to see them, but I am very busy all the time." When she had finished telling him about his friends, he relapsed into silence. He looked very tired and sad, and she knew that he was thinking about the wedding that was to take place to-morrow. After a while he said, very simply, "I am afraid I shall be very desolate, when my daughter is gone, Jessie."

"You must not look upon that as a loss. You are going to gain a son, not lose a daughter."

"I don't know about that, my dear; her home will no longer be with us—it is even best that it should not be. She will need a home of her own to develop all womanly and wifely qualities. That of itself will make a great difference in my life."

The lovers moved off into the next room, and the

murmur of their voices came through the half-open door. The heart of the father seemed to grow sadder as he listened to the sound.

"It is a great trial to give up our only one, Jessie," he said, with a faint sigh; "I know she is very far from being a perfect woman, but she has made our home very bright and cheerful, and I am afraid my wife and I will sink into old age when she is gone."

"Oh! no," exclaimed the young girl; "you have troops of friends—everybody in the city loves you; they will all pity your loneliness and come often to cheer you."

"Yes, dear, I think all my people do love me, but it is not quite the same kind of love that a daughter feels. You must grow a little older yourself, Jessie, before you can appreciate the different kinds of love and all the delicate shades. Some kinds leave one rather hungry, and some satisfy with a perfect fullness."

"I know that well," replied the girl in a sweet sympathetic tone; "and I think I know also how you feel to-night. The changes of life—the comings and the goings and the droppings out of sight—are desperately hard to bear; but somehow we get used to them."

"Yes, you are right, dear; we get used to them. We often think of Nature as a cruel step-mother, but there are times when she shows us the deep tenderness of a real mother. I must try to shake off this feeling of sadness which has taken possession of me to-night. Will you not go and play for me, dear?"

"Of course I will," she answered quickly, and seating herself at the piano, she began a gay waltz. Soon she heard Miss Hunter and Mr. Sage whirling around and laughing in the next room. When quite out of breath, they came in and stood by the piano.

"Jessie," said her friend, "this odious man has done nothing but compliment you for the last hour. I have been trying in vain to stop him; but he defies my authority, and laughs at my anguish."

"My daughter," said Mr. Hunter, "you must not talk in such a reckless manner. You have not been out of the room more than ten minutes."

"Well, it has been an hour to me, and a very stupid one too," she replied, laughing. Then going up to her father, she kissed him. "You dear old papa! I'm not half good enough for your daughter. You must adopt Jessie; she will suit you exactly."

"I wish I could," he answered.

"Say, Jessie," exclaimed Nettie; "stop your noise for a minute, and listen to me. Can't you come up, and look after this old couple when I'm gone?" There was not a trace of emotion in her voice.

Jessie lifted her hands from the keys of the piano, and said: "I should be a very poor substitute for you. They would feel the contrast, and that would be humiliating for me." Then the white fingers went back upon the keys, and another spirited waltz began.

"Now you are fishing for a compliment." But where, oh! where is mamma?" she added. "I must go and hunt her up." And she flitted out of the room, soon returning with her mother.

"Only think! I found her upstairs, contemplating the wedding dress with tears in her eyes." The mother looked at her daughter with a faint, sad smile. "Now it passes my comprehension," continued Nettie, "how any one can cry over so lovely a dress. I have really been compelled to put it out of sight because it filled my soul with such delight; I'm afraid I shall never be ible to keep my face straight when I get it on, I shall be so very, very happy."

"My daughter, you are very full of nonsense," said Mr. Hunter, shaking his head at her.

"Well, you know to-night is the crisis of the disease; to-morrow, about this time, I shall be on the road to recovery—I shall be Mrs. Sage. In a month, I shall be so sober you will not recognize me. Then you will long to have your silly little daughter back again. Alas! that human nature, even when it wears a surplice, should be so inconsistent!" She rushed up to her father, and kissed him several times. Mr. Sage looked at her much amused; she was bewitchingly pretty; her blonde hair was a maze of crimps around her small delicate face, and her blue eyes were dancing with fun and mischief.

"Do you take me for Bluebeard?" he asked very quietly, looking at her and smiling.

"Not the genuine old monster; he died long ago and was buried with proper ceremony. You are only one of his descendants, modified and refined by time and progress." Every one laughed. How was it possible to keep one's face sober in her presence?

"Stop your chatter, my dear, and listen to Jessie's music," said Mr. Hunter.

"I cannot; waltz music is like champagne; it always makes me talk."

"Please play something solemn, Jessie," requested Mrs. Hunter; "Nettie's high spirits jar upon me to-night."

Jessie Holcombe struck a few deep chords, and began the *Moonlight Sonata*. Every one was silent until she reached the end, and the last tones died away. Then

Miss Hunter turned to Mr. Sage with the question, "Don't you wish I could play like that?"

"I love you well enough just as you are," he replied. She got up, put her hand in his, and carried him off into the next room.

"You must not stop, Jessie," said Mr. Hunter; "it is very restful to listen to you, dear. I am too tired and sad to talk to-night. I am just in the mood to appreciate music." He lay back in his chair, and murmured to himself—

> "Music that gentler on the spirit lies,
> Than tired eye-lids upon tired eyes."

CHAPTER XXII.

"And therefore, if to love can be desert, I am not all unworthy."

A FEW hours later, Jessie Holcombe and Nettie Hunter were sitting in their dressing-gowns before a beautiful fire. They had extinguished the gas, and only the glow of the fire-light filled the room. It would have been difficult to find a greater contrast than these two girls presented as they sat upon the rug, brushing out their long soft hair. The face of Jessie Holcombe was as finely cut as an antique gem. The dark brown eyes were somewhat sad and dreamy; the brown hair which she was brushing fell over her shoulders in heavy masses, rippling and curling to its very ends.

The face of Nettie Hunter was fair and *piquante* and altogether bewitching from the play of smiles and dimples around a rosy mouth and clear blue eyes. Her hair was of that pale blonde shade which we often see on French dolls. It was naturally straight, but, by means of crimping pins and curling irons, it was made exquisitely fluffy, and formed a kind of halo around her small head. The friends might have sat to an artist as modern types of the Madonna and the Magdalen.

"Now, Jessie, I've ever so much to tell you," said Nettie. "I must really relieve myself by full confession before the dread to-morrow comes,"—and she gave a little gasp.

"Very well; make a clean breast of it," replied

Jessie, trying very hard not to laugh. "I am prepared to listen, if not to pronounce absolution. Go on."

"Well," continued the pretty penitent, "I will begin with the general confession—I've been a miserable sinner—I have flirted awfully. It has seemed such fun to carry on with gentlemen, bringing them by slow degrees to the point of making a declaration, then accepting the ring, and all the other gifts and attentions of a *fiancée*, and after due time, breaking off everything and settling up accounts. Now, I know you feel disgusted with me, Jessie. The truth is, I'm a little disgusted with myself, now it is all over; but I do insist there were lots of fun in it at the time. Sober damsels like you, Jessie, don't get much amusement out of maidenhood; it is the miserable sinners like me who drain the honeyed cup to the bottom." Here she laughed a wicked little laugh, and exclaimed, "Don't be shocked, dear; I don't believe after all that I am quite so bad as I seem to be. But let me go on with my confession. Well, papa used to lecture me and so did mamma about my awful levity, but somehow I could not stop flirting. Life didn't seem worth living without the excitement. The truth is, I didn't have anything else to do, and one must fill up the hours with something?"

"Yes," said Jessie, laughing; "you know the old couplet about Satan finding some mischief for idle hands to do."

"Then, if idleness is so dangerous, why don't girls have something to do after they leave school?" asked Nettie. "Dressing and making calls and going to parties—that's all they have to occupy them from year's end to year's end; as if their overflowing energies could be used up in that way! Well, Jessie, one day last summer, after the violent rupture of an engagement of only a month, papa sent for me into his study, and gave me a regular 'setting down,' as he called it. He told me emphatically that I was never again to engage myself to a man without intending to marry him. 'Understand me now,' he said, very sternly, even omitting to call me, dear, 'the next time you engage yourself, you shall marry the man, whether you really love him or not. I tell you this seriously, so you must take care. Even at the risk of forcing an odious marriage upon you, I shall keep my word.' Rather cruel language from a father, wasn't it? After that, I was very careful for a time. I became as demure as a pussy cat, and all the gentlemen began to wonder what had come over me. Some thought I was under conviction for my sins, and some thought that I was going into a decline. Just then Mr. Sage dropped down upon us. All the girls were in a flutter as soon as he appeared, and, Jessie, seriously I tell you, I was disgusted at the way they acted. I made up my mind that I would disappoint the whole crowd by taking him myself. I began very demurely, and watched him with interest as he approached nearer and nearer. Soon I really began to like him, for he is very handsome, and has fine manners and good sense, and has seen much of the world. By the time he proposed, I was a little unsettled myself, and it has been growing steadily ever since; and now I tell you truly, Jessie, I love him to the point of distraction. He seems to understand me, and knows how to get along with me better than either papa or mamma; and I think he appreciates my good qualities (here she indulged in a mocking little laugh), and really believes there is something to me. Now, this is serious, for I'm afraid he is deceived there. Jessie, I sometimes doubt whether there is anything at all to me. I am nothing more than a glass of syllabub, and it actually frightens me to think that Clarence may some day awaken to the shallowness of my nature. What shall I do, dear, if he does?"

Jessie smiled; she could not help it. There was a comic element even in Nettie's sober and solemn confessions.

" Wait till the time comes, and then you will be clever enough for the occasion," said Jessie.

" No, I won't; I feel as if my sins had found me out at last. I have made a jest of hearts, and now mine may have to suffer. Besides, I have not had the courage to tell him anything about all those miserable old engagements. How could I?"

" Well, he has probably heard enough about you to know that you have not been a model of propriety," said Jessie. " Perhaps he will feel flattered to count up your victims. It is like slaying a man-eating tiger. He will be proud of the feat."

They both laughed.

" You are making fun of me, Jessie. Please, don't do that, for I am really in earnest. I am dreadfully afraid that Clarence will find out everything, and will be angry with me, and not love me any more. I know he has not heard about my evil doings, for he despises gossip, and would not listen to it. Besides, he holds very absurd ideas about the clergy and—their daughters! I have recently found out that he is severely orthodox on this point, and it frightens me almost to death. " It would break my poor little heart!" She laid her hand upon her breast with a pretty gesture which left one in doubt whether she were in earnest or not. " Jessie," she continued, after a while, " there are ever so many boys in town who have love-letters from me. Ben

Thornton actually told me when I broke off my engagement with him, 'Never mind, I'll make you pay for it; I'll keep your love-letters, and send them as a wedding-present to your husband.' Do you think he will, Jessie?"

"Of course not. Mr. Thornton is a gentleman, and, though he might utter such a threat in a moment of anger, he is too honorable to carry it out."

"I don't know about that," said Nettie, shaking her head doubtfully; "he was dreadfully angry with me, and he has never spoken to me since. Somehow I am afraid of him."

The brushes went slowly through the shining locks, and there was silence for a time.

"Jessie," exclaimed the pretty penitent, "I cannot tell you how it scares me to think of taking a man's happiness into my keeping. What if I should not satisfy him? What if he should regret his choice when it was too late, and I should find it out? How terrible it would be! I don't know how I could go on living."

"I don't believe that you will ever make any discovery of that kind," said Jessie, surprised beyond measure to find that such serious thoughts were agitating the bosom of her friend. "Mr. Sage is very much in love with you, and I'm sure he will not criticise you severely. I daresay he will think everything you say and do exactly right."

"I hope so with all my heart. I shall try my best always to keep up the illusion. He is very kind and patient and good-tempered. That is better than genius —isn't it?"

"I think so," replied Jessie; "at least, it is a safer quality in a husband."

"Oh! yes; Clarence is all right," exclaimed Nettie;

"I'm not in any doubt about him—he has virtues enough for a dozen men; but I am afraid of myself—honestly and truly I am, Jessie. I have never meant to be quite as frivolous as I have always been, but it is like rolling a stone downhill—once get it started, and there is no stopping it. So it is with me. I have generally begun by being a little saucy and mischievous—you know I couldn't help that; it's my very nature, probably inherited from some great-great-aunt, or great-grandmother; then, as a man gets a little interested in one, the game becomes very absorbing. It is like cards, or anything else where delicate skill is combined with chance. Often a lucky meeting would favor the continuance of matters, or a neat little speech or gesture would entice the victim a little farther. Yes, it was the stone going downhill—I could not stop it. Now, the feeling often comes over me, shall I be able to stop it after I am married? I'm really in doubt about myself. What do you think of it, Jessie?"

"I don't know, Nettie. It is like asking my opinion about the climate of Mercury or Mars. My experience in love affairs has been very limited. You are more capable than I am of pronouncing upon your own case. Coquetry may become a dangerous habit, I suppose, like drinking or opium-eating. There is but one way to overcome such habits—that is, to struggle continually against them."

"Yes, I know, and yet I don't know. I have heard all that about fighting one's faults so often that it sounds very old and familiar, but I don't understand it in the least. I have no idea how to begin a struggle with myself. I can struggle with anybody else in the world; but, when I want to do anything, it does not seem possible for me to combat the wish myself."

"Then let us hope that your husband may be strong enough to struggle with you, when your wishes are wrong," said Jessie, smiling.

She could not believe that her friend was more than half in earnest in what she was saying.

"Mr. Sage looks as if he had a very strong will, and, if that is the case, you will soon learn to submit to his guidance. It is a comfortable thought that you have more confidence in him than you have in yourself."

"Yes, it is. Though I am such a tipsy little craft, I do believe that I have cast anchor in good solid ground. Jessie," she exclaimed, after a short pause, "I have really been a kind of Undine—a merry, sportive, soulless creature. Love has awakened me to a higher ideal of life. There is the growth of something new within me—the budding of a soul, perhaps." She laughed lightly, though her words were serious enough. "But I'm not half as happy as I used to be in the old days. The something new which has been born within me often makes me very uncomfortable. I suppose it is the conscience, which, you know, Shakespeare says 'makes cowards of us all.'" And she laughed again.

"Nettie, if I were in your place," said Jessie, "I would tell Mr. Sage candidly about all the past flirtations, the engagements, the love-letters, and everything else. Confess to him that you have been a dreadful little coquette. It may cost you a little effort, and it may shock him somewhat, but in the end it will be best."

"I can never, never do it," exclaimed Nettie, with a little gasp.

"But you will be ever so much more comfortable yourself. You acknowledge that you have a vague dread of revelations that may reach him in the course of time."

"I have!" she cried, with a half-comic, half-tragic

expression; "they are like horrible phantoms which murder sleep." Jessie laughed.

"I don't believe Mr. Sage will be very severe with you. He knows that you are a light-headed, light-hearted little creature, rather reckless in manner and conversation. He loves you just as you are, and will see that the fondness for flirtation is something which you will outgrow when life becomes more serious. He will pardon levity more readily than deception."

"But I have no intention of deceiving him. I shall simply be mum. My past does not belong to him. I suppose my future does—heigh-ho! But what right has he to go poking in the ashes of bygone years?"

"No right, perhaps, but, loving you as he does, every moment of your life possesses an interest for him," replied Jessie. "He will inevitably hear more or less from others. Chance words dropped in his presence may excite his curiosity. Anticipate such revelations by telling him frankly that you have been a little sinner Such a confession will strengthen his confidence."

"Almost thou persuadest me to do it," exclaimed Nettie Hunter. Soon she shook her head. "No, I cannot. The very thought of it makes me feel old and ugly. Jessie, one reason why I have always been so gay is because I have taken life easy, and have shirked disagreeable things. I am going to keep it up if I can."

"I'm afraid after a while you will have to abandon that smooth and flowery road," said Jessie; "most people have to climb a hill sometimes."

"I know it; and I have a vague prevision that some very steep and stony ones lie before me." Her face assumed a pensive expression. She had brushed out the crimps from her hair, and, drawing it down smooth over her ears, she twisted the mass into a small coil low down on the neck. Jessie scarcely recognized the little face; it looked plain and demure. Nettie caught a glimpse of it in the long looking-glass over the mantel-piece, and broke into a peal of laughter. How could she help it? There was something irresistibly comical in her new expression.

"Jessie," she exclaimed, "I shall comb my hair just so when I go to the confessional; and I shall put on one of mamma's plainest black dresses—the melancholy alpaca that she always wears to funerals. Then I shall fall upon my knees at Clarence's feet, and pour out the whole story of my folly. Don't you think he will be too much touched to be angry?" And the suppressed laughter came in little bubbles, as she buried her face in her hands.

Jessie joined in the laugh; she was too young and gay herself to be very serious with this charming little sinner. Human nature is very much like chemistry; each individual is a compound of good and bad qualities, mixed in proper proportions according to some unknown law of heredity. We do not expect to find the same chemical characteristics in chloride of sodium and sulphurated hydrogen. Then why should we be surprised that human beings differ so widely from each other? Why should we expect to find in every one the elements of character which we are conscious of possessing ourselves? Why should we feel annoyed to detect qualities wholly different from anything which our inner consciousness reveals to us as existing within ourselves? What we do not admire may be wholly admirable. What we do not love may be perfectly lovable. What we do not understand may have its noble uses in God's great universe. In her estimate of others, some sentiment of this kind was permanently present in Jessie Holcombe's heart, making her very broadly sympathetic. And so it was that her spontaneous laughter now mingled with Nettie's. At length, the latter looked up and said in her clear, incisive voice:

"Now, I know you have lost all hope of me. You must think me desperately wicked to laugh over such a serious matter."

"Indeed I don't, you did look very droll; I could not help laughing myself."

"Then you don't think it a sign of total depravity to go through life laughing instead of crying?" asked Nettie.

"No; I rather envy those who can laugh. I wish I were not so serious myself. Your sunny temperament is a rich dowry, my dear."

"Jessie," said the girl, "I tell you honestly and truly, I cannot help being what I am. Remembering papa's profession, I have often tried to be prim and proper, but there is a very fountain of mirth within me. The water is bubbling up all the time; I cannot stop it. I really do want to do right, but my spirits run away with me. Perhaps age and sorrow will change me."

"I hope not," said her friend; "if you were changed, you would no longer be yourself. I like you as you are."

"Jessie, dear, I have been in earnest to-night in all that I have said to you. I do want to be less frivolous —indeed I do."

"Have you ever talked with your mother about it, and asked her to help you?"

"Never! never!" exclaimed Nettie; "it would only fill her dear heart with anxiety; she would immediately think that I was going to die, if I began to talk anything but the very absurdest nonsense. No, I would never go to her with any confessions. I had rather go to papa, but he isn't a woman, you know, and might be perplexed; he is easily perplexed, dear man. No, Jessie, I will stick it out, and seek no confidant but you. After I am married I will understand Clarence better, and then I can judge whether he will care or not about my wicked little doings in the past. He may be much more interested in the science of banking, and hold my affairs in supreme indifference. One thing is certain— I shall never tell him a real black lie. I might tell a white one, or a gray one, but a real black one—Never! I would not do it to escape hanging."

Just then the tiny clock upon the mantel-piece struck one.

" We ought not to sit up any longer," said Jessie; " to-morrow will be a very tiresome day for you."

" I know it, dear," and again she gave a little gasp. " I would like to escape from it, if I only could. I've a great mind to run away, Jessie. I never thought myself capable of feeling as I do to-night. The *trousseau* isn't a bit of comfort. I am sorry for mamma, sorry for papa, sorry not to have made them more happy —and worst of all, I'm sorry that the beautiful, bright girlhood is forever over."

She burst into a hysterical laugh, as she bounded into the bed, and buried her head in the pillow.

The next evening, promptly at eight o'clock, the bridal procession walked up the aisle of St. Luke's Church, and the good Bishop tied the nuptial knot. Immediately after the ceremony, a large reception followed at the residence of the bride. Everybody of fashion—everybody of respectability, was present. The parlors were so thronged that the most intimate friends jostled against each other without recognition on either side.

Finally, when the bride had departed, when the crowd had freely partaken of refreshments, and were slipping quietly away, Jessie Holcombe attempted to cross the hall in the hope of getting upstairs. She was very tired and longed to escape from the noise and confusion and ceaseless chatter. She unexpectedly encountered a gentleman who showed an inclination to detain her.

"Good-evening, Miss Holcombe. I have been trying for hours to get near enough to speak to you, but the Fates have not been propitious."

"Good-evening, Mr. Brooks; I did not know that you were here. I hope you have enjoyed it."

"It is worse than a London ball in the height of the season. Miss Hunter has certainly given everybody an opportunity to see her and offer congratulations."

"Yes, you know how kind-hearted she is. She did not want to slight any one."

"It has been a crushing affair. If all these people are her friends, she has a good many more than the conventional five hundred. But you look tired. Can we not find a quiet place where we can sit down? I want to talk with you a few moments. Suppose we come in here?" And he moved towards a half-open door at the end of the hall.

They found themselves in the dining-room; the tables were cleared, the servants were gone, and the lights were turned down. Several weeks had passed since these two had met. They both recalled it now; it was a spot of burning consciousness in the memory of each; that evening when his eyes had flashed the passionate message from his heart.

"What had he to say to her at this late day?" she

sternly demanded of herself. She was a woman and could not put the question to him, but her manner was cold and haughty. If it had been possible, she would have broken away from him, but she did not wish to be rude, and she could not well decline to speak to him, since he was a guest of the house.

"Miss Holcombe," he said, "I am going away—I want to say good-bye to you."

She extended her hand—" Good-bye."

"But I am not going just yet. Can you not spare me a few minutes of your time? May I not sit down and rest a little while?" He seemed to be pained by her coldness.

"Excuse me," she said, "you look so hurried that I thought you wanted to catch the next train."

They both laughed. "Not so bad as that," he replied; "I am sorry to have a hurried, hunted manner, but I have been terribly driven of late. I have been attending to some business for my father, and have felt in a perfect fever to get through with it. But, Miss Holcombe, have you no curiosity to know where I am going?"

"To Europe, is it?" she asked, feeling her own heart sink as she put the question.

"Not quite so far as that; only to New York."

"A journey to New York! How pleasant that sounds!"

"Does it? Now to me it sounds very unpleasant just at this time; but I hope something pleasant may come of it. You think you would like it for yourself?"

"Indeed I would. I often long to break away from everything, and fly off in an aimless tangent. I have not thought much of an ultimate stopping-place, but New York might answer. It seems remote enough."

" You have never been there ? " he asked.

" No, Mr. Brooks, my knowledge of geography is exceedingly limited. I hope your own journey may be pleasant and successful."

" Thank you," he said; " your good wishes will insure me against all misfortune."

" I would not advise you to rely for safety upon my good wishes," she replied, laughing lightly. " It would be better to get out an accident policy, wouldn't it ? "

" That would argue that my life is worth something to somebody else. I am sorry not to have that flattering assurance. Your good wishes, Miss Holcombe, make it worth something to myself." After a short pause, he added, " I hope you will miss me a little."

" Perhaps I shall; I cannot tell until you are gone."

" And if you should find it out after I am gone, how am I to know? Do you think you could write a little note and tell me ? "

" That would scarcely be proper. A young lady must never violate the conventionalities, even to serve a friend."

" But if I wrote first, then the conventionalities would not be violated."

" But you will not do that, Mr. Brooks."

" Why ? " he asked. " Do you doubt my courage ? "

" No, I know that you are very bold, but I do not think you are bold enough to offend a lady." She was looking down at the withered bouquet she held in her hands. Unconsciously she was pulling the flowers to pieces.

" And why should she be offended ? "

" *Because*," she answered emphatically; then added, " Mr. Brooks, you have no right to expect a more satisfactory reason from a woman."

She looked at him with a clear, cold, fearless gaze. It seemed to her that he was trifling, and she longed to put an end to the interview.

"But, Miss Holcombe, I do not see why a letter should offend a lady, if it be written in a tone of admiration and respect."

"That depends on a great many other things. There are times, Mr. Brooks, when silence is much more effective than speech." Her words had a sharp, incisive ring that he understood.

"You are right, he said; "the hypothetical letter shall not be written; indeed there would be no occasion for writing it, if you would only say that you will miss me a little. Surely you remember all the pleasant rides and walks."

"Yes; but they may possibly be continued under another escort," she replied, smiling without pity.

"Now, that is a cruel blow to my self-love."

"I think you will survive it," she said, and her laugh sounded almost wicked.

"I do not know about that; I feel rather weak and tired to-night—quite unable to parry thrusts of any kind. The truth is my father has not been well of late, and I have been trying to assist him in getting through with some pressing business. I have been amazed to see the amount of work that he does."

"Don't you feel a little remorseful to go away and leave him?" she asked.

"Sometimes, perhaps," he replied, hesitating a moment; "but I assure you I cannot help it. I wish you would believe that something beckons me to arise, and go out of the old country into the new. Even my father now feels that it is altogether best. You must have a little confidence in my judgment, Miss Holcombe."

She smiled. "I have so much in the father's that it is hard to have any in the son's, when the two are opposed."

"And cannot you believe that I have inherited some of his good qualities?"

"I will try," she said, very simply; "it is pleasant to think well of every one."

"I am sorry it should cost you such an effort to think well of me." He tried to speak carelessly, but there was a passionate vibration in his tone which her ear detected. She did not dare to look up, knowing that his eyes were fixed upon her, and feeling that the safety of both depended upon her own coldness and self-control. She was very lovely, as she sat there, beside him in the dim light. Her dress fell around her like a soft white cloud, leaving only the beautiful face and arms and bust unveiled. Her lap was filled with the faded flowers that she had been pulling to pieces. Presently he said:

"There, leave that one for me; you have plucked the heart out of all the rest; spare that one."

And as he spoke, he extended his hand. But she only shook her head.

"No; I must keep this one as a souvenir of Nettie's wedding; it is a pale-eyed forget-me-not."

"That is why I would like it. Can you not give it to me?" His voice was full of tender pleading, but she hardened her heart, and answered, "No." He did not wonder that she was cold and cruel. What right had he to detain her, unless he meant to tell her all that was in his heart? More than once words of burning passion rose to his lips, but they remained unspoken. He remembered the promise given to his father—he must wait. He must go away and leave her to doubt his truth and honor. Since it was so, there was no use in detaining her any longer. He arose from his seat.

"Miss Holcombe, you look very tired; forgive me for keeping you so long. Alice wished me to give you a message. She wants to see you before you return to Redbank. Can you not go and see her to-morrow afternoon? She is at my father's."

"I will try, but I'm afraid that I shall be very busy to-morrow. I have promised Mrs. Hunter to assist her in putting things in order. You can guess what a task that will be."

"Well, at least I have delivered the message," he said, smiling; "you must not allow Alice to accuse me of forgetfulness. I shall not be on hand to defend myself."

"When do you leave, Mr. Brooks?" she asked.

"To-morrow morning at seven o'clock. Good-bye." He extended his hand coldly, as if it were only an ordinary parting.

"Good-bye!" she echoed, in a low tone. For a moment her hand rested in his; he did not allow himself to give it even the slightest pressure. Without another word or look, he turned and hurried away.

Could he only have guessed all the sorrow that awaited her during his brief absence, he would have folded her to his heart then and there, in spite of every pledge that had been spoken.

CHAPTER XXIII.

It was almost sunset the next afternoon, when Jessie Holcombe ascended the stone steps of Judge Brooks's residence. She was immediately shown upstairs, and Alice came forward with eager pleasure to meet her. She wore a long, dark dressing-gown, trimmed with fur, and a heavy shawl was thrown around her shoulders.

"Excuse me for not coming down, Jessie," she said, "but I took a severe cold last night, and have been suffering to-day with sore throat."

"I am very sorry," said Jessie, still holding the hand of her friend. "You must have found the reception very tiresome—everybody did—there was such a crush."

"Yes," replied Alice, "I'm not strong enough for such occasions; they exhaust me nervously. I have felt as limp as an old rag all day. But I went to please Waverley, and to have given him some pleasure is compensation after all."

As they spoke, they entered a beautiful airy sitting-room, richly furnished in dull old gold. A large bay-window, draped with delicate lace curtains, filled up one entire end; a *jardinière* of choice plants was standing there, and on them fell the last level rays of the setting sun. To Jessie's eye, it was the most beautiful room that she had ever seen, and an exclamation of delight burst from her lips.

"Yes, it is gorgeous," said Alice; "it is Waverley's

sitting-room—he furnished it himself. Those pictures on the wall are his own paintings, and he collected and arranged everything—rugs, skins, hangings and ornaments. It cost a pretty sum of money, I have heard. He insisted on my using it during his absence, but I feel like an intruder upon his privacy."—A grand piano stood near the centre of the room, but it was closed now, and the music was neatly piled upon the music-stand.—" There is his piano, and there are his books," said Alice, pointing to some shelves over which hung a rich Algerian scarf; " they are mostly in French, German, or Italian, so I cannot read them." Before seating herself, Jessie went around the room, and looked at the pictures; they were mostly landscapes—bits of bleak coast, and fair pastoral scenes, framed in by mountains. One picture especially chained her attention—a moonlight on the water, a boat with two occupants, a lady and a gentleman. The gentleman managed the oars, while the lady played upon the guitar, and the music of her voice seemed to be floating over the water.

" That is the Lake of Como," remarked Alice ; " I believe that is an incident in his own life, though he will not confess it. He always speaks of Como as heavenly. Here is a picture of the *Villa Serbelloni* where he stayed —it must be an enchanting spot." The girl took a quiet pride in pointing out the many beautiful things that were scattered around. Jessie could understand it. Was he not her affianced husband? And yet Jessie Holcombe recalled the expression of his eyes as he had looked into her face more than once, and the tender vibration of his voice as he had pleaded with her last night for that poor faded forget-me-not which she had at last thrown into the fire. What did it all mean? She could not make it out, and a sickening sensation came over her as she moved around his room, and gazed at the objects which his hands had touched only that morning.

"Come, let's sit down," she said; "you are not well, Alice, and it will not do for you to tire yourself." They drew two easy-chairs within the light of the bay-window and seated themselves.

"What in the world made Nettie Hunter invite every body in the city to her reception?" asked Alice in a slight tone of disgust; "it did seem to me that a few might have been comfortably spared."

Jessie smiled. "That is just Nettie's way—she likes everybody and everybody likes her; she wanted to give everybody a good time."

"Well, she did not succeed so far as I am concerned," said Alice. "Before I finally escaped, I felt as if I had been knocked down, trampled upon, and unmercifully beaten. I was never before in such a crowd and I hope never again to be victimized to such an extent."

"I suppose Mr. Hunter also felt it necessary to send out a large number of invitations," remarked Jessie; "you know clergymen belong to the public."

"Yes," exclaimed Alice; "every unwashed, unshaven creature who drops into a church, thinks himself entitled to the notice of the minister."

"Well, it ought to be so, dear; if they are truly the preachers of glad tidings to the people, as Christ was, they ought not to assume a social superiority."

"I'm sincerely glad I'm not a clergyman's daughter," said Alice; "I'm not at all democratic in my tastes, and some things would be dreadfully disagreeable. Nettie never seemed to care a fig for social distinctions."

"No, she has less pride and pretension about her than any girl I ever knew," replied Jessie; "I like that in her very much. She is always ready to give a cordial greeting to the very humblest person. I have seen her stop and chat with the old woman who sells pies at the corner of the street, and every ragged boy in town knows and admires her."

"Uncle thinks that she has married exceedingly well," Alice remarked after a short silence. "He says that Mr. Sage is a very superior young man, and that he is finely connected in New York. He represents a very strong banking-house, and will be a very rich man in course of time."

"I am glad—I think Nettie will enjoy being rich; she will not put on airs, as we used to say at school." And Jessie laughed.

"I dislike people who feel elevated when they have made a little money," said Alice; "as if that could really make them more important in the world."

"It does make them more important in the eyes of some people," replied Jessie. "It must be a very nice thing to have. I used to be perfectly indifferent to it; I did not even understand its value as a purchasing power; but of late, I have had glimpses of the many beautiful things which it can buy. It is not altogether 'filthy lucre.' See this lovely room, for instance. But for money, it would have been an unrealized dream. What a delight it must be to sit day after day in the midst of such surroundings—to drink in the warmth of sunshine that falls through such a film of lace, the fragrance of flowers so exquisitely arranged, the harmony of color that satisfies the senses as music does; and last of all to have such a splendid piano, well tuned and with a mighty volume of sound. Yes, I would like it all!"

And she indulged in a mocking little laugh as if oppressed by the futility of such wishes.

"Why, how worldly you are getting, Jessie!" exclaimed Alice; "I have always looked upon you as the simplest maiden on this green earth—one of the unconscious, unspoiled kind. Surely a residence of two days in this wicked old city has not corrupted you?"

Again Jessie laughed and shook her head. "Oh! no; I'm not utterly corrupted yet; and I'm only beginning to see some of the possibilities of existence. I think my sensuous side is just awakening. Never fear—it will have to go to sleep again. The prose of life is for me—not the poetry."

"You are wrong, then," said Alice; "you are the very one to get the poetry. But it has small connection with wealth. For instance, this room—it is not money that has made it beautiful, but good taste."

"The most refined taste without money would have been unavailing," replied Jessie. "Besides, the taste was trained and educated by advantages which could only be procured by wealth."

"How mercenary you are growing! You startle me," said Alice, breaking into a laugh, in which her friend heartily joined.

"No; I again repeat that I am only getting glimpses of possibilities. It is one thing to estimate wealth aright—it is another to barter one's higher nature for it. But really I must go—it will soon be dark."

"Do spend the night with me," pleaded Alice.

"I cannot, dear; I promised Mrs. Hunter that I would be back without fail."

"But I will send Harris with a message."

"That would not do. She expects me to return, and it would be cruel to disappoint her. Besides, they will both be so lonely to-night; the excitement is all over now, and the reaction has come. I must try to comfort them a little." She arose to go.

"Sit down just a minute," said Alice; "I want to say something to you. You will not mind? You will not get vexed with me?"

"Of course not. How could I ever get vexed with you, dear?" As she spoke, Jessie stooped and kissed the brow of her friend, and then added, "What is it? Tell me quickly. See how dark it is growing."

"Well, sit down; I cannot talk to you comfortably if you are standing up; you tower above me and overshadow me. Jessie dear, I must tell you something." She paused a moment; it evidently cost her an effort to speak. "I want you to know that I am not engaged to Waverley—I have never been really engaged to him—no rings have ever been exchanged between us. Uncle was not willing for us to pledge ourselves when we were very young; he required us to wait."

Jessie's heart gave a strange, wild bound, and the blood rushed to her face, but she was silent. It was almost dark in the room, and Alice could not see her emotion.

"Before Waverley went to Europe, there were some silly love scenes between us," Alice continued, "but neither of us were very deeply in earnest, and it is all over now. Both of us realize that we can never be anything nearer than cousins. I am dreadfully sorry to disappoint every one—mamma, uncle, the public at large, and you, too, dear." Alice smiled her sweet, sad smile that meant a great deal more than was expressed.

"Yes, it is an awful disappointment to me," said Jessie, struggling to be calm; "I had hoped to be your bridesmaid. It is a very interesting *rôle*."

"Is there no way of consoling you, dear?"

"Yes, you must marry somebody else."

The young girl shook her head, and said sadly:

"No, I shall never marry any one." After a moment she added, "I want you to know, Jessie, that Waverley is the soul of honor. I can never tell you how noble and delicate he has been in his conduct towards me. He has thought only of my feelings."

Jessie could not trust herself to speak. She understood well why Alice had made this confession, and her heart was full to overflowing.

"Jessie," said Alice, in a low, sad tone, "I would like to be a Vestal Virgin, if only there were a temple and an altar, and a fire to be kept forever burning; but not even that is left to us now; the fire has gone out long ago."

"Yes, dear, *that* fire; but there are many others that need to be kept up."

She spoke almost in a whisper; then she stooped and again kissed Alice. In a moment she was gone.

She descended the staircase rapidly, feeling hurried and excited, and anxious to escape notice. She wanted the cool, fresh air of evening to blow upon her heated face, and calm the fever in her veins. As she reached the lower hall, a gentleman entered the front door. It was impossible to avoid him. It was Judge Brooks; he recognized her, and came forward in his cordial way, exclaiming, "Why, Jessie, my dear, how glad I am to see you! Have you been up to call on Alice?"

"Yes, and I'm sorry to find her ill."

"It was that wedding fandango," he said, with an impatient expression, "she is getting to be a regular hot-house plant—a breath of cold air chills her. But I intend to keep her with me a while now, and have the attendance of a first-rate physician. We will cure her, if possible. We will hedge her around with orders and commandments. First of all, we forbid weddings in future; so you need not invite her to yours, my dear."

Jessie laughed, and remarked, "I was sorry not to see you last night; we hoped that you would honor the occasion by your presence."

"Thank you for missing me; but I am getting too old for such things."

"Oh! no, you are not; you must not speak of being old."

"I think you have sometimes reminded me of the fact," he said, smiling a little sadly.

"Then I was very rude and thoughtless, and hope you will forgive me."

"There is nothing to forgive, my dear. I *am* old—I feel it now, and am resigned."

She felt herself unequal to the task of talking to him, and made a movement towards the door.

"You are not going, are you?" he asked. "Spend the night with us."

"Thank you, but I cannot; I promised Mrs. Hunter to return, and I must not linger any longer; it is quite dark now."

"Yes, it is too late for you to go alone; I will accompany you to the rectory. But come in here a moment, and let me see you, Jessie."

She could not refuse; he took her hand in his, and led her into the large, brilliantly-lighted drawing-room. The young girl looked at him with a tender, intense gaze. Yes, he was changed; he had grown older; there were lines about the eyes and mouth which she had never noticed before, and she wondered if Waverley had grieved him so deeply as to add these furrrows to his face. Yes, it must be that. She could easily guess his disappointment in his son. It must be a cruel blow to nourish hopes and expectations for years, to work hard for their final accomplishment, and then to have them swept away as rubbish by a careless hand. She could scarcely forgive the young man, and yet she could not find it in her heart to condemn him. He was a noble fellow, and she blamed herself for being so cold and cruel as to refuse him that poor faded forget-me-not. Well, it could not be helped now. Some day, perhaps, he would return, and she would not be so unbending in her pride. These thoughts passed rapidly through her mind, as the Judge moved the chairs and found a comfortable seat for her.

"Jessie, my dear," he said, lingering fondly on the name, "I wish you would come and stay awhile with Alice. It would cheer her immensely, and me, too. We are rather a melancholy couple to be left to our own devices."

"You are very kind, but I cannot," said the young girl, shrinking from the thought of accepting his hospitality.

"May I ask why?" and he looked at her intently as if determined to read her very soul; then he added, "You must not be afraid that I will persecute you, Jessie. That is all over now. I am convinced of my folly. It is only necessary to look at you, my dear, in order to realize that you are beyond my reach. You are blossoming into greater loveliness every day, like a flower that keeps opening wider and wider to the sunlight. It is not for my old hand to pluck it. I must leave it for some one younger and more worthy."

Jessie was inexpressibly touched by his words and manner; a vivid blush spread over her face as she said: "You must not talk so; there is no one on earth half so worthy as yourself. I feel it more and more every day. It would be a noble task in life to make you happy—if only I could succeed; but I know that I should fail," and she shook her head sadly.

"Yes, you would fail, Jessie. There is a brighter destiny in store for you, my child."

"Please don't say another word!" she exclaimed, raising her hand imploringly; "I will not have you making predictions about me—I am content to wait."

"I know it, dear," he replied, slowly and solemnly. "I will not utter a single prediction, but I see it all like a beautiful vision, and, Jessie, my darling, I am content—I would not have it otherwise if I could."

The tears were gathering in her eyes; she could not sit there any longer and hear him talk in this way. She arose to her feet, exclaiming, hoarsely, "I must go; I cannot stay another minute."

"I am going with you," he said.

"No, no; please don't—please don't," and again she raised her hand with an imploring gesture. "I am not at all afraid to go alone. It is not far."

"I cannot allow it, my dear," he replied, reaching for his hat.

"Then let Harris go with me," she pleaded. The old servant was moving about at the lower end of the hall. Hearing his name spoken, he approached at once.

"Harris," said the young lady, "get your hat and accompany me to the rectory. Your master wishes to go, but he is tired, and I cannot consent for him to go out again on my account. Good-night," and she extended her hand to the Judge. He took it and held it for a moment.

"Good-night, and God bless you!" he said.

CHAPTER XXIV.

ALTHOUGH it was only the first of March, signs of spring were already beginning to appear on all sides. The fruit trees were in blossom, and a delicate mist of green hovered over the distant woods. The songs of happy birds were heard again; the coo of the turtle-dove and the whistle of the partridge came floating on the soft, sweet air. At Redbank the negroes were cleaning up the fields and lighting bonfires in all directions; the odor of burning brush was mingled with the odor of the earth, freshly upturned by the plow. A faint, smoky haze hung in the atmosphere, lending to all objects that dimness of outline which is so enchanting to the eye and to the imagination.

The sun was mounting higher and higher every day, and his generous rays were warming the world into life and beauty. All living creatures felt the impulse to step out of doors and bask in the genial heat.

Jessie Holcombe was again at Redbank. On her return from the city, after a visit of several weeks, she had been glad to find every one well, and the machinery of life moving on quietly and smoothly. Harry had come back during her absence, and fallen into the old habits of eating, sleeping, hunting and lounging around. He looked dejected, and Jessie feared that he was recovering from a prolonged period of dissipation, but she said nothing. She pitied him more than ever, because he appeared less light-hearted and gay, and was evidently struggling with a very real trouble—a haunting phantom that would not be downed.

One afternoon, she was sitting out on the piazza in the warm sunshine, reading, when her brother came sauntering up the steps in a listless fashion, and approaching the joggling-board, threw himself down upon it at full length. He pulled his hat over his eyes to shut out the dazzling light, and in a little while he seemed to be sleeping. Jessie did not notice him, but continued to read. Half an hour passed without a word, when at length Harry pushed back his hat, and said :

" What are you reading, Jessie ? You appear to be perfectly absorbed."

" 'Alton Locke,' " she replied, looking up for a moment from the page ; " have you read it ? "

" Only glanced at it ; it is not a very cheerful production," he answered ; " how do you like it ? "

" I find it rather interesting ; but I do not know much about that Chartist movement, and, perhaps, I do not give the actors enough of my sympathy. The truth is, I don't like political agitators."

" There the woman spoke ! " he exclaimed impatiently.

" But governments seem somewhat sacred to me," she said ; " they are symbols of the law which rules the Universe. Men should respect them. Agitation often brings far greater evils than it remedies."

" Nonsense ! You don't know what you are talking about. Human governments are made by men, and they have the faults and failings that men have. Only agitation and actual insurrection can force the governors to attend to the sufferings of the governed." He spoke with a passionate indignation that was not usual with him.

"But when the agitation or insurrection is suppressed by arms, and the leaders are led off to execution, while the helpless followers are shut up in prison, where is the benefit?" she asked.

"Even then public opinion is more or less affected by the new ideas, and the governing classes are compelled to modify their tyrannical proceedings. Without such struggles on the part of the people, all governments would crystallize into absolute despotism. It is surprising how soon the possession of power makes a man a tyrant. Let a man rise from the ranks as did Cromwell or Napoleon, and just as soon as he becomes a master, he begins to forge chains for the people."

"Then the evil lies deeper—it is inherent in human nature," she said, with a quiet smile; "men must become better themselves, if they would have better governments."

"That will be a mighty slow process," he exclaimed in a tone of disgust; "at the present rate of progress, it will take several great cycles before men cease to enjoy tyrannizing over their fellow-men. Before that blessed era arrives, I'm afraid our planet will be as cold and desolate as the moon."

"I don't believe that," she said, shaking her head; "we do advance a little, century by century. After a while, we will abandon those old methods of insurrection and revolution."

"I only hope we may," he replied; "but you and I will not live to see it. War is an ugly thing for a nation as well as for an individual. It is like waiting to get dreadfully sick and then taking a lot of nasty medicine. There are laws of health, which, if followed, would prevent people from getting sick at all. I think the people of a country ought to take more trouble to find out what the rascally politicians are about, and nip their schemes in the bud. Every man ought to own a powerful telescope and keep it turned right upon Washington all the time. Men are altogether too careless about public affairs until a crisis comes; then they kick up a dreadful row, which often ends in smoke, defeat, and humiliation, as our war did. What did the great mass of Southerners know about the real, true cause of the war? What did they know about the relative strength of the sections? Absolutely nothing. A few politicians managed the whole business, and, like stupid sheep, we followed them. Now we are turned out of our 'green pastures beside the still waters,' and have to roam the mountain-sides in search of a few stray blades of grass. I tell you, it is devilish hard."

"You are getting too deep for me, Harry," said the girl, turning again to her book. She did not care to discuss anything connected with the war. For a time she went on with her reading, but presently he again interrupted her.

"Jessie, do you believe there is another life after this one?"

She was startled by the question as well as the tone in which it was spoken.

"Of course, I do," she replied; "did we not say the creed together at our mother's knee: '*I believe in the Holy Ghost; the holy Catholic Church; the Communion of Saints; the Forgiveness of Sins; the Resurrection of the Body; and the Life Everlasting?*'"

"Oh, yes, we said it often enough, but it was so much Sanscrit to me. Saying a thing isn't always believing it, by a long shot."

"Harry dear, it grieves me to hear you talk so," she said.

"I know it, Jessie; you were always a good little girl. But how can I believe a thing if I can't, I'd like to know. For my part, I believe that death is an eternal and dreamless sleep—that alone will be a compensation for all the ills of life. When night comes, I like to wrap my blanket around me and forget everything in sleep; it is compensation for all the fatigues and mistakes of the day. So death will come to us and close our eyes forever."

"Oh, Harry, you are a real pagan!" she exclaimed, looking at him sorrowfully.

"No, I'm worse than that," he answered; "most of the pagans believed in a spiritual life beyond the grave. Those people whom we stigmatize nowadays as heathen, believe in a hereafter of some kind. The ancient Greeks believed in a Styx to be crossed, a grim tribunal to be faced, a trial by judges, and an award of happiness or misery. I rather like their faith; it was founded on right and justice. A fellow got what he deserved. Now with Christianity it is different: it is the sneaking, long-faced, psalm-singing creatures who go right to heaven when they die, provided they can swallow the whole Thirty-nine Articles without making a wry face."

"That's not Christianity," said Jessie, shaking her head; "you are mistaken, if you think so. To be a Christian is to be like Christ, and we are told that He went about doing good, and preaching the beautiful doctrine that God is our Great Father, and all men are brothers."

"Those who call themselves His people are mighty little like Him nowadays. They are just as selfish and greedy after the good things of the world as all the rest of us. I wish to goodness that I had lived in the time of those old Greeks. They were fine fellows: they had respect for strength, valor, and beauty. They did not think much of business and money-making; they left that dirty work to slaves. In these latter days of the glorious nineteenth century, no man succeeds in life who does not go into some kind of business and make a big pile of money—the more the better. It fills me with disgust. I could live for something really worth living for, and die for something really worth dying for, but I shall never stand behind a counter, and sell needles and pins, and spools of cotton; I'll take to the woods first, and live on nuts and berries."

He was silent for a few moments and then he sat upright, and exclaimed : " Jessie, I was born several thousand years too late. What shall I do ? I don't seem to fit into this present civilization. I ought to have been with Leonidas and his Spartans at Thermopylæ; I could have been of some use there. That bit of fighting was fine!"

Jessie looked up from her book and smiled. In a way, she knew that he was right; he was capable of splendid flashes of heroism. He would make a fine soldier, or a fine sailor; he could hunt bears in the Rocky Mountains, or sail to the North Pole; but he could not run a mill, or manage a store, or direct a bank, so there was but small use for him in these modern times.

"Yes, I know what you mean, Harry," she said, in her sweet, sympathetic voice; " there is a great charm in that old Greek life. Sometimes I, too, feel that their civilization was higher than ours. We seem more material in our aims, and less intellectual and æsthetic; but one cannot tell—behind all their love of the beautiful, there must have been much ghastly suffering. Think of the Helotes."

"So there is now," he replied, " and the world is more than two thousand years older. If the teachings of Christ had been followed, human suffering would have been eliminated by this time."

"I think not," she said; "suffering is so closely connected with ignorance, and men grow wise very slowly. Each new human life begins at the beginning, and must learn for itself, through its own experience, and the span is very short. But we cannot settle these things, Harry, and it does no good to talk about them. The age of Greek civilization is past; you were not permitted to live then, and you are permitted to live now. Try to make something noble out of your life, even if you have fallen upon evil times. If you would only go to work in earnest, you would not be worried by all these questions. We are hedged around with awful mysteries, but, after all, some things are very plain. We are set in the midst of duties, and our happiness lies in doing them."

"I don't agree with you there," he replied. "We are not fixed in the soil by roots with nothing to do but grow. We are left to develop our own roots, and find a spot to fix ourselves in, and then get our proper nourishment; and I tell you it is devilish hard to do. Sometimes we are even torn up after we are firmly planted, and seemed to be growing pretty fair. No, Jessie, I can't agree with you—nothing's plain in this world —everything is in a muddle. Now, for a personal application : look at me, I don't know what to do, nor where to go. I haven't talents, as they call them, and I haven't energy, and I haven't money. What's to be done with such a fellow? There is no place for him in the universe, and the best thing for him is to fall asleep."

"No! no!" exclaimed Jessie, "the best thing is to struggle to develop energy and talent. You cannot guess what is in you until you begin the fight with life.

Half the pleasure of living comes from the determination never to give up—never to be conquered in the battle. If one thing fails, try another. Men have made themselves great and strong in that way."

"Well, we will think about it," he said, as he again extended himself upon the joggling-board. "It sounds good and wise, but I daresay there's a flaw somewhere in the argument—there generally is in all advice;" and he laughed quietly to himself. Jessie went back to her book, but the interest was gone, and she turned the pages very slowly. Soon Harry again interrupted her —his mind was evidently full of thoughts this afternoon.

"Jessie, do you know what I would do if I were rich?"

She smiled and replied, "No, I haven't the least idea. Tell me."

"Well, I would travel. It is my opinion that there is more fun in travelling than in anything else in the world."

"It is very possible to travel without a great deal of money—at least for a man," she said. "You might buy a monkey and go round the world with him."

"Gracious! what plebeian notions you have! When I start on my travels, I wish to go *en prince*—with a retinue and plenty of money to give to the beggars. I would like especially to go to Rome and stand among the crumbling columns of the Forum, and to Greece and walk over the plains of Marathon. Yes, with a big pile of money, one can make life jolly enough. Why did a wise Providence permit my fortune to be swept away by the calamity of war? I'm rather inclined to question the wisdom of that particular Providence."

"There are hundreds of acres of land in the Far West

waiting to be settled," said Jessie; "why don't you go and claim your inheritance? It is worth money now, and will be worth still more in the course of time."

"It is almost as much of a desert as Sahara," he exclaimed impatiently; "by Jupiter, I'm not going to work it. I'll starve first. But I'd just like to know who it is that has cheated me out of my own lawful possessions. If I could only find the particular individual, I would be very apt to put a bullet into his head. Why am I turned almost penniless upon the world?" He looked up at his sister, as if demanding a reply.

She shook her head and said, "I cannot answer any of your questions, Harry. But I do believe, if you would go to work at something, many of them would be answered for you. We are told that it is the idle who are full of perplexities and doubts. When one is very busy, mists and fogs and clouds disappear, and there is a general clearing up of the mental weather."

"You are a wise little puss, Jessie, and I've a vague feeling that you are right, but your prescription is devilish hard to take. The only law which I find fulfilled in my being is the law of inertia." Jessie laughed. "It is a property of matter which is only overcome by the application of some external force," he continued. "If a fellow gives me a kick, my inertia is slightly overcome; it takes nothing less."

"Then you ought to hire somebody to kick you continually," said Jessie, again laughing; "suppose you get Mike—he has nothing in particular to do. Take him around with you and have him administer the required number of kicks every day."

"That wouldn't answer," he replied, "for the momentum excited by each one of his kicks would all be expended in kicking him back again."

"Oh! Harry, Harry, I have no philosophy deep enough to reach your case," she exclaimed; "you don't believe in anything but inertia and sleep. What a creed for an American! I had rather be a Hindoo and worship Juggernaut."

"You are right," he said, laughing; "but here comes Sugar-plum. We'll leave metaphysics for the present." As Lilian approached the joggling-board on which he lay, he looked up at her. "Come here, Pet, and let me put my naughty head in your lap.—There, that's ever so nice. Now, run your fingers through my hair, and see if you can't make things pleasanter for me." She did as he requested, and he caught her little hand more than once and kissed it. "Nice little hand! dear little hand!" he murmured, softly; "I wonder who is going to win it some day. I'd like to kick him, whoever he is."

"Why, Uncle Hal, my hand is always going to belong to me," she said, laughing at his words.

"No, it isn't," he answered, kissing it again. "You'll be giving it away to some confounded, good-for-nothing, impudent fellow in a few years, and I'm angry with him right now. He doesn't deserve it in the least—the sweetest little hand that ever was made! Don't you ever get married, dear; men are awful old humbugs. There is nothing sweet in the whole round world but little girls. They are the salt that keeps the Universe from corruption."

She pinched his ear, and told him to hush talking, and go to sleep right away. She played with his soft curls, and rocked him gently up and down upon the joggling-board, and sang a low cradle-song whenever he stirred.

Jessie went on with her book until the hour of sunset.

Then she closed it and fixed her eyes upon the splendors of the west. As she watched the brilliant clouds, she thought, "How nice it would be to have a little boat like Hiawatha's and sail away into the sunset. It would be beautiful to go home that way."

Harry still slept on, and Lilian sat patiently holding his head and stroking his hair. Jessie knew that the child must be tired, but she could not find it in her heart to arouse the sleeper. If sleep were indeed so beautiful to him, then let him sleep. She listened to his heavy breathing with a sad heart. Poor Harry! what was to become of him? Would he go on living this aimless, wretched life for twenty, thirty, fifty years, perhaps, before the Eternal Sleep for which he sighed came to him? The thought was full of pain, and tears gathered in her eyes.—Finally, the young man stirred, yawned, stretched his limbs, and slowly came back to himself.

"Why, Pet," he cried, "you must be tired! How long have I been sleeping?"

"Ever and ever and ever so long," she answered, drawing a deep breath; "but I didn't mind."

"Thank you, darling, for holding my good-for-nothing head," he said, lifting her in his arms and kissing her; "now, come, and let's joggle away the old tired." He bounded upon the board, and began to spring up and down with her.

"Come, Jessie, and join us. Let's play that we are children again, and have a real, good, old-fashioned romp."

She did not reply, so he approached the chair in which she was sitting. He saw the tears in her eyes. "Why, what are you crying about? Have the sorrows of 'Alton Locke' opened the fountain of your tears? I'll fling the old book away, if you are going to spoil your eyes over it."

"I am not thinking of 'Alton Locke,'" she replied; "there are sources of grief nearer home."

"Dear, sweet little goose," he said, stooping and kissing her, "I'm not worth a briny jewel from those glorious eyes. Cheer up! I expect to be President of the United States in a few years, and you shall preside over the White House, since a certain young lady declines the exalted destiny. So do come and have a joggle with Lilian and me. It takes at least three to make it real lively."

"No, I do not feel like it, dear; you must excuse me to-night." Soon she got up and went into the house. The joggling went on with ever-increasing hilarity. As Jessie listened to the shouts and laughter, she wondered anew at the strange and wayward character of her brother, and her heart grew sadder and sadder with a vague dread of the future.

CHAPTER XXV.

"WELL, Pet, how is Lady Coraline to-day?" asked Harry as Lilian entered the back-parlor, one afternoon, with her doll in her arms.

"She is not at all well," said the child, assuming a very solemn air; "she has the mumps and the measles and scarlet-fever."

"What! all three?"

"Yes," the little mother answered.

"Why, that is a dreadful complication! Bring her here and let me see her. It is well that I'm a first-rate doctor, isn't it?" he said.

Lilian assented with a nod of the head.

The young man felt the pulse of the doll, and examined her arms and neck with care.

"Yes," he finally said, "she is very ill—there is really occasion for anxiety. You must put her to bed immediately. It will not do for you to drag her around through the cold, damp halls."

"Can I put her to bed in here?" asked the child; "I don't want to go upstairs to play. I want to stay where you are."

"Oh! yes; make her bed there on the end of the sofa, and I will prepare some medicine for her." He took a little bottle of homeopathic pellets from his pocket and counted out six of them. "Here, give her one of these every half-hour, and bathe her head with cold water. You had better keep a wet cloth on it all the while."

For ten or fifteen minutes, Lilian was very busy following his directions. She undressed the doll, made a nice bed for her on the end of the sofa, gave a pill as prescribed, looking at the clock carefully to note the exact time and then placed a damp cloth on the little patient's head. Harry watched her as she went through the whole performance with a serious air of maternal solicitude. He had nothing to do but to watch her. It was pouring rain, so no one could get out of the house, and his paper-back novel did not interest him. Jessie came into the room after a time, and, seating herself at the piano, began to play some solemn kind of music which formed a good accompaniment to the rain that was driving violently against the window-panes. Harry rocked lazily backwards and forwards before the fire ; it was comfortable to have a roof over one's head on such a day—comfortable to have a blazing fire and a rocking-chair—comfortable to have nothing to do but watch the beautiful child as she moved noiselessly around the bed of the sick doll. When her motherly attendance was at an end, she came and stood beside Harry's chair ; he put out his arm and drew her to him.

"My darling, do you love me?" he asked.

She threw her arms impulsively around his neck—"Better than anybody in the whole world," she said with emphasis.

"That is right—I want somebody to love me just that way—better than anyone else in the whole world." She smoothed back the hair from his high, white brow, and kissed him again and again.

"And are you going to love me always?" he asked.

"Always! always! as long as I live," she replied.

"Even if I go away?"

"Don't I always love you when you go away?" she

said, a little reproachfully; "and don't I love you when you come back? Nobody is ever so glad to see you as I am."

"That is true," he replied.

"And when you are gone, I don't forget you either. Every night when I say my prayers, I always say, 'God bless Uncle Hal and bring him back again!' And I say it over twice, to be very sure that God hears me. You know He might be listening to some other little girl's prayer, and not hear me the first time."

"Yes," he whispered, "always say it over twice, and then He will know that you are really in earnest."

Again she kissed him.

"But, darling, if I went away and never came back any more, do you think you could go on loving me always?" he asked.

"Always! always!" she said, emphatically; "but you will come back, I know. You must come back."

"Why?" he asked.

"Because I could not bear it!—to have you never come back any more." And the tears came into her eyes. "You will come back—won't you?"

"Perhaps," he answered; "if you want me very much. We will see about that."

"But when are you going."

"I cannot tell you yet," he said, a little absently.

She nestled her head close up to his, and began to cry very softly. He took her into his lap.

"There—that will not do, at all—you must not cry. Go and see about Lady Coraline. It is time to give her another pill. She will require very careful nursing, you know, for she is very ill."

The child dried her eyes with the end of her apron, got down from his lap, and went to the sofa where the doll lay. Soon she exclaimed, "Lady Coraline is ever so much better, Uncle Hal; she says her head does not ache a bit now. I'm sure her fever is going off."

"I think so," he replied. "Give her another pill."

When the directions had been followed, she returned and got into his lap again. Jessie, from her seat at the piano, could hear them talking softly to each other as they rocked back and forth. She was accustomed to see them play in this manner; but, somehow, to-day their words made a deep impression upon her, and her heart felt unutterably sad as she struck the chords of the *Sonata Pathétique*. Just then the Colonel entered the back-door, and went storming through the hall. He had not been able to find his umbrella, and had got wet in his journey to the stable. He declared emphatically that he would break a certain good-for-nothing fellow's head, if the said individual did not stop meddling with his possessions.

"How cross father is to-day!" said Lilian, snuggling up closer still to Uncle Hal.

"Never mind," was the reply, "it is all on account of cotton. The price is down and is going lower still every day. He made a mistake in not selling when the price was up. It is enough to make him cross."

"Have you had the umbrella, Hal?" asked Jessie.

"No, my dear; I never use an umbrella. I do not consider my cranium too sacred to be rained upon."

The storm continued without abatement. It had now lasted for several days, and had been increasing in violence each day. Jessie played throughout the long dull afternoon, and Harry and Lilian seemed to fall asleep in the deep comfortable rocking-chair before the fire. Towards night there was a slight lull in the storm; the rain fell more gently, as if the end were near at hand.

At the supper-table, the Colonel expressed himself as glad, very glad, that there were some indications of clearing.

"I have felt a little anxious about the mill," he remarked; "the fall of water has been very great in the last three days. Peyton tells me that all the streams are up higher than he has ever known them. It is almost impossible to get to the Quarter—the branch is like a river. I do hope it is over now. I'm glad that nothing is planted yet awhile."

"It seems to me that we have had a great deal of rain this winter—more than usual, have we not?" said Jessie.

"I don't know about that. The storms have continued longer, perhaps, but I don't suppose the actual rain-fall has been much greater," replied the Colonel.

"I never in my life saw it rain harder than it has done this afternoon," said Mrs. Winston. "It has made me very restless and nervous."

"It affected me in the same way," remarked Jessie; "I have felt quite wretched. I hope it is over at last."

"Now it has been delightfully soothing to me," declared Harry. "Pet and I have had a charming nap in the big rocking-chair, haven't we, darling?"

"Yes, but I don't like the rain," replied the child.

"Well, I have been thinking about the mill the whole afternoon," said the Colonel.

"Then, you had better send down right away, and see if everything is right," Mrs. Winston answered, in a tone which showed that she shared his anxiety.

"I will go for you, sir," said Harry. Now, it always annoyed the Colonel to be obliged to accept any favor from his brother-in-law. He generally treated the young man with lordly indifference; and, without even looking up from his plate or even expressing any thanks for the offer, he coldly replied—" I do not think I need your services in the least. Old Burch has a little intelligence, and I imagine he will know how to manage the gates, if the pond is too full."

" Well, for my part, I have a very poor opinion of Mr. Burch's intelligence," said Mrs. Winston. " To me he seems slow and stupid. If you have any anxiety whatever about the mill, do let Harry ride down and see about it. There is a lull now, and he can get back by bed-time."

"I am at your service," the young man remarked. " I don't profess to have any great amount of intelligence, but what I have is at your disposal."

The Colonel did not like this speech—he seldom liked any speech of Harry's, and answered rather haughtily :

"If I should ever happen to want your services, I will let you know."

The young man colored slightly, but made no response.

"Well, I do not believe that the rain is over yet," said Mrs. Winston, "and it seems very foolish to run any risks with the mill. The pond must be very full now, and if it begins to rain again there may be more danger than you apprehend. I wish you would let Harry go."

The Colonel was silent, and no one else seemed disposed to continue the conversation.

After they had arisen from the table, and the Colonel had departed to the library, Harry went out on the piazza, and looked at the sky. When he re-entered, he said, carelessly, " The rain is not over yet. There is a very ugly-looking cloud rising in the south-east. We shall probably have a thunder-storm. Listen ! that's thunder now,"

Yes, it was muttering far away in the distance. Jessie and her brother went into the back-parlor as usual.

"Play for me, Jessie," said the young man; and she again went to the piano, glad to drive away the painful thoughts that were oppressing her heart.

The storm came on slowly—a faint flash of lightning now and then, and a low rumble of thunder. Eleanor had carried off Lilian to the nursery to be put to bed, and the house was very still. Within an hour, the rain began to fall again—the storm was gathering force. Soon blinding sheets of water descended. The wind arose and drove it violently against the house, and the crash of thunder overhead became more and more terrific.

At bed-time, the brother and sister went upstairs, kissing each other in silence at the head of the steps. On entering her room, Jessie threw off her dress, and put on a wrapper; then, seating herself in front of the fire, she began to read. She knew that she would not be able to sleep, if she went to bed; a strange, restless feeling possessed her. The wind was now blowing a perfect gale, and peal after peal of thunder rent the air. This continued for an hour or two. It seemed even longer to Jessie as she sat in the loneliness of her room.

Suddenly she heard a soft step on the stairs. She listened intently. Some one went to Harry's room and knocked. The knock was repeated several times before he was aroused. Jessie moved quietly to her own door, and, opening it, listened almost breathless. Yes, it was Eleanor, and the girl guessed her mission!

Eleanor was standing motionless at the end of the upper hall, waiting to speak to Harry. "Yes, in a minute," he called from his room.

Soon he came to the door and opened it. He had

been asleep, and now was only half dressed, and looked wild and tumbled. " What is it, Eleanor ? " he asked.

" Harry dear," she said, " I am so sorry to disturb you, but do you think you could get to the mill in this awful storm? The Colonel is half crazy—he is sure everything will be swept away, if the rain continues much longer. It seems terrible to think of your going out, but you know, dear, we would be utterly ruined if anything were to happen to the mill."

" I understand," said the young man ; " yes, I think I can get there—I'll try anyway. I will put on my clothes and be down in a minute. Get the lantern for me, please, and a rubber coat—mine is in the hall-closet downstairs. There is no time to be lost." He closed the door and Eleanor descended the steps. When, at the end of a few moments, he came out in the hall, Jessie sprang forward to meet him.

" Oh ! Harry, please don't go ! " she said, in a beseeching tone ; " it is an awful night—I am sure something dreadful will happen to you, dear."

He looked at her with a flash of determination in his eyes,—" Eleanor has asked me to go, and I am going," he said ; " it is not much that I can do for her, and she has done a great deal for me."

" But, Harry, darling, you are risking your life. Please, don't go."

" My life is not worth much," he answered ; " it is only fit for a bad job like this." And again his eyes gleamed with a fierce purpose.

Jessie's face was ghastly white as she turned it up to her brother's and implored him. " Harry, *don't go!* The Colonel refused your offer at supper-time,—it is not fair to send you now. Only listen to the thunder ! and the rain is fearful ! Don't go, Harry ! " And she hung upon his arm.

He bent down and kissed her. "Good-bye. Kiss Lilian for me and don't let her forget me," he whispered.

"Oh! Harry! Only listen to the storm—don't go! *don't go,* darling."

Gently he loosened her hold upon him.

"I must, Jessie," he said, and hurried down the steps.

Eleanor met him and gave him the lantern, and helped him put on the rubber boots and coat. "Come back as soon as you can," she said.

"I will. Now go to bed—I'll do all I can, you may be sure." He opened the outside door; a blinding gust of wind and rain blew in. He staggered for a moment, but, grasping the lantern firmly and gathering his coat around him, he closed the door and was gone. Jessie heard it all. She went back softly to her room, threw herself upon her knees, burying her face in her hands. This, then, was the end. She had not thought that it was so near at hand.

On leaving the house, Harry Holcombe went immediately to the stable and saddled his horse. "Come, Dandy, we are in for it now," he said, as he mounted and dashed off in the blinding rain; he held his lantern far above his head, for the darkness was intense. Down the red lane he plunged. He must go to the Quarter and get Mose to accompany him. Mose was a powerful negro, almost a giant in size and strength; he had always had the care of the mill until a few months ago, when the Colonel had displaced him on account of some suspicion of dishonesty. For a while, Harry had overlooked him, but the young man had not found the business at all to his mind, and had thrown it up. He and the negro were much attached to each other, and he knew that Mose would follow him through thunder and tempest.

The brook over which he had helped Lilian on that day, so long ago, was now raging wildly across the lane. It had swept away the log that had served for a bridge, torn up the fences, and spread havoc all around.

The young man buried his spurs into the dripping flanks of the horse and plunged in; after a desperate struggle of ten or fifteen minutes, the panting animal landed his rider on the opposite bank, and on they dashed again. When he reached the Quarter, Harry pulled up in front of Mose's cabin, and kicked with all his might against the door, shouting at the top of his voice,

"Mose! Mose! wake up!"

In a few moments, the negro was at the door.

"De Lord hab marcy 'pon me! What is de matter, Marse Harry?" he exclaimed.

"Put on your clothes this minute, and come with me to the mill!"

"De gracious Lord! I don't want to go out in dis storm," said the negro, rolling his eyes until nothing but the whites could be seen.

"I don't care whether you want to go or not; you are going. Do you suppose I like it any better than you do? Come, you've got a mule, haven't you?"

Mose hesitated, reluctant to confess that he owned such a piece of property.

"Yes, dar in dat out-house. I'se comin', Marse Harry." And he disappeared in his cabin. When he came out he was enveloped in an old rubber blanket with a hole in the middle, through which his great woolly head was thrust.

"That will do," said Harry; "now get your mule, quick as a flash of lightning."

The negro obeyed, and in a few minutes the two were moving along rapidly in the darkness.

The storm grew wilder and wilder every moment; the wind went rushing through the trees, snapping off the branches and hurling them madly in every direction. The glare of lightning and crash of thunder was almost continuous.

"Marse Harry," said the negro, "I do declar' dat dis is jes' awful. Did ole marster send you?——"

"That's none of your business," the young man answered, "we've got to save that mill if possible."

"I'se mighty fear'd dat de bridge is gone by dis time; ef dat's de case, we can't never git cross dat creek —'tain't no use to try."

"We'll try for all that," was the answer; "you can do what I can do, and I am determined to save that mill in spite of all the devils out to-night."

Soon they heard the roar of the dam above the noise of the tempest, and Mose exclaimed:

"Well, de mill ain't gone yet, nohow, case I hears de water fallin' over de dam. Marse Harry, 'tain't my opinion dat Ole Burch knows anything 't all 'bout managin' dat mill 'cept de grindin' of de corn. He ain't got much sense anyways."

Harry made no response to these remarks, but rode on in silence. When the creek was reached, he held his lantern aloft and uttered an exclamation of relief. The bridge was still standing, though the water was rushing on both sides of the rustic structure, far out of the natural banks of the creek. The riders both dashed boldly in; the water was not very deep nor the current strong, and the good animals bore them safely across, and then scrambled up the muddy slope to the miller's house. There was not a sign of life to be seen anywhere—no light within the rude dwelling; the stupid old miller was in bed and asleep, unmindful of the danger that threatened his home and family. The raging storm, the rising water, death and destruction, were not even visions of unconscious slumber. Harry felt a sentiment of pity and disgust for the low nature that could sleep in the midst of such awful surroundings. He kicked loudly against the house, and called out until hoarse, but it was long before he could arouse Old Burch.

"He mus' be dead!" exclaimed Mose, more than once, before a frowsy head was finally thrust through the half-open door, and a voice demanded:

"What under hell is the matter?"

"Get out of that house this minute, you confounded old sinner," shouted Harry; "the pond is rising an inch a minute; for heaven's sake come and help us, or everything will be washed away. How under the sun could you go to bed such a night as this? Haven't you sense enough to know that the mill is in danger, and your old carcass, too? Come, right away! Have you opened a single one of the gates?"

The old man looked dazed, and confessed that he had not. He had retired to rest before the storm began, and had been sleeping so soundly that he had heard nothing.

"Have you got any brandy in there?" asked Harry.

"Not a drop," was the reply.

"Well, have your wife get right up and make us some strong coffee; we are wet and cold, and tired."

The three men were soon in the mill at work over the gates. The water of the pond dashed with such violence against the sides of the building that it swayed back and forth with a terrible warning motion. They scarcely hoped to save it; the water was already two feet deep on the lower floor. They found the gates harder to move than they had anticipated, for the flood-trash had gathered in a heap in front of them, and the current was swift and strong against them. At length, Mose, the great brawny negro, by means of his ponderous strength, succeeded in raising three of them, and the water dashed madly through, relieving the immense pressure against the sides of the mill-house. They gave themselves no rest, even when this was accomplished with crowbars and beams they worked on for another half-hour, until two other gates were raised. The three men were utterly exhausted by this time, and Harry sent Burch for the coffee, which they all drank with eagerness, finding themselves warmed and refreshed by the smoking beverage.

The storm had now begun to abate; the wind had fallen, and the thunder was rolling away in the distance, proclaiming that the battle was ended and the forces withdrawn; the rain was falling with a soft patter as if its strength was spent. Harry threw himself down upon a high pile of grain bags, out of reach of the water, which had now almost disappeared from the floor of the building. He was very tired, and quite ready to rest a while, and thought of his good bed at home and heaps of soft blankets with a longing heart. Mose approached his young master and lay down quietly at his feet.

"Well, old fellow, this hasn't been a bad night's work, has it?" asked Harry, slapping the negro on the back. Despite the difference in color, there was a pleasant *camaraderie* between them, and each had great respect for the good qualities of the other.

Mose laughed and said, "Marse Harry, I tell you what, you'se got a heap o' grit. I'd never hab come froo dem dark woods an' cross dat yonder creek, ef you hadn' bin wid me. To tell you de truf, I don't like to go out sich nights as dis. I'd a heap radder be at home in bed, kivered up warm."

"Is that so?" asked Harry with a laugh. "Now, Mose, I thought you were a very brave fellow—ready for anything. I brought you along purposely to take care of me. After all, it wasn't much worse than a 'possum hunt."

"Bless de good Lord, Marse Harry, you donno what you'se talkin' 'bout; a possum hunt is jes' fun, an' dere sartinly wasn't much fun 'bout dat ride—'twas a rale tarnation ride."

"Well, it wasn't very lively, that's the truth, Mose, and I'm glad it is over. I wish I was back again at home in bed. Go, bring us a little more coffee, Burch, and then I'll start."

"Why, Marse Harry, you isn't gwine to start back 'fore day, is you?" asked the negro, rolling his eyes with an expression of alarm and horror.

"I am that," said the young man; "the Colonel will want to know that everything is all right, and there is no use staying here now. You can remain and attend to things—you understand the business thoroughly. You can let the water run off till day, perhaps; then you had better close the gates. You don't want the pond to get too low, you know."

"Yes, sar," replied Mose, "I knows all 'bout it, and I'll tend to it all right. Fur my part, I'se glad to stay here. I thinks you had better stay, too, Marse Harry."

"No, I'm wet and cold, and I had better get home as soon as possible. I'm not as tough as you are, Mose, and this night's work may cost me a spell of sickness. I feel as if I had a chill now."

"You'd better go to old Burch's house and warm

yourself, Marse Harry, an' git some dry clothes," said the negro.

The young man laughed. " I hardly think his clothes would fit me, and I'm sure I would not like to try them. And I don't feel like invading his private sanctum. No, I had better go back home ; the storm is over."

By this time the rain had entirely ceased. Harry went to the door and looked out. Yes, the clouds were breaking away in the west, and a few pale stars were shining dimly through their ragged edges. He pulled out his watch and looked at it. "Three o'clock," he said ; " why, I shall have time to get back home and have a good nap before breakfast."

" I declar', 'fore de Lord, I wouldn't go ef I was you," said the negro ; " dat creek must be a sight higher dan 'twas 'fore we crossed it, Marse Harry. We'se let off a heap o' water from out'n dis mill-pond. I wish you wouldn't go, Marse Harry. 'Tain't safe, 'cordin' to my 'pinion."

" Pshaw! the water has run off by this time. The bridge is still standing—I can see the white railing. Besides, Dandy can swim like a fish."

Just at this moment, Burch brought the hot coffee, and Harry drank several cups of it. " I wish to goodness you had some whiskey, Burch," he said ; " are you sure you cannot find a drop in your house ? Here, I will pay you well for it," and he put his hand into his pocket and drew out some shining quarters.

The man shook his head. " Not a darned drop ! " he replied ; "I drank the very last glass just now," and he laughed.

"You confounded old cheat!" exclaimed Harry. " If you had only let me have it, I might have been saved from this chill that is on me. Go to the devil this minute."

The man laughed as he turned away, and Mose, too, chuckled at the clever trick. "I thought you asked for brandy," said Burch; "I ain't had none of that truck in my house for many a year."

"You know well enough what I meant," replied Harry; "you are a confounded brute, not fit to live. Get out of my sight!"

In spite of the ague that had seized him, he felt happy and elated to have accomplished the task that Eleanor had given him. It would be good news to carry back to her that he had saved the mill. He was not utterly good-for-nothing; there were times when his courage and determination came in "pretty handy," as the negroes say. Perhaps Alice Brooks might hear of what he had done, and feel a pang of regret that she had cast away his love so coldly. These thoughts filled his heart.

"Go and bring my horse immediately, Mose," he said, staggering to his feet.

The negro obeyed; but when he saw his young master mount into the saddle, he gave utterance to another protest.

"Marse Harry, I wish you wouldn't go. It's mos' day now, an' I declar', 'fore God, I don't think you'se fitten to swim dat creek." Harry laughed in his usual light way.

"I've done worse things than that, Mose, and I'll do them again. Good-bye, I'll see you in the morning. You shall be well paid, old fellow, for this night's job, if I have to bankrupt myself to meet the claim."

"I'se not de least bit fear'd 'bout dat; you'se always a gentleman, Marse Harry. Nobody knows dat better'n I do." Mose stood and watched him until he disappeared in the darkness.

CHAPTER XXVI.

THE day dawned gray and cold and cheerless. Jessie Holcombe awaked from her troubled sleep with a deep feeling of utter wretchedness. She looked at the clock —it was late—almost breakfast-time. She hurriedly threw on a dressing-gown, and went to Harry's door, and rapped several times; there was no answer, and she softly turned the bolt, hoping to find him in bed and asleep. He was not there; everything was just as he had left it the night before, and she smiled sadly at the signs of his carelessness all around. With a sickening sense of loss, she returned to her room and finished dressing. As the last garment was hastily put on, she heard the breakfast-bell ringing in the distance. It died away like an echo. The house was unnaturally still; not even from the nursery, where the baby and Lilian were accustomed to noisy romps every morning, did there come the faintest sound of life.

When Jessie entered the dining-room, the Colonel and Eleanor were both already there, looking much as usual; a bright fire was burning on the hearth, and the girl approached it with a feeling of relief. The flames went roaring and crackling up the chimney, like a lively household god whose presence is potent to dispel all gloomy forebodings.

"Well, good-morning, Jessie," said the Colonel, "you are a late bird, it seems to me. I have been up ever so long; I have been down to the mill and everything is all right—that is, as far as I could judge. The water was up tremendously high last night; I could plainly see the line on the house, but the gates had been opened and the pond was well down. I did not attempt to cross the bridge, for the water is very high on this side of it. It has torn away the banks for fifty feet at least, and the whole force of the current is sweeping across the road. I'm glad of it, for the bridge is safe, and I sha'n't have to rebuild that. A few wagon-loads of dirt will repair the bank. I'm a good deal better off this morning than I expected to be last night at bed-time. I was sure that the mill would go. If it had gone, it would be all over with us, Eleanor. It is just as much as I can do to keep my head above the water now. I feel immensely relieved."

"Has Harry returned yet?" asked the girl.

"No, not yet; he probably stayed to breakfast at the miller's; he must have been tired out. Reuben told me that he stopped at the Quarter last night, and got Mose and took him along. Mose wasn't back either, when Reuben left the Quarter. I suppose we shall have a full report from Harry and Mose both in the course of an hour or two. It may be even longer than that before they can get across the creek."

When the meal was ended, Jessie went to her room and seated herself at the window which overlooked the long avenue. Her heart was still sick and heavy. She took up the dainty heap of Eleanor's shawl and tried to find some interest in the delicate crochet-work, but all in vain; her eyes wandered from the white meshes. She was looking and waiting for the gallant young horseman who had so often come galloping up the road to Redbank.

The morning wore slowly away. The sun had come out at last, and the vapor was lazily ascending from the damp earth to join the great masses of gray clouds that floated overhead. Jessie was growing more and more impatient every moment. She felt that she must go down and inquire if any news had come, and was folding up her work, when Lizzie glided into the room with a frightened expression upon her face.

"What is the matter, Lizzie?" exclaimed Jessie with white, dry lips; "you look as if something had happened. Tell me this minute; don't you see I cannot wait."

The girl hesitated, and then said: "Uncle Mose is down-stairs in de liberry wid ole Marster, an' I'se bin listenin' at de door. I'se afear'd dat something has happened to Marse Harry, Miss Jessie. Mose, he says, dat arter dey had saved de mill, Marse Harry, he 'sisted on comin' right back home to tell you all, and Mose, he's a fear'd that Marse Harry is drowned."

Jessie Holcombe gave a piteous groan, and buried her face in her hands. The negro girl stood beside her young mistress, silent and motionless. She had the fine instinct of her race, and knew that it was useless to speak another word, or offer any sympathy; she knew also that her presence was a kind of mute comfort, so she did not withdraw. After a while, Jessie got up, and slowly went downstairs to the library; but there was nothing more to learn.

The Colonel and Eleanor were both there; they had already heard the tale of Mose to the very end, but the negro repeated it all to the young lady, telling every-thing with vivid effect in his homely way, from the moment he had been aroused by the kick of Marse Harry against his door, to the time when he had held Dandy by the bridle, and seen the young man mount and ride away in the darkness. That was enough. Who could not guess the dreadful sequel?

With effort Jessie found her way back to her room, and lay down upon the bed. She heard the Colonel in his high sharp voice giving orders to the group of negro men who had collected in the yard, and she knew well that they were going out to begin the search. She heard the old spring-wagon rattle down the avenue. A dull pain seized her—head-ache and heart-ache in one; but she could not weep a single tear.

At dinner-time, Lizzie brought her a cup of strong coffee, which she tried to drink in response to the mute entreaties of the maid. More than once during the afternoon she fell into a troubled sleep, and almost immediately awoke with a violent start. Would the long hours of this awful day never, never pass?

It was almost night when she heard the sound of wheels and voices at the front door. It was not necessary to arise, and go downstairs, and ask questions; she knew perfectly well that they had found his body, and were bringing him home. Yes, they were laying him out in the parlor, and busy feet were moving here and there over the house. They would all try to make it comfortable for him now—even the Colonel. In the midst of her bitter anguish, she felt a joy and pride in what her brother had done. It was a noble thing to ride out at midnight in the wild storm, and save the tottering mill, and, perhaps, the miller and his family, too; and these words of our Saviour came into her mind, "Greater love hath no man than this, that a man lay down his life for his friends." If there were indeed merit in such love, Harry might wear the white robe and the crown. At this thought, the tears began to flow softly down her cheeks, and peace and comfort came to her broken heart.

Another hour or two passed, when she heard the knob of her door gently turn. A little figure glided in, and coming close up to the bed, whispered faintly, "Aunty, are you asleep?"

"No, darling," she answered, "what is it?"

"May I get up beside you?"

"Yes, dear."

The child climbed on the bed, and nestled up to her. The little hands were very cold, and the breath came in quick gasps like sobs. Jessie drew the blanket over the little form, and clasped it to her own heart. "What is it, darling?" she asked more than once, but Lilian gave no answer. It was not strange that she was mute and cold—she had seen them bring him into the house, had looked upon his white face, and knew that it was her Uncle Hal. No one was thinking of her, and she had stood at the window and watched it all. She had heard them whisper that he was dead, and now her little heart was breaking. She knew what it was to be dead, for she had seen her little sister years ago lying still and white in a coffin, and they had covered her up in the ground; she knew exactly where the little mound was in the corner of the garden; she had often looked at it with a strange awe. She had waited at first for the baby sister to come back and play with her again. This, then, was what Uncle Hal meant yesterday when he had said that he was going away, and might never return any more. Again and again the child shivered from head to foot, and violent sobs convulsed her delicate form.

"What is it, darling? What is it?" Jessie asked, but no response came.

Lilian only nestled closer and closer up to the young girl's heart. And so the hours passed by, and, at last, they fell asleep in each other's arms.

The next morning when Jessie awoke, she felt calm and strong, and equal to the burden that had fallen upon her. The grand words of the poet were in her heart and on her lips:

> "But, peace : I must not quarrel with the will
> Of higher dispensation, which herein
> Haply had ends above my reach to know."

The young life that had gone out so suddenly had, in its way, been noble and joyous, and worthy to be rekindled in some other sphere.

Who could tell how high it had already soared above the stars? How vain and presumptuous it is for us to hold the scales and try to weigh out human merit! The heroic deed may flash from some despised and unknown source. We little know the latent force in human souls; then let us lay our fingers on fault-finding lips and wait the end before we call any man great, or good, or happy.

The day was clear and beautiful, and the young girl stood at the open window and drank in great draughts of the sweet spring air. The world was too lovely for grief; death seemed to be something belonging to its sublime order, something to be accepted with faith, like the darkness of night; something which would be understood in the fulness of time. The more Jessie thought of Harry's death, the more she schooled herself to bear it with calmness and resignation. It was surely for the best, since it had terminated a career which might have moved onward into deeper suffering. His was an untamed nature, which would always have fretted itself against restraint and the severe bondage of labor. He had arrayed himself with proud defiance against the fiat of nature: "In the sweat of thy face shalt thou eat bread."

Jessie dreaded to meet the Colonel and Eleanor, and lingered as long as possible beside the open window; but when she descended they greeted her tenderly, each one giving her a good-morning kiss. The Colonel was white and subdued, and drank his coffee in silence; Eleanor looked old and gray, and wore an expression of despair that pierced Jessie to the soul.

After breakfast, as the girl arose to leave the room, Eleanor reached out her hand and said, "Jessie, don't go upstairs again, please; stay with me, darling, I want to talk to you. I feel so miserable that I must have you near me, or my heart will break."

They went together into the back-parlor, and sat down, side by side.

"Jessie," said Eleanor, "I shall never, never forgive myself. I sent him out in the storm—his death is my work—I have killed my brother! It is no use to deny it—I am a guilty murderer."

Her eyes were full of unutterable agony as she slowly spoke these words.

"I heard you, dear, entreat him not to go; one word from me would have sent him back to bed and sleep, and I would not speak it. I am amazed now at my own hard-hearted cruelty."

Jessie put her arm lovingly around her sister. "Well, dear, it is all over now and cannot be helped. You must not grieve over him with this sting of remorse in your heart."

"I cannot help it, dear child. My whole life is made up of mistakes, and this is the most terrible one of all. I would be glad to die this moment, if I could only undo the work of that night, and have him back with us again. I never knew before how well I loved him. There was so much that was good and noble in him.—I always felt it, and I kept hoping that the time would come when some kind of congenial work would present itself. He was not lacking in energy,—it was a purpose that he wanted, a noble aim in life. I wish that Alice Brooks had consented to marry him; she might have made a man of him; but I suppose I have no right to blame her for preferring her cousin. Oh! life is so hard."

"Eleanor," said Jessie in a sweet, solemn tone, "you find it hard, because you have no faith. If you would only look up out of the darkness into the light!"

"Where is the light?" she asked, helplessly; "I cannot see it dear."

"If we would live aright, Eleanor, we must believe in the loving Father, who is guiding us. When we place our hand in His, like little children, we can walk in safety, but not till then."

"But I cannot find His hand, it does not reach down to me."

"Yes, it does, dear, perhaps you will find it after awhile."

"Perhaps I shall," she said in a faint voice; "all these sorrows must be sent for some purpose. I have been so proud and wilful in the past, perhaps I needed the discipline. My spirit is utterly broken now."

Jessie could not reply; she was weeping softly.

After a few moments, Eleanor continued: "Jessie, the Colonel feels very badly about it—I have never seen him so remorseful before—so full of self-reproach and regret. You must not be too hard on him, dear."

"I do not mean to be hard on any one," said the young girl, "you misunderstand me if you think that there is any bitterness whatever in my heart against either you or him. You could not foresee the disaster, nor could he, when he started on his journey back. Death comes to all. Harry must have died sometime as did Richard and father and mother. This was the appointed time and way. I should be miserable, if I felt otherwise. I am glad that it was bravely and nobly done. Ever since I can remember, Eleanor, I have felt anxious about him. There was a dashing recklessness in his nature that always threatened some tragic end. He did not value his life. My heart aches with a sense of loss, for I loved him truly, and shall miss him more than I can bear to think of, but I have no anger against you or the Colonel. I know that Harry was glad to do something for you, so you must not grieve for him in this hopeless way."

"Jessie, you are a noble girl," said Eleanor, clasping her sister's hand in both of her own. "Your words have given me comfort. I will try to look up and take courage and be strong. I will lie down here on the sofa and rest awhile; I could not sleep last night, and to-day I feel so tired and ill that I cannot sit up any longer."

Jessie arranged the pillows for her, and laid a warm blanket over her; then she herself lay back and rested in the great rocking-chair in which Harry had sat with Lilian that rainy day. Feet were moving about softly in the next room where his body lay, and voices were talking in subdued tones.

Jessie knew that the negro women had come from the Quarter to see him. The door was partially open, and she heard what they were saying to each other.

"Well, I never did have anything tuck de bref out'n my body as dis has," said Aunt Lucy; "I tell you

I could scarcely git up here to de house, yet I jes' had to come. Marse Harry, he allus was kin' an' good to me an' Reuben. When Reuben cut his foot so bad las' year, 'twas Marse Harry dat tended to it, day arter day, fur nigh on to a month, a-washin' it, an' bindin' it up jes, as handy as a woman."

" Yes, he was mighty good when dar was trouble round," said Rena. " When de baby got burnt up, he was de fust one to git to de house, and he try his best to keep me quite, an' hol' me back, when I catch up de corpse an' run up here to mistis."

" He fotched me quinine his own se'f, when I was sick in de beginnin' o' las' summer," said Rose; " an' he come right up to de bed an' made me take it, too, 'case he knowed I'd throw it away soon as he was gone, ef he didn't make me swallow it 'fore his very eyes."

"Yes, he had a mighty good heart, even ef he did get drunk sometimes," said Aunt Lucy, shaking her head and sighing; "he was better to everybody else den he was to hissef. He never 'peared to care much fur hissef, somehow. When I used to talk to him 'bout his way o' handlin' a gun, he'd allus say, ' Well, Aunt Lucy, I'se not much account no way—mighty few folks would grieve over me, ef I did happen to blow my brains out some day.' Dem was jes' his words, 'fore de Lord. Well, I know dere's a good many a-grievin' over him on dis plantation to-day. I'se never seen old marster so quiet in all my born days."

" I hope he's in de lan' o' promise now," said Aunt Nancy, with a doubtful groan and a solemn shake of the head. They all groaned in chorus. Presently they shuffled out, and went off together down the red lane to the Quarter. Their words had carried comfort to Jessie's sad heart, for she loved to think of her brother as full of sympathy for the poor and afflicted. This was the active virtue on which Christ had himself pronounced the blessing of eternal life. She was not orthodox—this simple Southern maiden. To her intelligence it seemed better to love one's neighbor and help him in this world than to hold fast to the doctrine of eternal damnation in the next.

Late that afternoon, Jessie went softly into the room where her brother lay. She had not dared to trust herself to look upon him until now. No one had thought to close the blinds, and the pale evening light fell upon the shrouded form. She approached the bier, and drew aside the sheet that covered him from sight. Cold, still, and beautiful he lay, with a smile of perfect peace upon his lips.

> "His palms were folded on his breast,
> There was no other thing expressed
> But long disquiet merged in rest."

"O Harry! Harry! my brother! my brother! where are you now?" she sobbed in the bitterness of her grief. "Are all the questions answered for you, dear? Is life better than you thought?—And God more merciful?"

The next day Mr. and Mrs. Hunter arrived, and many other friends from the city and all the surrounding country. Far and wide his gallant deed was known, and every one now had a kind word for Harry Holcombe. We always delight to honor one when dead, however we may regard him when living. It is a trait of human nature, not altogether commendable. A little of the kindness expended on the lifeless remains would, perhaps, have warmed the heart before it ceased to beat, and have made the world a fairer dwelling-place.

A grave had been dug for him in a quiet corner of the beautiful cemetery of the city. There they laid him to rest, and there we will leave him to his long sleep. Before many months had passed a slender cross of white marble marked the spot, and on it these words were deeply cut:

"Greater love hath no man than this, that a man lay down his life for his friends."

CHAPTER XXVII.

There was one member of the family at Redbank upon whom the death of Harry had fallen with crushing weight—this was Lilian. Too young to realize his faults or to criticise his actions, she had only felt the charm of his gay and affectionate nature.

She had returned his playful fondness with a passionate admiration and love which was rooted in the very depths of her being. During those first sad days she had been very quiet and composed, indulging in no sobs nor tears. During the preparations for the burial, during the funeral, and the last solemn rite, when " dust is given back to dust," she had moved around like one dazed or stunned. No one but Jessie guessed the agony through which the young soul was passing. Night after night, the small, white-robed figure appeared beside the young girl's bed, and begged to be taken in ; night after night, the cold little hands were clasped around her neck, and the dry little lips were pressed to her cheek. Lilian was drooping like a blighted flower ; dark circles were settling around her eyes, and an insidious languor seemed to be slowly creeping over her. Often she would come and lay her head against Jessie's shoulder, and whisper : " Aunty, I am so tired ! " Then the girl would take her in her arms and talk with her, or read to her, or tell her stories. Jessie knew well that the little heart was aching, and she bravely laid aside her own grief to minister to the silent suffering of the child. It was well that it was so; otherwise she might herself have grown morbid and despairing over all the mysteries of life and death, for the pain of bereavement was not lessened day by day. From her soul the cry often went out—

"Oh! for the touch of a vanished hand,
And the sound of a voice that is still!"

There were moments when resignation forsook her, and she yearned unutterably for the bright presence that had departed forever. But now these feelings must be locked up out of sight; it was no time for selfish indulgence in the luxury of grief; another sweet young life was threatened, and every one was soon awake to the danger. Mrs. Winston, with an anxious heart, gave every leisure moment to her child; she took her in her arms and carried her from place to place during the busy morning hours, demanding assistance in the pantry, in the kitchen, in the garden, in the smoke-house, whenever there was anything that the little one could do. She had Reuben make a tiny garden for her, and plant it with flower-seeds; she had Rena bring the little chickens for her to look at and admire. Even the self-centred Colonel aroused himself to amuse this drooping child, whose step each day was growing feebler, and whose eyes were dim with unwept tears. He went to the city and bought playthings for her—and pets without number; now it was a bird, now a dog, and last of all, he bought a pony for her and took her with him to ride, reviving his old-time gallantry for her sweet sake. Lilian made no response whatever to these efforts; her thoughts seemed far away in some shadowy land, searching forever for the lost one. She never spoke the name of her Uncle Hal to any one, not even to Jessie when she nestled in her arms at night and patiently waited for sleep to come. The young girl wondered more and more at this, and felt that if she could once get the child to talk about Harry, relief would come from this unnatural listlessness and self-control. At length, one evening after supper, when they were in the back parlor, and Lilian was in her lap, while they rocked backwards and forwards in the dear old rocking-chair, and talked softly together, Jessie said, "Darling, wouldn't you like me to tell you something about Uncle Hal? You know he and I were little children together, and we used to play all kinds of funny games. Shall I tell you about them?"

There was a little shiver as if some sore spot had been touched, and then the whispered answer came, "Yes."

This was the beginning of many stories about the childhood of Jessie and her brother. Evening after evening, the girl patiently went over these tales, painting every scene with a careful hand, and trying hard to keep Lilian's interest well sustained. Soon the child began to ask questions and to fill in the little voids which the aunt's memory sometimes unconsciously made. Often the two indulged in a little soft laughter over the childish pranks of the brother and sister. With the quick eye of love, Jessie began to note a change for the better—a slowly awakening interest in other things, and an ever-increasing inclination to talk about Uncle Hal in a natural way, as if he were only absent for a few weeks, and would walk in upon them unexpectedly some day. The beautiful cool spring days favored this return to health. The warm weather seemed to delay its coming purposely to advance the recovery of this little child, whom every one watched with an anxious heart.

Something good came to each member of the family from this patient and unselfish devotion to Lilian. They grew more tender and considerate in manner—less self-absorbed, and less careless of the little blossoms that were blooming in the old home. Master Francis, who was growing into a stout, noisy boy, was given a place at the table and in the family gatherings. He soon learned to contribute his mite to the entertainment of the household. Eleanor grew daily in sweetness under this discipline of unselfish effort. The old despairing expression left her eyes. A holy peace seemed to be descending upon her troubled soul. She gave herself no time to spend in introspection—no time to brood over the mistakes of the past—no time to waste in vain regrets over ungathered fruit. The Colonel, too, was changed; he was gentler and kindlier to every one—even to the dogs. Before him was ever present that gallant act which had saved him from irretrievable loss—that gallant soul which he had so lightly valued because of some flaws upon its purity. Verily, in dying, one sometimes accomplishes the very thing in which one fails while living.

The glorious May days had come again, and the world was a marvel of beauty. One afternoon, when the leaves and flowers were dancing joyously in the fresh breeze, and the mocking-birds were filling the air with music, Lizzie put her head through the half-open door of Jessie's room and said—

"Miss Jessie, dere's a gentleman in the parlor wants to see you."

"Who is it, Lizzie?" asked the young lady.

"I dunno; Uncle Oliver, he tole me to tell you."

Before descending, Jessie glanced from the window,

and saw the gray horses of Judge Brooks standing at the front door.

"It is the Judge," she said to herself, smiling at the thought of seeing her old friend again.

The long agony through which she had been living had almost deadened the other feelings of her heart, and she did not now dread to meet her former lover, and face the dim shadow of a new relationship.

She glided quickly down the long staircase. As she entered the parlor, Waverley Brooks came forward to meet her.

She gave him her hand, and a faint color came into her cheeks. The young man was hardly prepared for the change in her appearance; the long black robe, the pure pale face, the large, sad eyes, told a tale of patient suffering, and he felt his heart beat with a quick throb of pity and love. He longed to take this delicate creature in his strong arms, and henceforth protect her from all the rough winds of heaven.

"Mr. Brooks," she said, "I am very glad to see you. I did not know you had returned. I saw those beautiful gray horses at the door, and expected to meet your father."

"And you are disappointed?" he asked, a slight shadow passing over his face.

"Shall I speak the truth?" she said, her color deepening under his intense gaze.

"Yes: the truth, the whole truth, and nothing but the truth."

"Well, yes; I am a little disappointed." And she smiled faintly, feeling how much easier it would be to face an interview with the father than with the son.

She had an uncomfortable sense of helplessness in the presence of Waverley Brooks; she knew that he mastered her with his clear gray eyes and determined will. Already she was fluttering strangely, and she could neither control the quick beating of her heart, nor the tide of color that it kept sending into her face.

"Am I always to stand in my father's shadow, Miss Holcombe?" he asked, with a touch of impatience in his tone.

"I thought you had just stepped out of it into the sunshine, Mr. Brooks," she replied, smiling at his annoyance. It placed her a little more at ease to see him on the verge of losing his temper. "Your journey North has been successful, I am sure."

"Why do you think so?"

"Because you have the indefinable air of success around you."

"Have I? Your eye is quick to read character, Miss Holcombe. Well, I will acknowledge to you that I have realized my most extravagant hopes. Your good wishes proved a powerful talisman."

"I imagine it was your determined efforts rather than my good wishes."

"Don't destroy that beautiful illusion, please; allow me to believe in something outside myself."

She felt vexed at the embarrassment that was again taking possession of her and tried in vain to shake it off. She did not dare to lift her eyes, and found no ready response to his words

"Miss Holcombe," said he, after a moment's pause, "may I offer you my deepest sympathy; I cannot tell you how grieved I am at the great sorrow that has come to you."

She raised her hand with that imploring gesture which she so often made, and said, hoarsely,

"Don't speak of it, please—I cannot bear it. I am

very grateful for your sympathy; we have received kind words from every one, but that cannot restore the lost."

He longed to say more—to tell her that her sorrow was his own—that he wished to help her bear it and all the other troubles of life, but a feeling akin to awe restrained him. How could he speak of love to this pure nun-like creature, whose grief seemed to make her sacred? The words died upon his lips, and the silence was becoming oppressive, when she said,—" Tell me about your journey North, and what you saw and enjoyed."

"Then you do feel a little interest in me?" he asked, a slight flush of pleasure coming into his face.

" How can you doubt it?"

" I have doubted it a great deal, and these doubts have made me very wretched, in spite of all other successes."

"Doubts generally make people wretched," she said, very simply, as if speaking of religious doubts; "it is much better to cast them to the wind and have faith."

"And will you let me have faith? Will you let me believe in the possibility of realizing my dearest wish?"

She felt the color warming and dyeing her face. "How can I guess what that may be?" she said, looking up at him, but her eyes immediately fell, and the blush on cheek and brow deepened.

"May I tell you?" he asked; "will you pardon me if I am too bold? I would not for the world offend you." Again the feeling of awe came over him as if he were treading on holy ground. She drooped her head in silence. He arose from his seat and approached her; unconsciously she also arose as if his visit were at an end, and nothing remained but to say good-bye. He reached out his hand and whispered softly, "Jessie, look up at me. You know that I love you."

She could not speak; her heart was full to overflowing. She extended her hand and laid it in his. He clasped it firmly for a moment, then drawing her very tenderly to his heart, he stooped, and kissed her again and again. They were silent for a little while then Waverley said, "Go and get your hat, Jessie, and we will drive."

She flitted away and soon returned, prepared to accompany him. He assisted her into the carriage, then, taking his seat beside her, he gave the command to the coachman.

"Not by the mill," she whispered, as they left the avenue. The horses turned into the opposite road, and trotted swiftly over the smooth white sand. Waverley Brooks held her little ungloved hand in his under the snowy afghan; that was enough for the present to content him.

As the horses dashed on, and the soft spring air fanned her cheek, Jessie Holcombe thought of that ride with the Judge so long ago. She remembered how hard it had been to resist his pleading—how lonely she had felt that day, how hungry for love, and how weary of the struggle of life. She shuddered to think that she might have been the wife of another—the wife of Waverley's father. Only her true heart and her strong sense of right, had saved her from such a fate. By failing to obey this deep womanly instinct, many a sweet maiden has lost forever the chance of entering the paradise of perfect love.

When they had returned home and were again in the parlor, he took the hand of Jessie in his, and said, "May I not now speak to Colonel Winston and your sister? I would like to tell them all about it and secure their approval."

"No, not yet, please let us wait a while, until I get a little used to it myself. It does not seem quite right for me to be so happy,"—and the tears came into her eyes. "Besides, I cannot think of leaving Eleanor and Lilian for a long time—they would miss me so. I must stay with them, and try to comfort them."

"Do you imagine that I shall listen to that argument, or be content to wait long? Jessie, you belong to me now. Do you realize that I shall determine some things for you?"

She looked at him with surprise.

"Perhaps I shall dispute that, if you are inclined to tyrannize."

"I shall not tyrannize, but you are mine now, and I shall take care of your health and happiness. I shall not allow you to sacrifice yourself for any one."

"Except for Mr. Waverley Brooks," she said, with a radiant smile, which he reflected.

"Except for Mr. Waverley Brooks. That is just how matters stand," he answered. "Your sister may have had claims upon you in the past, but they are now swallowed up—utterly devoured, by my own."

"I don't think that I am quite prepared to acknowledge that. Perhaps I have reserved a small amount of myself for private jurisdiction?"

"Not an ounce of flesh, not a drop of blood—you are wholly mine. Now, don't deny it, for it is so." He paused a moment, and clasped her hand more tightly in both of his own, before he added:

"I want to tell you another thing, Jessie—my mind is quite made up, I will not swerve an inch; it is this,— I must take you away from Redbank just as soon as possible; the place is full of sad memories for you—you are not strong; you are more shattered by all this sorrow than you realize. I wish that you would go with me to-day!" His voice was very tender and pleading.

"What do you mean?" she asked, amazed at so unreasonable a request.

"Go with me to my father's house, and stay until you are ready to be married. I cannot bear to leave you here!"

She shook her head. "You know it is impossible for me to grant such a request."

"Well, I cannot wait long—a very few weeks must satisfy you."

"But I cannot leave Eleanor," she answered entreatingly; "you do not know how much she needs me—her heart is almost broken."

"She has her husband and her children; she must find her comfort in them."

"I did not think that you could be so hard. I must reconsider the matter; it may be necessary to cancel the contract," she said, smiling faintly.

"You cannot," he replied, "you are mine; no power on earth nor in heaven shall take you from me."

"Hush! do not talk so. It is blasphemy," she whispered, almost frightened at the vehemence of his manner and tone.

"No, it is not blasphemy. Living or dead, Jessie, you will always be mine to love, honor, and cherish. Can you not measure your own love that way?"

"Yes, I think so."

"Jessie," he continued, softly, "I could love you

with the breadth of heaven betwixt us. During all these weeks, I have waited, waited, waited, because my father wished it and exacted a promise from me. He wanted to test my feelings for you, knowing that I had failed towards Alice. My love for you has grown stronger day by day, until it has become an all-consuming passion. I could not trust myself to say what might happen if you trifled with me."

"I have no intention of trifling with you; I do love you with all my heart," she said, simply, her sweet eyes confessing the fact as well as her sweet lips. "Since we have been parted I, too, have weighed my love for you, and I know that it fills my whole being. I could not live without you." She turned her face up to his, that he might read her whole soul and see that she had spoken truly.

"Thank you," he said, in a low tone. For a few moments they sat in silence. "It is very hard to leave you, Jessie, but I must go now," he said, at length. "I will see you again to-morrow, and every day until you are ready to follow me 'over the hills and far away.' I shall tell my father and Alice about our engagement to-night. And, Jessie, I want you to come to my father's house for a while, and make acquaintance with your future home and new relatives. They already know and love you, but this act of mine has made a little difference." Yes, she knew that well, and she did not wish to meet them just yet—these new relatives. She looked at him and shook her head.

"Not to please me?" he said; "surely you will do it for my sake?"

"I will think about it; indeed I cannot promise now. I wish you would give me a little time to get used to it all. It seems so strange that you should have such a claim upon me, such a power over me. Only a few months ago, I had not even seen you."

"Yes, it is strange," he answered, smiling at the sweet confusion of her face; "but the strangeness will soon wear off, when we are always together. Jessie, I shall be busy in the city the whole of next week, and I must have you with me. I shall not be able to drive out here every day, will you not come to my father's house."

"Oh, I cannot, I cannot! You must not ask me. The very thought of it makes me feel unhappy. I am not quite ready to meet those new relatives."

"But I shall be with you. Come, say that you will go, and do not keep me in suspense."

"I am truly sorry to detain you, but I cannot give you any promise now."

"Yes, I must have it before I go."

"I am afraid you are a little selfish," she whispered, softly.

"Yes; I confess that I am—every man is; do give me your consent before I go."

Jessie bowed her head silently. He could not know how much it cost her to give this tacit consent.

"And you will also promise to be married very soon?" he pleaded.

She did not reply, and he continued:

"Well, I shall be sure to have my way. As compensation for all this haste, I have a delightful surprise in store for you, when we are married."

"What is it?" she asked, quickly.

"You must wait," he replied, laughing at her eagerness; "perhaps curiosity may make you willing to hasten the happy event."

"I think not," she said.

"We will see. Good-bye—I must go now." And again he drew her to his heart, and kissed her upon brow, cheek, and lips.

She watched the gray horses drive away. Then she sat down quietly in the gathering darkness to think over her great happiness.

CHAPTER XXVIII.

WAVERLEY BROOKS came again the next afternoon, and the pleasant drive was repeated. On the third day, he insisted upon informing the Colonel and Mrs. Winston of the engagement between himself and Jessie. They were both exceedingly surprised at the announcement.

"I can hardly believe it!" exclaimed the Colonel. He just did save himself from adding, "I thought you were going to marry your cousin." However, instead of this unbecoming remark, he said, "Why, Mr. Brooks, it seems to me that you are hardly acquainted with Miss Holcombe. I am afraid you are acting too hastily. One ought to think a long time before getting married. It is rather a serious matter, you know."

The young gentleman smiled quietly. "I have been thinking of it almost steadily for about six months, Colonel. Isn't that long enough? The very first time I met Miss Holcombe, I made up my mind that she, and no other woman, was to be my wife."

"Well, I'm immensely surprised," again exclaimed the Colonel, almost whistling at the thought of all the queer unexpected things that do happen in this world. "Why, Mr. Brooks, I thought you were going to marry Miss Alice." To save his soul, the Colonel could not help uttering those words. In fact, he seemed entitled to some explanation from a gentleman who could so boldly disappoint public expectation and marry the wrong girl.

The young man coolly replied, " Yes, that was the general opinion, but I could not marry a lady who flatly and persistently refused me. Besides, after an absence of three years, I found my own affections cooled down to a cousinly temperature.

" In spite of your doubts, Colonel, I consider myself very well acquainted with Miss Holcombe. I saw a great deal of her last fall when she repeatedly visited my cousin at The Grove. I find that she suits me in every respect. I have asked her to marry me, and she has consented. We only await your approval and that of Mrs. Winston. My own relatives are perfectly satisfied with my choice."

" Well, Mr. Brooks," said the Colonel, " I have no right and no inclination to disapprove of your conduct, but, all the same, I'm immensely surprised."

" I'm glad to have surprised some one," the young man remarked ; " my own family have foreseen it for a long time, so they say. One does not wish to be perfectly transparent. I want the credit of a little self-control. I have always rather prided myself that I did not ' wear my heart upon my sleeve for daws to peck at.'"

" Well, I hope you are worthy of such a wife as Jessie Holcombe," said the Colonel ; " she is one of the sweetest women that God ever made."

"I am aware of that," replied the young man, " and I trust that I am not altogether undeserving of her love."

" I hardly know how we shall manage to live without Jessie," said Mrs. Winston, who had felt too surprised and grieved at the announcement of the engagement to utter a single word until now.

" That will be a great deal easier for you than it would be for me. I find her presence so essential to my happiness that I shall give her only a few weeks for possible regrets."

At this moment, Jessie entered the room. The Colonel had sent for her; he wanted confirmation from her own lips of this strange fact. He could not really believe that she was engaged to this young man, and contemplated leaving Redbank for another home. With a blushing face, she answered questions and received congratulations.

"Now, Mrs. Winston," said Waverly, "I have a rather obstinate young lady here to deal with, and I want to appeal to you. I will make a clear statement of some facts, and add an appendix of my wishes. First, for the facts : the summer is near at hand; Redbank is not altogether healthy during the hot season ; Jessie is far from strong, and needs a change of climate to restore her bloom. Now for the wishes ! I want to be married just as soon as possible, within two or three weeks—say the first of June. I want to take Jessie and give her a breath of mountain air before the summer comes. I would also like to have her go with me, after a few days, to my father's house, and remain there until the wedding. My aunt and cousin are both there, and I wish my future wife to live *en famille* with us all for awhile." This plan did not altogether please the future wife, but Waverley was determined to have his own way, and so he triumphed over all opposition.

It was impossible for him to understand Jessie's reluctance to meet the members of his family, and it was equally impossible for her to explain her feelings. She had an ill-defined conviction that they all felt more or less sore about this new departure. Then and there, she made up her mind that Waverley Brooks should never know anything about his father's attachment to her. This was her only mental reservation, and it cost her conscientious nature some few pangs; but she feared that it might permanently disturb the confidential relations of father and son. No one outside her own family had ever suspected the ardent admiration of the Judge for Miss Holcombe, and no one but Eleanor knew positively of his offer and its rejection.

When, a few days later, the carriage stopped at the door of the Judge's residence, and Jessie and Waverley alighted and ascended the broad steps, there was a painful quickening of the young girl's pulse. When she entered the great drawing-room, brilliant with light and color, upon the arm of her promised husband, she was conscious of an emotion of embarrassment and constraint. Mrs. Brooks, Alice, and the Judge awaited them, and Jessie fancied that the welcome of each one of them wanted some of the old cordiality. She did not wonder at it, but she was too delicately strung not to feel a pang of regret at having done anything to wound these three dear friends. Mrs. Brooks was far from satisfied with the new arrangement; she blamed Alice for coldness and Waverley for faithlessness, and rather suspected Jessie of a little feminine coquetry. The young gentleman had been too great a match for her to resign willingly the rightful claim of her daughter. She had never before in her life experienced so bitter a disappointment, and she had not sufficient tact to conceal it from the eyes of the world. With quick intuition, Jessie read the feelings of this lady as easily as if they had been reflected in a mirror.

The manner of Alice was also somewhat constrained, for she had suffered keenly from her mother's reproaches, she also had some sense of humiliation in the thought that the world would look upon her as a forsaken maiden. Besides all this, her heart was deeply wounded by the death of Harry Holcombe. She now realized that she had loved him well, and that no new affection could ever supplant the old. Life stretched before her like a melancholy waste, and her depression was apparent to all. The Judge suffered silently from the surrender of his most cherished hopes, but he was too strong and noble a man to bear any evidence of such suffering in face or manner. After the first greetings had been passed, Waverley stood in front of Judge Brooks, with Jessie on his arm, and said, "Well, father, you are satisfied with my choice, are you not?" He smiled as he put the question, but at heart he was very eager for his father's approval. The Judge looked at his new daughter for a few moments, and she felt the color come into her face.

"I think she will do, my son," he replied slowly, a glow of tenderness lighting his eyes; "she is tall enough for even such a great fellow as yourself, and her complexion and hair contrast well with yours. We will try to like her for your sake, and perhaps, in the course of time, we will discover that she has a little merit of her own. Are you sure that you like each other well enough to be married? You know marriage is a very serious matter."

"I think I like her," said the young man.

"And how is it with you, Jessie?" asked the Judge.

"I think I like him a little," replied the girl, feeling the warm color driving in waves over her face. "You know one cannot tell exactly until afterwards. He may not be as good as I think him. It is just possible that I may be deceived."

"Well," said the Judge, "I want you both to understand that, if you find out you have made a mistake, you need not come to me to get a divorce for you."

"Now, that is too bad," remarked Jessie, "we quite counted on you to help us, if we became dissatisfied. You are a great lawyer and a great judge, and are accustomed to manage such affairs successfully."

They were all smiling now.

"I wish at once to undeceive you, Miss Holcombe, if you are putting your trust in me. I shall not aid you in the least."

"Well, we understand that now," said Waverley, "and we promise not to trouble you in case of disaffection. Now, Jessie, tell me what you think of him," and the young man motioned towards his father. "Do you think you are going to like him, and get on well with him?"

She drew a long breath and exclaimed—"I am so thankful that he is not a mother-in-law! I shall try very hard not to quarrel with him."

"And what are you going to call him?" asked Waverley.

"*The Judge*, of course."

"No; that will provoke a quarrel immediately," said the elderly gentleman; "I will not be called *The Judge* in my own house; it is sufficiently annoying to have no other name outside of it. I wish a more respectful appellation from my son's wife."

"What could be more respectful than *The Judge*," Jessie replied; "it is almost an acknowledgment that you are the best and wisest judge in all the world. Surely such a distinction ought to satisfy you."

"No, it does not by any means."

"Then what must she call you?" asked Waverley;

"I have some little influence over her, and I will do my best to have her respect your wishes."

"Never mind now, I will give her a lesson after a while," said the Judge; "you had better go and prepare yourselves for dinner now. I see Harris hovering around as if impatient to make an important announcement."

When they were again in the drawing-room, Judge Brooks called Jessie to come and sit beside him. She obeyed, and he drew a piece of paper and a pencil from his pocket, and wrote down a word.

"Now spell that for me," he said, in a tone of authority. She began in a pretty, childish way to call the letters f-a-t-h-e-r.

"Now what does that spell?" he asked.

She looked up at him and shook her head, saying simply, "The word is too hard for me yet a while. You must wait until I am older."

"You do not know your lesson," he said, severely; "and, furthermore, I'm afraid that you are a very obstinate girl. You can go now, but to-morrow I shall expect you to do better."

She arose, and Waverley beckoned her to a seat beside him, taking her hand in his. Mrs. Brooks looked at the Judge and said, "Charles you are not a very old man, but do you know, I sometimes see signs of approaching dotage."

"Do you, Kate? Well, I'm very sorry."

Alice came and sat down near him. "Uncle Charles," she said, "it is a beautiful dotage. I like that playful mood in you better than any other. It is ever so much nicer than your wise mood, or your silent mood, or your gloomy mood, or your stern mood. You shall be just as doty as you please, you dear, darling old uncle."

He took her little hand in his, and carried it tenderly to his lips—" Thank you, my dear."

He loved this gentle niece—she had been always the nearest equivalent to a daughter that he had ever known.

Alice continued, " Uncle Charles, I know that you and Jessie are going to get on splendidly together, and you must never have a single regret." How little she guessed the heart-ache beneath that broad expanse of immaculate linen ! " Jessie," she called across the room, " I am so glad to have you in the family. It is a new element which will favor a better rearrangement and recomposition of the old elements. You will brighten up Uncle Charles—he has been awfully glum of late—now don't deny it! " and she stroked his hand tenderly. " Then you will keep mamma from nodding over her patchwork. She will not confess that she ever does really nod, but I assure you I have occasionally heard something very much like a little snore."

" Alice, my dear, will you please confine yourself to the truth when you undertake to report my doings," said the mother.

" And you will stimulate me, Jessie, to exert myself a little for the entertainment of others. I, for one, am willing to confess my sins. I have been lazy and good-for-nothing of late, and anybody but dear good Uncle Charles would have kicked me out of the house."

" I am glad you have such an excellent opinion of me, Alice," replied Jessie; "I will try not to disappoint your expectations, dear."

" But I haven't finished enumerating my expectations yet. Last of all, but by no means least, I trust you will take that unruly young gentleman in hand, and prevent him from being so unbearably cross."

"Heigh-ho!" exclaimed Waverley, "What is that you say? You cannot possibly refer to me; I was never cross in all my life. Don't believe her, Jessie; it is a libellous attack without foundation and without provocation."

"Alas! thou dost not know thyself, my cousin!" said Alice, laughing. "Why, only this morning I heard you storming furiously out in the hall, because you could not find your gloves. I wanted to be sure that it was really you, and not some escaped lunatic, so I opened the door softly and peeped out. Yes, there was no mistaking your identity;—you are not so small as to hide away from sight like a pin; there you were in all your monstrous height and breadth, raging and foaming at the mouth."

"For heaven's sake do have some slight regard for the truth, Alice!" cried the young man, turning somewhat red in the face; "you must have been dreaming or seeing visions. For a long time I have suspected you of having optical illusions,—now I'm sure of it."

"No, she was not dreaming, nor having optical illusions either," said Mrs. Brooks, laughing at Waverley's discomfiture; "you were positively and dangerously cross. I trembled for Harris's head. And it was all because you could not start off to Redbank as soon as you desired. My dear sir, your temper has not been angelic of late, and we hope that Jessie will take you in hand."

Jessie shook her head. "I am afraid that my influence is not going to prove very strong. He often shows an inclination to have his own way, and I can do nothing with him."

"Well," remarked the Judge, "it is said that every man is born again when he gets married. Now, Jessie, I want you to see that Waverley is born right this time —with all proper tendencies and impulses. Discipline him freely during his childhood, and take a little of the wilfulness out of him. I turn him over to you, my dear."

"I will try my best," she replied, "but I know he will be difficult to manage."

"I daresay I shall be benefited by the discipline of living with her," Waverley coolly remarked. "They say that women are very hard to get along with."

"Now, you invented that saying, Waverley," exclaimed Alice; "nobody ever said such a thing but yourself."

The young man pretended to ignore this accusation and continued: "They say that women require a lot of petting and caressing, and coaxing and humoring, otherwise they retire into a little den all their own and pout! You know that is a well-established historical fact, Alice. And, furthermore, I myself have seen you through the key-hole of your den, I have seen you pouting until your cheeks looked like the old pictures of Boreas."

"Well, Waverley Brooks, I would never have suspected you of peeping through a key-hole; I am thoroughly shocked!" said Alice.

"Oh! it was when I was a very small boy; I have outgrown such habits now; but, all the same, I believe in pouting, and I daresay Jessie is a perfect mistress of the accomplishment. I do not want to make the mistake of believing her better than the rest of the sex. It is well to begin with a low opinion, and gradually have it improve than to reverse the order."

"Jessie, I would not allow him to talk so disrespectfully about me, if I were in your place," said Alice.

"I cannot help it, dear," replied Jessie, "he will do as he pleases."

"Yes, I am going to carry her right off this very minute," said Waverley. "You are all beginning to undermine my authority. Come, Jessie, I want you to go upstairs and see my own special sitting-room and belongings."

"Prepare yourself for a disappointment, young gentleman!" exclaimed Alice, with a wicked little laugh; "Jessie has already been in that room, and inspected all your pet possessions."

"When, I would like to know?" he asked, somewhat annoyed.

"On the very day you left for New York, last February—the day after Nettie Hunter's wedding. Jessie called on me, and I was wicked enough to take her into your precious sanctum. How we did go round that room, and talk about you! We commented very freely on your extravagance, your effeminate tastes, and fondness for Oriental luxury; also your passion for rowing by moonlight, and having young ladies play on the guitar and sing to you, in order to make the exercise less laborious."

Waverley looked at Jessie with a crestfallen air, and asked, "Is that true, Jessie? I require confirmation of every statement Alice makes."

"I'm afraid it is true, Waverley," said his *fiancée*; "but, never mind, I shall enjoy seeing it again, with you as a guide. I daresay Alice gave me much false information which you will be able to correct."

"Thank you both for your high opinion of me," exclaimed Alice, trying to suppress her inclination to laugh.

"Well, come, Jessie," said the young man, "I shall lose my temper, if I stay any longer in the room with that provoking young female," nodding towards his cousin. When they entered the sanctum, which was now brilliantly lighted, Waverley turned and asked, "How do you like it, Jessie?"

"I think it is the most beautiful room that I have ever seen."

"Do you, indeed? Now, that is flattering!"

"Yes; but I see you have made some changes, and the gaslight makes a difference. It does not look like the same room that I saw with Alice, so you need not feel vexed that I have already seen it."

"Is it less beautiful?" he asked.

"No, it is far more beautiful." She was silent for a moment, then added, "And your presence gives it a glory that it did not have before."

"Thank you," he said, gazing into her eyes with a look that was full of tenderness and love; "I am glad to have you feel that my presence makes a difference. Yours would glorify a desert for me."

"Thank you; but, please don't be extravagant. My faith in you will be lessened if you talk too wildly."

"I will remember that and try to moderate my raptures."

"When I entered this room before," said Jessie, "it was near sunset, and there was a wonderfully brilliant glow upon everything. After the sun was quite gone, the room seemed still to retain the rays of light. I think you have managed to produce the effect of perpetual sunshine."

"And you found that out yourself?" he asked.

"It was not hard to find out," she replied.

"Well, that is just what I aimed at when I furnished the room. The truth is, Jessie, I have been rather blue sometimes since I came home. I seemed to be disappointing everybody at such a rate that I felt disgusted with myself, and I determined to fit up this room so as to counteract the mood. I have not admitted a single blue tone in anything—everywhere you will find glorious yellow, which is my favorite color. I am going to dress you up in yellow after awhile, Jessie. I do not like those black dresses at all, and, after we are married, I shall beg you to burn them all up. I detest black—unless it is velvet."

"You know why I wear them, dear," she whispered, with a tone of sadness in her voice.

"But, my darling, I don't want you to express your grief that way," he said, very tenderly. "Indeed, I don't want you to grieve any more. I shall try very hard to make you forget all that is sad in your past life."

Ah! how little he guessed her love for Harry, and the dull heart-ache she often felt, when she thought of him lying in his coffin still and cold under the grass. She replied very gently:

"I know that you will do all that you can to make me happy, and I do not think you will find it a very hard task; but you must not be vexed, if I sometimes remember those whom I have loved and lost."

He put his arm around her, and after a moment said: "But you will be willing to give up the black dresses and crape veils?"

"I shall be very willing to wear whatever you like, Waverley," she answered, returning his half-smile.

"That's a good girl," he whispered, caressingly. "Jessie, I want you to have more color; you are often very pale, and black increases the pallor. It is charming, to see you blush; it gives you the last perfect touch."

She responded to this by a vivid color, which the young man immediately commended. Though exacting in some respects, and fond of having his own way, Waverley Brooks was a model lover. He was cool and quiet; he was never familiar—he never demanded kisses, nor caresses, nor even endearing epithets as his rightful claim; he rather asked for sympathy and intellectual companionship from the woman whom he loved, and he did this in a boyish way which gave a great charm to his manly and dignified manners.

Soon he began to show Jessie his art treasures, telling her where each picture, or vase, or enamelled plate was bought, and under what circumstances. His eyes glowed with delight at her appreciation of everything and her perfect understanding of his tastes. "Jessie, it makes me so happy to have you sympathize with me in my passion for beautiful things. Father has rather a contempt for this room; he says it looks as if a sentimental, luxurious woman had furnished it. He would like to see a great desk in the centre, with piles of law-books bound in calf upon it, and, perhaps, a bust or two of Roman jurists on the top of those shelves. Aunt Kate is scarcely more merciful toward my weaknesses. Alice is a little better, but she lacks genuine enthusiasm for everything except good literature. I have so wanted some one to understand this side of my nature, for it is a very big part of my inmost self."

He handled the beautiful vases with tenderness, and pointed out their artistic merits; he showed her his etchings and engravings, and found her quick to choose the best in everything. He told her about his pictures —when and how they were painted. When he came to the "moonlight on the water," he flushed slightly, and said, "Do you recognize anybody there?"

"I think I do; it is you who are rowing, is it not?"

"Yes, that is a bit of my own life, Jessie. I came

very near falling in love with that girl. She was English, and an awfully sweet blossom. My engagement with Alice saved me. It would have been a dreadful mistake, for she was very English in her tastes and feelings, and could never have been transplanted to America. When I found out that I was becoming too much interested, I packed my valise and took to flight. So you see I did not really fall in love, and that incident was not included in my confession at The Grove last fall."

"It is rather a suspicious circumstance that you should have omitted it," said Jessie, smiling. "Are you sure that you have entirely recovered from it now? It would be painful to have a rival, even though she were three thousand miles away."

"Never fear," he replied, "you have no rival on this green earth; I have entirely recovered from all my previous attachments; and I shall turn this picture to the wall."

"No, you won't. I like it very much—the landscape is charming, and the girl is not so very bad."

"Sometime, I will paint her out and put you in her place."

"No, I would not like that; it would destroy the verities. You are quite welcome to all the pleasant things in your past, Waverley. I shall not vex you by my jealousies. It is enough that you have chosen me for your wife. I shall try to be worthy in every way."

"You are that already, my darling," he said. "I have had my fancies as other men have them, but now the passion of my life has come. You seem to be a very part of myself, Jessie; you like what I like, and your thoughts fit into mine. I cannot bear to have you away from me—I feel incomplete and wretched without you." Pausing a moment, he slowly repeated the lines,—

> "Unless you can muse in a crowd all day
>   On the absent face that fixed you;
> Unless you can love as the angels may
>   With the breadth of heaven betwixt you;"

"You know the words,—don't you?" he asked.

"Oh! yes," she said, quickly adding the remainder of the verse,—

> "Unless you can dream that his faith is fast,
>   Through behoving and unbehoving;
> Unless you can *die* when the dream is past,—
>   Oh! never call it loving."

"Yes, that is it," he said in a low, tender tone, drawing her to him. They stood silently for a few moments, looking into each other's eyes, as if trying to measure the heights and depths of their love and happiness.

"And, Jessie, I am so fond of travel too," he continued in his eager, joyous way; "you see my tastes are awfully Bohemian, but I cannot help it. I do hope you will sympathize with me in that, too; sometimes, we will tear up and go to Europe for a few months or years, just as we like. You will not mind it, will you?"

"Mind it, dear!" she exclaimed, her eyes dancing with delight; "I shall like it more than tongue can tell. For years it has been my waking dream. But we must not make too many plans; let's just live along day after day, loving each other better and better all the while, and not thinking much about the future."

"But I must build my *châteaux en Espagne*," he said, "and you will have to help me carry brick and mortar up the hill. I always have at least two or three castles on hand at the same time, and I'm awful glad to have somebody to assist in making the plans."

She laughed. It pleased and surprised her to find so much boyish enthusiasm under an exterior which had always impressed her as rather cold and proud and self-sufficient. She responded promptly to this new demand upon her sympathy.

"I shall like to help you about *everything*, dear,— only the future is so full of unexpected things that one sometimes feels punished for daring to plan it according to one's own wishes."

"I don't," he said, quickly, with a self-confident smile; "I like unexpected things; often they are far better than the things we plan for ourselves. For instance, you are an unexpected gift, my darling, and nothing half so beautiful has ever happened to me before; in my wildest dreams, I have never imagined that my wife would be so sweet and perfect as yourself."

She expressed her thanks for such a tribute by smiles instead of words. It was easy to see that he knew but little of disappointment and sorrow. It did her good to be in the presence of this strong, healthful, hopeful temperament; it counteracted the slight tendency to melancholy which lurked in her nature.

"Now, go and play for me, dearest," she said, "and I will sit here in this beautiful chair. I long to hear that grand piano in this large, airy room."

He obeyed, choosing the music that he loved best, feeling confident that it would satisfy her own taste. She rested her head against the soft cushion, and gave herself up to the delight of roaming in the dream-land of love.

CHAPTER XXIX.

EVERY evening Jessie had her spelling lesson with the Judge, but the word seemed always too difficult for her to pronounce. Only after the wedding was over, and she stood with her hand in his, ready to say the last good-bye, could she command her lips to call him father.

Mrs. Brooks, as she watched this evening lesson, thought them very silly and childish, and wondered what they would do next; but Alice and Waverley got much quiet amusement out of their sparkling nonsense. The young man, especially, looked on with delight to see his father unbend and become gay and playful in the presence of Jessie. He was not familiar with this paternal mood, and began to have a vague idea that the girl, so soon to be his wife, possessed some wonderful power to call out whatever was sweetest and best in others. He watched her with a lover's eye, and saw that she was growing more beautiful every day. Sometimes he wondered if she could indeed be human, like other women. No, she was divine; and he smiled to himself, for he well knew that it was his own hand that daily poured out the glass of nectar for her lips.

One evening, by some chance, the Judge and Jessie found themselves alone in the great drawing-room. The young girl's fingers were busy with some delicate sewing, while the gentleman was slowly cutting and turning the leaves of a newly-arrived magazine. Suddenly he laid aside his book, and turning to her said, "Jessie, my dear, I wish you would tell me something about the Colonel and your sister—I mean something about their business affairs. I'm afraid they are getting into trouble, are they not?"

"I am afraid so myself," she answered, sadly, "but I know very little about it; they are both so proud and reserved."

Then she told him about the mortgage on Redbank. The Judge was surprised, and remained silent a long time, as if pondering some weighty question of the law. At length he spoke—"Jessie, I think I must go to the assistance of the Colonel. With all his faults, he is a fine old fellow, and must not be driven to the wall. I do not like to think that he will ever be compelled to give up his plantation—it would be a deep humiliation for him. Like every father, he wants to leave his estate intact for his son to inherit, and to lose Redbank would be a blow to his love as well as to his pride. I will see him and talk with him as soon as you and Waverley are out of the way. You two lovers keep me in such a perpetual turmoil and flutter, that I am quite unfit for anything but dallying and talking nonsense."

"How good and generous you are!" cried the girl, the tears springing to her eyes.

"If I helped them out of their troubles, would it make you happier, my dear?" he asked.

"Ever so much happier!" she said, laying down her work, and clasping her hands imploringly. "I cannot tell you how it grieves me to think of them."

"It shall be done," he replied in a low, emphatic tone, adding after a few moments: "It will be, perhaps, some little compensation to them for losing you. Since their loss is our gain, it is only fair that we should be willing to settle up accounts, and make

things square and even." After a while, he continued—
" Jessie, I imagine that if you were put up in the market of Stamboul, like the Greek Slave, you would bring several thousand dollars. What do you think of it?"

" What put that idea into your head?" she said, breaking into a laugh.

" Have you never thought of your market value?" he asked, joining in her mirth.

" Never! never! I did not even fancy that girls possessed any market value nowadays. I thought it was the gentlemen who were valuable, and every woman was expected to pay the man a price for taking her. Isn't it so?"

"In some countries, perhaps," he said, "but happily not in ours."

" Ah! you need not say that. You know perfectly well that a handsome *dot* makes a girl wonderfully attractive, even in this land of the free and home of the brave."

" Perhaps you are right. I cannot find it in my heart to disagree with any statement that you may make."

" I feel very sorry not to bring Waverley a dower worthy of his acceptance," she remarked, with a little truthful ring in her voice, as if she meant what she said.

"Nonsense, my dear; he has a great deal more now than he knows what to do with. I only hope you will save him from being ruined by having too much money; that will be far better than bringing him any more."

Then they fell into a long silence, which was broken at last by the gentleman.

" Jessie," he said, " I do think your sister and the children ought to get away from Redbank this summer. The place is very unhealthy. That old mill-pond is a fertile source of disease to all the country around."

"How I wish they could go away!" she replied, "but I am afraid it is quite impossible."

"Why should it be impossible?"

"Because they have no money. They are waiting for the ship to come in, and it sails very slowly."

"Then you and I will play the part of Zephyrus and Eolus; we will blow with all our might, and make the ship move faster."

"That would be splendid!" she cried, her eyes glowing with happiness. "It is delightful to be in partnership with a real divinity like yourself."

"I like the partnership myself," he said, with a quiet smile; "to be associated with a divinity makes one almost divine. Now, listen to my plea. The first of July, perhaps earlier, I am going to take Kate and Alice with me to the Virginia Springs. Your sister and the children must go with us: I shall not accept any excuses. The children will amuse Alice, and prevent us old people from sinking into family dulness and hopeless dotage. You know I have already shown signs of the approach of that disease."

Jessie looked up at him with grateful tears in her eyes. "Thank you! thank you!" she whispered. "You are the best and noblest man that I have ever known."

"Except Waverley," he answered, a tender expression coming into his face.

"I cannot even except him," she said, dropping her eyes; "a part of the love and confidence I give him is for your sake. I accept him on trust because he is your son. Are you not satisfied?"

"I am more than satisfied, Jessie," he whispered in a low tone.

The silence that fell upon them was broken by the entrance of Waverley.

"Come here, my son," said the Judge.

The young man obeyed, and stood before his father as if awaiting commands.

"I want to thank you for this sweet daughter that you have given me. I am willing to acknowledge that, at one time, it did not seem easy to relinquish other plans, but that is all over now, and this new arrangement grows more and more pleasant every day. It makes me proud of you, Waverley, to see how wisely you have chosen your wife. My son, I give you my blessing,"—and the Judge extended his hand. The young man clasped it in both of his, and in a voice full of emotion, said,

"Thank you, my father."

A few weeks later, Waverley Brooks and his wife were standing on the deck of an ocean steamer, bound for Europe.

They were nearing the coast of Ireland; it was just after dinner, and they had been enjoying a brisk promenade. Now they had paused beside the railing to look out over the sea, and to drink in great draughts of salt air which was blowing stiffly from the west and driving them rapidly towards the Old World.

"Do you like it, Jessie?" he whispered softly, clasping her hand more tightly within his own.

"How can you ask?" she answered, looking up at him with a great love in her eyes. "It is all so beautiful! so beautiful!"

Her voice died away in the vain attempt to give expression to the happiness that filled her soul to overflowing.

THE END.

From the Press of the Arena Publishing Company.

COPLEY SQUARE SERIES — Continued.

IV. Esau; or, The Banker's Victim.

"ESAU" is the title of a new book by Dr. T. A. BLAND. It is a political novel of purpose and power. As a romance it is fascinating; as a history of a mortgage it is tragic; and as an *expose* of the financial policy of the old parties it is clear and forcible. It is a timely and valuable campaign book.

Price, single copy, 25 cents; per hundred, $12.50.

V. The People's Cause.

CONTENTS:

1. The Threefold Contention of Industry.
   Gen. J. B. Weaver, Presidential Nominee of People's Party.
2. The Negro Question in the South.
   Hon. Thos. E. Watson, M. C. from Georgia.
3. The Menace of Plutocracy. *B. O. Flower, Editor of "The Arena."*
4. The Communism of Capital. *Hon. John Davis, M. C. from Kansas.*
5. The Pending Presidential Campaign. *Hon. J. H. Kyle, State Senator from South Dakota; Thos. E. Watson, M. C. from Georgia.*

Price, 25 cents a copy; per hundred, $10.

For sale by all booksellers. Sent postpaid upon receipt of the price.

Arena Publishing Company,

Copley Square, BOSTON, MASS.

From the Press of the Arena Publishing Company.

The Rise of the Swiss Republic.
By W. D. MCCRACKAN, A. M.

It contains over four hundred pages, printed from new and handsome type, on a fine quality of heavy paper. The margins are wide, and the volume is richly bound in cloth.

Price, postpaid, $3.00.

Sultan to Sultan.
By M. FRENCH-SHELDON (Bebe Bwana).

Being a thrilling account of a remarkable expedition to the Masai and other hostile tribes of East Africa, which was planned and commanded by this intrepid woman. **A Sumptuous Volume of Travels.** Handsomely illustrated; printed on coated paper and richly bound in African red silk-finished cloth.

Price, postpaid, $5.00.

The League of the Iroquois.
By BENJAMIN HATHAWAY.

It is instinct with good taste and poetic feeling, affluent of picturesque description and graceful portraiture, and its versification is fairly melodious. — *Harper's Magazine.*

Has the charm of Longfellow's "Hiawatha." — *Albany Evening Journal.*

Of rare excellence and beauty. — *American Wesleyan.*

Evinces fine qualities of imagination, and is distinguished by remarkable grace and fluency. — *Boston Gazette.*

The publication of this poem alone may well serve as a mile-post in marking the pathway of American literature. The work is a marvel of legendary lore, and will be appreciated by every earnest reader. — *Boston Times.*

Price, postpaid, cloth, $1.00; Red Line edition, $1.50.

For sale by all booksellers. Sent postpaid upon receipt of the price.

Arena Publishing Company,
Copley Square,   BOSTON, MASS.

BOOKS

From the Press of the Arena Publishing Company.

Jason Edwards: An Average Man.

By HAMLIN GARLAND. A powerful and realistic story of to-day. Price: paper, 50 cents; cloth, $1.00.

Who Lies? An Interrogation.

By BLUM and ALEXANDER. A book that is well worth reading. Price: paper, 50 cents; cloth, $1.00.

Main Travelled Roads.

Six Mississippi Valley stories. By HAMLIN GARLAND.

"The sturdy spirit of true democracy runs through this book."— *Review of Reviews.*

Price: paper, 50 cents; cloth, $1.00.

Irrepressible Conflict Between Two World-Theories.

By Rev. MINOT J. SAVAGE. The most powerful presentation of Theistic Evolution *versus* Orthodoxy that has ever appeared. Price: paper, 50 cents; cloth, $1.00.

For sale by all booksellers. Sent postpaid upon receipt of the price.

Arena Publishing Company,

Copley Square,   BOSTON, MASS.

From the Press of the Arena Publishing Company.

The Dream Child.
A fascinating romance of two worlds. By FLORENCE HUNTLEY. Price: paper, 50 cents; cloth, $1.00.

A Mute Confessor.
The romance of a Southern town. By WILL N. HARBEN, author of "White Marie," "Almost Persuaded," etc. Price: paper, 50 cents; cloth, $1.00.

Redbank; Life on a Southern Plantation.
By M. L. COWLES. A typical Southern story by a Southern woman. Price: paper, 00; cloth, $1.00.

Psychics. Facts and Theories.
By Rev. MINOT J. SAVAGE. A thoughtful discussion of Psychical problems. Price: paper, 50 cents; cloth, $1.00.

Civilization's Inferno: Studies in the Social Cellar.
By B. O. FLOWER. I. Introductory chapter. II. Society's Exiles. III. Two Hours in the Social Cellar. IV. The Democracy of Darkness. V. Why the Ishmaelites Multiply. VI. The Froth and the Dregs. VII. A Pilgrimage and a Vision. VIII. Some Facts and a Question. IX. What of the Morrow? Price: paper, 50 cents; cloth, $1.00.

For sale by all booksellers. Sent postpaid upon receipt of the price.

Arena Publishing Company,

Copley Square,   BOSTON, MASS.

BOOKS

From the Press of the Arena Publishing Company.

The Rise of the Swiss Republic.

By W. D. MCCRACKAN, A. M.

It contains over four hundred pages, printed from new and handsome type, on a fine quality of heavy paper. The margins are wide, and the volume is richly bound in cloth.

Price, postpaid, $3.00.

Sultan to Sultan.

By M. FRENCH-SHELDON (Bebe Bwana).

Being a thrilling account of a remarkable expedition to the Masai and other hostile tribes of East Africa, which was planned and commanded by this intrepid woman. **A Sumptuous Volume of Travels.** Handsomely illustrated; printed on coated paper and richly bound in African red silk-finished cloth.

Price, postpaid, $5.00.

The League of the Iroquois.

By BENJAMIN HATHAWAY.

It is instinct with good taste and poetic feeling, affluent of picturesque description and graceful portraiture, and its versification is fairly melodious. — *Harper's Magazine.*

Has the charm of Longfellow's "Hiawatha." — *Albany Evening Journal.*

Of rare excellence and beauty. — *American Wesleyan.*

Evinces fine qualities of imagination, and is distinguished by remarkable grace and fluency. — *Boston Gazette.*

The publication of this poem alone may well serve as a mile-post in marking the pathway of American literature. The work is a marvel of legendary lore, and will be appreciated by every earnest reader. — *Boston Times.*

Price, postpaid, cloth, $1.00; Red Line edition, $1.50.

For sale by all booksellers. Sent postpaid upon receipt of the price.

Arena Publishing Company,

Copley Square,   BOSTON, MASS.

From the Press of the Arena Publishing Company.

Songs.
By NEITH BOYCE. Illustrated with original drawings by ETHELWYN WELLS CONREY. A beautiful gift book. Bound in white and gold. Price, postpaid, $1.25.

The Finished Creation, and Other Poems.
By BENJAMIN HATHAWAY, author of "The League of the Iroquois," "Art Life," and other Poems. Handsomely bound in white parchment vellum, stamped in silver. Price, postpaid, $1.25.

Wit and Humor of the Bible.
By Rev. MARION D. SHUTTER, D.D. A brilliant and reverent treatise. Published only in cloth. Price, postpaid, $1.50.

Son of Man; or, Sequel to Evolution.
By CELESTIA ROOT LANG. Published only in cloth.

> This work, in many respects, very remarkably discusses the next step in the Evolution of Man. It is in perfect touch with advanced Christian Evolutionary thought, but takes a step beyond the present position of Religion Leaders.

Price, postpaid, $1.25.

For sale by all booksellers. Sent postpaid upon receipt of the price.

Arena Publishing Company,
Copley Square,   BOSTON, MASS.

From the Press of the Arena Publishing Company.

Along Shore with a Man of War.

By MARGUERITE DICKINS. A delightful story of travel, delightfully told, handsomely illustrated, and beautifully bound. Price, postpaid, $1.50.

Evolution.

Popular lectures by leading thinkers, delivered before the Brooklyn Ethical Association. This work is of inestimable value to the general reader who is interested in Evolution as applied to religious, scientific, and social themes. It is the joint work of a number of the foremost thinkers in America to-day. One volume, handsome cloth, illustrated, complete index. 408 pp. Price, postpaid, $2.00.

Sociology.

Popular lectures by eminent thinkers, delivered before the Brooklyn Ethical Association. This work is a companion volume to "Evolution," and presents the best thought of representative thinkers on social evolution. One volume, handsome cloth, with diagram and complete index. 412 pp. Price, postpaid, $2.00.

For sale by all booksellers. Sent postpaid upon receipt of the price.

Arena Publishing Company,

Copley Square,   BOSTON, MASS.

From the Press of the Arena Publishing Company.

Jason Edwards: An Average Man.

By HAMLIN GARLAND. A powerful and realistic story of to-day. Price: paper, 50 cents; cloth, $1.00.

Who Lies? An Interrogation.

By BLUM and ALEXANDER. A book that is well worth reading. Price: paper, 50 cents; cloth, $1.00.

Main Travelled Roads.

Six Mississippi Valley stories. By HAMLIN GARLAND.

"The sturdy spirit of true democracy runs through this book."— *Review of Reviews.*

Price: paper, 50 cents; cloth, $1.00.

Irrepressible Conflict Between Two World-Theories.

By Rev. MINOT J. SAVAGE. The most powerful presentation of Theistic Evolution *versus* Orthodoxy that has ever appeared. Price: paper, 50 cents; cloth, $1.00.

For sale by all booksellers. Sent postpaid upon receipt of the price.

Arena Publishing Company,

Copley Square,   BOSTON, MASS.

BOOKS

From the Press of the Arena Publishing Company.

Along Shore with a Man of War.

By MARGUERITE DICKINS. A delightful story of travel, delightfully told, handsomely illustrated, and beautifully bound. Price, postpaid, $1.50.

Evolution.

Popular lectures by leading thinkers, delivered before the Brooklyn Ethical Association. This work is of inestimable value to the general reader who is interested in Evolution as applied to religious, scientific, and social themes. It is the joint work of a number of the foremost thinkers in America to-day. One volume, handsome cloth, illustrated, complete index. 408 pp. Price, postpaid, $2.00.

Sociology.

Popular lectures by eminent thinkers, delivered before the Brooklyn Ethical Association. This work is a companion volume to "Evolution," and presents the best thought of representative thinkers on social evolution. One volume, handsome cloth, with diagram and complete index. 412 pp. Price, postpaid, $2.00.

For sale by all booksellers. Sent postpaid upon receipt of the price.

Arena Publishing Company,

Copley Square,   BOSTON, MASS.

From the Press of the Arena Publishing Company.

COPLEY SQUARE SERIES.

I. **Bond-Holders and Bread-Winners.**
By S. S. KING, Esq., Kansas City, Kansas. The most powerful book of the year. Its argument is irresistible. You should read it.
> President L. L. POLK, National F. A. and I. U., says: "It should be placed in the hands of every voter of this country."

Price, postpaid, 25 cents; per hundred, $12.50.

II. **Money, Land, and Transportation.**
> CONTENTS:
> 1. A New Declaration of Rights. *Hamlin Garland.*
> 2. The Farmer, Investor, and the Railway. *C. Wood Davis.*
> 3. The Independent Party and Money at Cost. *R. B. Hassell.*

Price, single copy, 25 cents; per hundred, $10.

III. **Industrial Freedom.** The Triple Demand of Labor.
> CONTENTS:
> 1. The Money Question. *Hon. John Davis.*
> 2. The Sub-Treasury Plan. *C. C. Post.*
> 3. The Railroad Problem. *C. Wood Davis and Ex-Gov. Lionel A. Sheldon.*

Price, single copy, 25 cents; per hundred, $10.

For sale by all booksellers. Sent postpaid upon receipt of the price.

Arena Publishing Company,

Copley Square,   BOSTON, MASS.

From the Press of the Arena Publishing Company.

Is This Your Son, My Lord?
By HELEN H. GARDENER. The most powerful novel written by an American. A terrible *expose* of conventional immorality and hypocrisy. Price: paper, 50 cents; cloth, $1.00.

Pray You, Sir, Whose Daughter?
By HELEN H. GARDENER. A brilliant novel of to-day, dealing with social purity and the "age of consent" laws. Price: paper, 50 cents; cloth, $1.00.

A Spoil of Office.
A novel. By HAMLIN GARLAND. The truest picture of Western life that has appeared in American fiction. Price: paper, 50 cents; cloth, $1.00.

Lessons Learned from Other Lives.
By B. O. FLOWER.

There are fourteen biographies in this volume, dealing with the lives of Seneca and Epictetus, the great Roman philosophers; Joan of Arc, the warrior maid; Henry Clay, the statesman; Edwin Booth and Joseph Jefferson, the actors; John Howard Payne, William Cullen Bryant, Edgar Allan Poe, Alice and Phœbe Cary, and John G. Whittier, the poets; Alfred Russell Wallace, the scientist; Victor Hugo, the many-sided man of genius.

"The book sparkles with literary jewels." — *Christian Leader*, Cincinnati, Ohio.

Price: paper, 50 cents; cloth. $1.00.

For sale by all booksellers. Sent postpaid upon receipt of the price.

Arena Publishing Company,
Copley Square,   BOSTON, MASS.

From the Press of the Arena Publishing Company.

Songs.
By NEITH BOYCE. Illustrated with original drawings by ETHELWYN WELLS CONREY. A beautiful gift book. Bound in white and gold. Price, postpaid, $1.25.

The Finished Creation, and Other Poems.
By BENJAMIN HATHAWAY, author of "The League of the Iroquois," "Art Life," and other Poems. Handsomely bound in white parchment vellum, stamped in silver. Price, postpaid, $1.25.

Wit and Humor of the Bible.
By Rev. MARION D. SHUTTER, D.D. A brilliant and reverent treatise. Published only in cloth. Price, postpaid, $1.50.

Son of Man; or, Sequel to Evolution.
By CELESTIA ROOT LANG. Published only in cloth.

> This work, in many respects, very remarkably discusses the next step in the Evolution of Man. It is in perfect touch with advanced Christian Evolutionary thought, but takes a step beyond the present position of Religion Leaders.

Price, postpaid, $1.25.

For sale by all booksellers. Sent postpaid upon receipt of the price.

Arena Publishing Company,

Copley Square,   BOSTON, MASS.

BOOKS

From the Press of the Arena Publishing Company.

Is This Your Son, My Lord?
By HELEN H. GARDENER. The most powerful novel written by an American. A terrible *expose* of conventional immorality and hypocrisy. Price: paper, 50 cents; cloth, $1.00.

Pray You, Sir, Whose Daughter?
By HELEN H. GARDENER. A brilliant novel of to-day, dealing with social purity and the "age of consent" laws. Price: paper, 50 cents; cloth, $1.00.

A Spoil of Office.
A novel. By HAMLIN GARLAND. The truest picture of Western life that has appeared in American fiction. Price: paper, 50 cents; cloth, $1.00.

Lessons Learned from Other Lives.
By B. O. FLOWER.

There are fourteen biographies in this volume, dealing with the lives of Seneca and Epictetus, the great Roman philosophers; Joan of Arc, the warrior maid; Henry Clay, the statesman; Edwin Booth and Joseph Jefferson, the actors; John Howard Payne, William Cullen Bryant, Edgar Allan Poe, Alice and Phœbe Cary, and John G. Whittier, the poets; Alfred Russell Wallace, the scientist; Victor Hugo, the many-sided man of genius.

"The book sparkles with literary jewels." — *Christian Leader*, Cincinnati, Ohio.

Price: paper, 50 cents; cloth. $1.00.

For sale by all booksellers. Sent postpaid upon receipt of the price.

Arena Publishing Company,
Copley Square,   BOSTON, MASS.

From the Press of the Arena Publishing Company.

The Dream Child.
A fascinating romance of two worlds. By FLORENCE HUNTLEY. Price: paper, 50 cents; cloth, $1.00.

A Mute Confessor.
The romance of a Southern town. By WILL N. HARBEN, author of "White Marie," "Almost Persuaded," etc. Price: paper, 50 cents; cloth, $1.00.

Redbank; Life on a Southern Plantation.
By M. L. COWLES. A typical Southern story by a Southern woman. Price: paper, 00; cloth, $1.00.

Psychics. Facts and Theories.
By Rev. MINOT J. SAVAGE. A thoughtful discussion of Psychical problems. Price: paper, 50 cents; cloth, $1.00.

Civilization's Inferno: Studies in the Social Cellar.
By B. O. FLOWER. I. Introductory chapter. II. Society's Exiles. III. Two Hours in the Social Cellar. IV. The Democracy of Darkness. V. Why the Ishmaelites Multiply. VI. The Froth and the Dregs. VII. A Pilgrimage and a Vision. VIII. Some Facts and a Question. IX. What of the Morrow? Price: paper, 50 cents; cloth, $1.00.

For sale by all booksellers. Sent postpaid upon receipt of the price.

Arena Publishing Company,

Copley Square,   BOSTON, MASS.

www.ingramcontent.com/pod-product-compliance
Lightning Source LLC
Chambersburg PA
CBHW030357230426
43664CB00007BB/635